FROM
Limelight

A Scottish Film Book

TO
Satellite

EDITED BY

Eddie Dick

BRITISH FILM INSTITUTE
bfi

SCOTTISH FILM COUNCIL
sfc

The publishers thank Scottish Television for their
financial contribution to the production of this book.

Designed by James Hutcheson and Paul Keir, Wide Art, Edinburgh.
Typeset in Baskerville by Hewer Text Composition Services, Edinburgh.
Printed in Great Britain by Courier International, Tiptree, Essex.

Cover illustrations

(front, clockwise) *Floodtide, My Childhood, Never Say Never Again, Mary of Scotland*

(back, clockwise) *Master of Ballantrae, The Courier, Ashes, Silent Scream,*
Mackendrick directing *Whisky Galore!*

British Library Cataloguing in Publication Data
Dick, Eddie
   From limelight to satellite : a Scottish film book.
   1. Scottish cinema films, history
   I. Title
   791.4309411

   ISBN 0-85170-281-3
   ISBN 0-85170-282-1 pbk

Contents

For Linda

Foreword

Scotland has made many distinguished and lasting contributions to the culture of the United Kingdom. Her poets and novelists, painters and musicians are justly renowned throughout Europe. Yet sadly, the major impact Scotland has had on the moving image – certainly no less distinguished and equally lasting – has failed somehow to achieve the international recognition it so richly deserves. One need only think of the superb documentary tradition, the immensely popular feature films of recent years and the inventiveness and skill which individual Scots have brought to the film industry over many decades to realise that a new view, a new appreciation, is indeed long overdue.

From Limelight to Satellite provides that new view by bringing together and examining in depth some of the most enduring and significant aspects of Scottish cinema. The film makers and broadcasters, journalists and critics, academics and researchers who are gathered in these pages represent contemporary opinion at its best and most informed. Never before has there been such a wide ranging Scottish film publication, so carefully put together, so profusely illustrated.

The book has come into being through collaboration between the British Film Institute and the newly independent Scottish Film Council. It is a partnership which, as Chairman of the BFI's Board of Governors and an 'honorary Scot' by virtue of my new island home, I find both welcome and gratifying.

From Limelight to Satellite will, I feel sure, give enormous pleasure, providing much food for thought, not just in Scotland but wherever it is read. Its profundity and the discussion it will undoubtedly provoke should contribute immeasurably to the further development of Scottish film and help elevate this long underrated but crucial element in the country's artistic heritage to its full and deserved status in the cinema of the new Europe.

Richard Attenborough

Introduction

Eddie Dick

From Limelight to Satellite, as its title suggests, looks at Scottish films from the earliest days to the present. From the times when the pictures meant rows of wooden benches in tented booths and the limelight dangerously illuminating the flammable nitrate to now, when satellite footprints stamp their shapes across a Scotland that is suddenly, again, part of Europe.

This book is written for moviegoers who are not only interested in watching films but reading about them, about the delights and difficulties of making and understanding movies. As well as entertaining and informing through the words, *Limelight* offers a visual richness which is unique for a Scottish film book. You will see stills from films which have disappeared, images from some of your favourite Scottish movies (and others you'd prefer to forget) and pictures from films which you may have missed.

Limelight is a book which will challenge and intrigue, particularly at a time when questions of Scottish identity and the related issues of filmmaking and culture in a small country jostle to the foreground.

What it is and what it is not

> I propose the following definition of the nation: it is an imagined political community . . . *imagined* because the members of even the smallest nation will never know most of their fellow-members, meet them, or even hear of them, yet in the minds of each lives the image of their communion.
>
> (*Imagined Communities*, Benedict Anderson)

From Limelight to Satellite discusses film in the context of Scotland. Clearly, the imagined Scotland is not *imaginary*; what we collectively remember or forget, the geographical space we occupy, the institutions which support and control us – these and many other things operate powerfully on our daily lives to make us what we think we are. The imagining is not an illusion; being Scottish might be a pain or a pleasure but it is *real*.

What is discussed, implicitly or explicitly, in each of the controbutions to *Limelight* is what happens when the words *Scottish* and *film* are brought together. How rich or poverty-stricken the imaginings have been since the cameras started to roll. The possibility of cinema in a small country. The kinds of Scotland we can see on our cinema and television screens, courtesy of Scottish filmmakers and those of other countries. The histories and future options which have to be confronted. The pleasure of seeing ourselves in ways which break the kitsch stereotypes which bedevilled the past and sour the present.

If the word *Scottish* is a problem, so is the word *film*. Gone are the easy days where it was possible to speak only of darkened picture houses and whirling celluloid. This book takes a fairly pragmatic attitude towards the problem. If it was shot on celluloid and seen as a film, it is one – irrespective if it was experienced in a cinema or at home on broadcast TV or video. As film and TV technologically converge, the remaining differences will principally interest historians and accountants. Partly for historical reasons, and partly because of practicalities, *Limelight* concentrates on cinema.

In a book packed with argument, analysis, memory and opinion – as well as (170) film stills – the pressure on space demands that the editor be brief. I will be, but *From Limelight to Satellite* is a unique publication and that status calls for some explanation so that readers may appreciate what this book is and, just as important, what it is not. It is *not* a definitive history of film in Scotland. It is a gathering of essays and pictures which form a historical and contemporary mosaic of Scottish film. A *kind* of mosaic in which each piece makes its individual sense but where the totality blends into a fuller impression of film in Scotland. Inevitably, there are gaps.

Some are omissions which are created by the absence of basic research. The filmography in the book shows how much contemporary work needs to be done on feature films. The tragically large number of films which do not physically exist any more and remain merely as enigmatic titles in a catalogue means that it is only possible to speculate on these films and their audiences' reactions. In addition, the fundamental research into documentary and television film remains to be done.

Some gaps occur because I felt that the basic work has been done elsewhere. For example, Forsyth Hardy's *John Grierson, a Documentary biography* deals more fully with Grierson and his influence than could have been attempted in *Limelight*. Hardy's more recent *Scotland in Film* gives a semi-autobiographical chronology of sixty years of documentaries and feature films; *Limelight* opts for a broad base of insight from a variety of informed writers. What is lost by not having a single voice telling the story is more than offset by having a diversity of current opinion.

That very diversity means that *Limelight* does not have a 'line' leading to set conclusions. The influential ground-breaking work done by Colin McArthur's *Scotch Reels* was marred by offering judgements on representations of Scotland whose incisiveness depended on their partiality. What was said was not wrong but could not be extended to all the available films.

The Essays

The importance of the ways we see ourselves and are seen by others – and the historical relevance of *Scotch Reels* in understanding film in Scotland – leads to the placing of John Caughie's 'Representing Scotland' at the beginning of *Limelight*.

Writing with cool insight which masks his passionate concern, he recasts the issue of representations so that it cuts into the heart of things now. He not only looks at what happens on the screen but places those images in historical and industrial contexts which allow us an optimistic glimpse of the potential of a film culture in Scotland.

The next five articles are mainly historical. David Hutchison's contribution is aptly named 'Flickering Light'. The limited number of silent films still available and the large number which are lost forever mean that no general light can be shed on the area; David Hutchison limits his occasionally scathing comments to the particular evidence offered by the few remaining features and some of the more interesting of the less well-known documentaries.

Adrienne Scullion's piece shifts the attention to audiences during one of the peaks of Scottish cinema-going. She examines some of the principal aspects of mainstream and alternative cinema, some of the commercial and political concerns against the social background of Scotland in the thirties. Neil Blain's 'A Scotland As Good As Any Other' is a witty contemporary sweep across some notable documentary output from a forty-five year period. Some of the films were embarrassing failures, others were substantial successes both in Scotland and abroad. In 'Hollywood Comes to the Highlands', David Bruce discusses issues affecting the establishment of a Scottish film 'industry'. He outlines the lessons to be learned from a mid-forties experience to question the equation between 'industry' and 'studio'. 'Family Pictures' by Andrew Young is an affectionate account of two of Scotland's picture-house families, the Singletons and the Pooles. 'Family Pictures' is an album of cinema memories, with revealing insights of showmanship and business.

Colin McArthur deals with the successes and failures of the 'glam' side of exhibition at the Edinburgh International Film Festival.

The five articles which follow look at individual filmmakers and their films. Murray Grigor's and Chris Rush's contributions complement each other well. Murray Grigor's article on *Whisky Galore!* is what he calls 'an unfashionably unashamedly auteurist piece' on the first feature of that talented but neglected filmmaker Sandy Mackendrick. We move from an Ealing Studios comedy in the rain-battered Barra of 1948 to the dapple-weathered Orkney of 1988 in *Venus Peter*. Murray Grigor's piece is an admiration of Mackendrick written from the perspective of an experienced filmmaker; Chris Rush's article sketches the sharp learning curve of an outsider. Essentially a masterly wordsmith, Chris Rush describes the translation of his book *A Twelvemonth and a Day* into the film *Venus Peter* and the shocks, delights and despair he experienced

11

as he participated in and watched the process.

Shock was the initial reaction, too, for Andrew Noble when he first saw Bill Douglas's *Trilogy*. This time, however, the shock was one of recognition which Andrew Noble analyses for us as he writes of three masterpieces of filmmaking. Bill Forsyth has been much written about and little understood. Alan Hunter provides us with one of the best pieces so far on this pre-eminent Scottish filmmaker. Those who think of Forsyth as the whimsical comedian are in for a surprise. John Millar's celebration of Sean Connery as the only Scottish superstar provides a fitting closure before we move into considerations of the film industry.

'Pictures in a Small Country' is by Ian Lockerbie who was the first chairman of the increasingly influential Scottish Film Production Fund. A retrospective and speculation for the future, this article examines the rationale for the Fund and its potential roles. Charlie Gormley assesses 'The Impact of Channel Four' in an iconoclastic article which balances reflections on his own films with insider talk on the effects of Channel Four on film production in Scotland. The managerial insider, Gus Macdonald in 'Fiction Friction', gives some hard figures on television's filmmaking and, possibly, some even harder truths to cope with. From the view with franchised broadcast TV, we are moved by Robin McPherson in 'Declarations of Independence' to a position of considering the shifting nature of the 'independent' producer.

In coming to the final article, we have travelled from representations to historical considerations through aspects of audiences, filmmaking and filmmakers, engaged with money and industry and come back to representations again. Philip Schlesinger's 'Scotland, Europe and Identity' looks at the external influences on national identity and speculates on what these might mean for image-making.

Janet McBain's 'Scotland in Feature Films, a Filmography' is one of the sections of *Limelight* which will give the book a lasting shelf-life. It is the first time that a Scottish filmography of this kind has been published and the fact that it is illustrated gives added value. The commonsense which pervades *Limelight* influences the filmography. Readers should read the criteria for inclusion before dipping in to search for a title.

Limelight is a major Scottish Film Council venture into book publishing. We extend our grateful thanks to the British Film Institute for their necessary and appreciated support.

Representing Scotland: New Questions for Scottish Cinema

John Caughie

To begin with a banality: the 1980s was a decade of considerable change for Scottish film production. To be more precise: in the 1980s, working both in cinema and in television, a group of Scottish filmmakers and Scottish independent production companies (still not much more than a handful) gave Scottish film production a public visibility of a kind it did not have before. Since much of this visibility has been on television the question of a Scottish *cinema* still remains – an actually existing Scottish cinema, that is, like the German, or Canadian or even Québecois cinema, with its own national and even international audience, a cinema which is no longer synonymous with the films of Bill Forsyth. Such a cinema, which, for a moment of over-expectation at the beginning of the eighties seemed imminent, has not yet materialised in any complete cultural sense. But, in an industrial sense, Scottish film production (even if it is not yet a true industry) does seem to be at work and expanding. It is no longer exceptional to see a Scottish film in the single play slot on BBC television; Scottish films and programmes may not constitute a due proportion of Channel Four schedules, but they are at least there; Scottish Television has established *Taggart* as a network crime series with a national and even international audience (he may be a stereotype, but he's our stereotype); and, if one is alert, one may, from time to time and for short runs, see Scottish feature films in the cinema – even, locally, in the case of *Venus Peter* for example, in the *commercial* cinema.

This diversity of mixed blessings in itself means that questions of representation have to be asked in a much more complex way than when, less than a decade ago, Scottish cinema could be simplified, abstracted and categorised in critical and historical research, and when representations were something that other people did to us. In this essay, I am interested in exploiting both senses of the term 'representation': the figurative sense, familiar to cultural criticism, of image and identity; but also the institutional sense, familiar to political

13

discourses, of proportionality, representativeness and participation. That's to say, I am interested not just in the increasingly diverse ways in which Scotland is represented, but also in how the many possible diversities which constitute nationality are, or can be, represented (in the participatory sense) in what we are probably not yet ready to call 'the Scottish film industry'. Thus, looking positively into the 1990s, representation raises questions not just of national identities, but also structural questions of participation, access and training.

Scotch Reels

At the risk of opening old wounds, I want to start in a fairly personal way from 'Scotch Reels', an event which was mounted at the Edinburgh Film Festival in August 1982, and from the book *Scotch Reels*, edited by Colin McArthur, which was published to coincide with the event. As one of the organisers of the event and a contributor to the book, I am wary of attributing too much significance to 'Scotch Reels'. There had been significant events before – most notably 'Cinema in a Small Country' 1977, and a series of seminars called 'Film Bang', an important attempt by independent filmmakers to kick-start Scottish film culture into existence – and there have been events since – a conference on Scottish/Québecois culture at Stirling University in 1987. But 'Scotch Reels' does seem important as a particular moment at which the idea of a Scottish cinema began to take on some material force for many people who had not hitherto been directly involved in its production. More than that, in the event and the publication, 'Scotch Reels' did articulate a coherent cultural analysis of the representation of Scotland in film and television. However preliminary, polemical and 'of its time' that analysis may now seem, it will be difficult for any new analysis to ignore it.

The event sent waves of resentment, bordering on fury, not only through large tracts of the institutionalised Scottish film establishment, who were always meant to be infuriated, but also through the paths and byways of the independent production sector, who were meant to be the allies with whom broad alliances were made. It was partly this shock to the system which gave the event some lasting significance and which placed the terms of the critique, for better or worse, into the routine vocabulary of cultural and critical discussions of Scottish cinema and television.

At the simplest, and most readily appropriable level, 'Scotch Reels' identified a set of relatively consistent discourses which informed the representation of Scottishness, defining the images of Scotland which could slip comfortably into the national imaginary as familiar identities, and into the national and international image markets as tradeable symbolic goods. These representations reproduced and, in cinema particularly, often refreshed the identities by which we are invited to recognise our difference and our status as a great wee nation. Unfortunately in the case of Scotland, it was argued, they

14

Lochaber no More

The tartan epitome of Scotland as loss, defeat and the divided community. One of a popular series of postcards showing the departure of the impossibly romantic Bonnie Prince.

were almost entirely regressive, launching their appeal from a vanished or vanishing past. It is perhaps a measure of their simplicity, but also of their seductive explanatory power, that the governing discourses can be identified quite schematically: 'tartanry', 'kailyard', 'Clydeside'. But behind the litany of what Colin McArthur called 'discursive positions' there was an historical analysis which tied the position to its source, and found there the real social, economic, political and cultural tensions which the mythological discourse served to efface. It may be useful to summarise the analysis very briefly, focussing on the historical moments which give them their meaning.

'Tartanry' takes Culloden as its privileged moment: a moment recast as an epic of tragic loss and triumphal defeat, which is able to forget, with mythic amnesia, the actual historical tensions involved in the replacement of an absolutist, historically anachronistic and economically unproductive feudal system with a relatively productive free range agrarian system. If, economically, the epic transformation is tied to the industrial revolution, culturally, it is tied to the Romanticism which sought wildness in the now empty landscapes of one of the last 'wildernesses' of Europe, emptied by Cumberland and the Clearances, and filled, by Scott and MacPherson, with wild, charismatic men and fey, elusive women. Almost invisible behind the tartan monster which stalks High Street souvenir shops and Hollywood movies are real epic confrontations between progress and tradition, nature and culture, rationality and romance.

The privileged moment of the 'kailyard' mythology is probably the Great Disruption of the Church of Scotland in 1843, a social as well as religious disruption involving issues of local democracy, moral authority and social welfare which left traces within the stable communities of the small townships well into the twentieth century. Of less epic resonance than the clash of nature and culture embodied by images of Romantic

This postcard, dating from 1915, shows a caricature whose aggression and ridiculousness is far removed the sad wistfulness of Charles Edward Stewart.

One of Cynicus' gentler depictions of Scottish hypocrisy. Cynicus was Martin Anderson (1854–1932) who was often dismissed as an eccentric but his biting and sometimes cruel satires on Scottish life and types were very popular at the turn of the century.

wildness, the imagery and imaginary of the kailyard is domesticated and social, concerned with a real disturbance, but moderated by the couthy and benign view from the manse window. The kailyard passes into popular culture most famously or notoriously through Harry Lauder, though he was only more consciously comic than J M Barrie who had been almost as popular on the American lecture circuit only a few decades earlier. Less aggressive than tartanry, the kailyard may be every bit as stifling, though there is no reason why it should not also echo with the real divisions in the community which first gave it life.

'Clydesideism' is the mythology of the Scottish twentieth century, the discourse which seems currently most potent, and not yet universally acknowledged as mythology. The gritty hardness of urban life parades itself as an antidote in the real world of today to all those legends of tartanry and couthy tales of kailyard. It turns out, nevertheless, in most of its available forms, to be just another mythology: a modernised myth of male industrial labour, with its appurtenances of labour, pub and football field alive and in place, surfacing, for example, in the celebration of a 'real Glasgow' beneath the yuppie surface of shopping malls and Garden Festival and City of Culture. As 'real' productive industrial labour (the culturally inscribed 'masculine domain') disappears into consumption (the 'feminine domain'), the myth becomes more desperate; and when masculinity can no longer define itself in 'hard work' it increasingly identifies itself with the 'hard man' for whom anguish, cynicism and violence are the only ways to recover the lost dignity of labour.

Each of these discourses plays out an epic transformation rendered as a loss: a loss of pre-capitalist natural order; a loss of the pre-industrial natural and self-regulating community; and finally a loss of industry itself, and with it a loss of 'natural masculinity'. Each of the discourses also looked back with a specifically masculine yearning, calling on women to give body to the romance of nature, to the desire for a bewitchment which went beyond the prosaic rationality of a domesticated enlightenment, or to the need for confirmation in the uncertainties of post-industrial manhood. It was the consistency of currents such as these running across the discourses, rather than the somewhat too neat categories of 'tartanry', 'kailyard' and 'clydeside' themselves, which gave force to the analysis, avoiding a simple reductiveness, and preventing the response that, 'Actually, no one really takes tartanry seriously anymore'. It was never necessary to take the worst excesses of the discourses seriously to be a part of their discursive world, a world which opened easily on to the past but which had difficulty finding a way into the future. Cairns Craig identified the regressiveness as a kind of freezing of cultural assets which contemporary expression had to unbind:

For the problem that these mythic structures have left to twentieth-century Scottish art is that there are no tools which the artists can inherit from the past which are not tainted, warped, blunted by the uses to which they have been put. The speech of Lowland Scotland, the landscape of the Highlands have become clichés which need to acquire a new historical significance before they can be released into the onward flow of the present from the frozen worlds of their myths of historical irrelevance. And what that historical significance needs, of course, if it is to come into being, is a sense of the nation's particular and individual development, both past and future. (*Scotch Reels*, pp 14-15)

The Big Man directed by David Leland and starring Liam Neeson as the unemployed miner turned bare-knuckle boxer, Danny Scoular. Based on William McIlvaney's novel, the film opened the Edinburgh International Film Festival in 1990 to mixed reviews. With Scots reduced to comic turns or minor roles, *The Big Man* epitomised the hard-man stereotype, the weak film industry base in Scotland and the continuing difficulty of talking about a 'Scottish' feature film.

The analysis and the critique of representations met a number of quite important requirements. It did work as an interpretative tool when applied to popular cinema, and its interpretations were less concerned to castigate representations for their false consciousness and bad faith than to investigate them for their history. It did attempt to trace problems and blockages to the fault-lines in the culture rather than to seek excuses in the vulgarity of a popular commercial cinema. And it was interested, perhaps somewhat academically, in those popular films in which the historical and cultural tensions could be argued to show through, and perhaps undermine, the mythologies in which they were cast: *The Maggie*, for instance, or *The Gorbals Story*, or even (or particularly) *Brigadoon*.

But more than that, 'Scotch Reels', as an event, and as itself a 'discursive position', did attempt to construct a practical critique, albeit from an ultimately theoretical position. Though the analysis has been taken up as a critical instrument for understanding representations of Scotland in popular film and television, the event and the publication were meant to be more than that. They were meant to be an *intervention*. Though the organisers may have had a rather idealized conception of the practicalities of production, we did see ourselves engaging with Scottish filmmakers in a positive, rather than a negative way, and the critique, not just of the culture but of the institutions which administered it (most notably the Scottish Film Council), was meant to open the way towards a progressive future by exposing the obstacles in the past. From the cooler and wearier vantage point of the nineties, it may be hard to imagine our surprise to find that many of the filmmakers did not welcome our engagement or our intervention.

What was wrong?

I should say here that I am replaying 'Scotch Reels' for two quite distinct reasons. The first is quite simply to recover a cultural and historical framework which, taken in quite broad terms, does still provide a base point for the critical analysis of Scottish film and television. The second, in a way quite contrary to the first, is to lay the ghost to rest. While the cultural analysis which 'Scotch Reels' articulated (and which, through the accompanying publication, has become a kind of critical and educational orthodoxy) still seems necessary as a way of seeing representations in a cultural-historical context, it no longer seems adequate as a way of thinking about a

EALING STUDIOS present
A MICHAEL BALCON PRODUCTION
PAUL DOUGLAS in
THE 'MAGGIE'
G.F.D. RELEASE   CERTIFICATE 'U'

The Maggie is a classic Ealing comedy by the director of *Whisky Galore*, Alexander Mackendrick who was born of Scottish parents in the USA. It is an important film for an American Scot, pitting as it does American commerce and rationalism against Scottish sleekitness and relaxed honesty. Here Calvin B Marshall (Paul Douglas) marches in fury away from the Skipper (Alex Mackenzie), the Wee Boy (Tommy Kearins) and the Engineer (Abe Barker).

more extensive Scottish film culture only eight years later. The point of referring back to 'Scotch Reels' is both to re-insert what was valuable about it, and to try to go beyond it: to use its base point as a way of measuring the ground that has been covered since 1982, and to note the shift in the conditions which make a different kind of engagement necessary. To do this it may be useful to enumerate quite briefly some of the inadequacies of both the analysis and the event, without in any sense renouncing the achievements or apologising for the attempt.

The first and most immediate problem was one of tact and timing. 'Scotch Reels' happened three months before Channel Four opened. Many of the filmmakers were already working on projects for the Channel, including at least one film, Charlie Gormley's *Living Apart Together*, which was scheduled for cinema release. For the first time ever, a generation of Scottish filmmakers sensed an opening through which they could enter the mainstream, getting out from under the sponsored film, and showing their work, as Scottish filmmakers and programme producers, to a national UK audience. Guarded optimism about the possibility of independent Scottish filmmaking was in the

18

air. Then suddenly, like buses and taxis, there were intellectuals and academics all over the place when you no longer really needed one – where had they been with their interventions when you had been waiting all these years at a bus stop in the wilderness? More than that, and more materially, the intellectuals, in their radical aspiration, were taking up the cause of the low budget, collectively inspired Workshop Movement, and were arguing for a share of the very limited resources of the newly established Scottish Film Production Fund, intended for film development, to be allocated to the development of a Scottish Workshop sector. So not only the cultural credibility, but also the pittance of indigenous funding, seemed under attack. In this context, it was not surprising that relationships were strained.

Scotch Myths, made in 1980 by Barbara and Murray Grigor. A *cause celebre* of Scottish representations, this Channel 4 film provoked passionate debate. It was congratulated for peeling back the mystifying layers of tartan which swathed Scottish images and was rebuked for being half in love with the kitsch it exposed.

While these relational strains are hardly of historic significance, they do point to some elements which have bearing on subsequent developments in the eighties. In the first place, the 'Scotch Reels' organizers completely underestimated the significance of Channel Four for Scottish filmmaking, not simply its direct significance as a commissioning agency, but its importance in establishing a climate in which independent Scottish (and regional) film production became viable – and therefore fundable. But it still seems important to have opened the question of the workshop sector and its relationship to more established independent producers, a question which was not addressed satisfactorily then, and has still not been properly resolved. 'Scotch Reels' did open lines of communication which began to break down the isolation from each other of filmmaking and cultural criticism and to open the way to a more inclusive concept of a Scottish film culture, one which would include educational and critical work as well as production.

But in terms of theory and critique, the 'Scotch Reels' analysis bore the mark of some of the developments in film theory in the seventies, a period of considerable energy and excitement, but also of some fairly reductive dogma. In hindsight, it is possible to see how that reductiveness gave a hard edge to the initial polemic but, at the same time, limited the scope of the analysis for a more complex representational field. The most damaging single hostage which 'Scotch reels' gave to fortune was the admission that the Bill Douglas *Trilogy* (*My Childhood*, *My Ain Folk*, and *My Way Home*) had not been included because it did not fit the analysis. (The *Trilogy* was discussed in a second event at the Festival the following year.) The analysis, in other words, inherited from structuralism a desire for clean, discernible categories which could be used to organize the heterogeneity of representation. It had little purchase on films which danced to a different discourse. Nor had it thought through divisions within the neat 'discursive positions' – the implications for the homogeneity of kailyard, for instance, of the anti-kailyard discourse of Scottish novelists Hay and Brown and their tortured dissections of deformed sexuality and patriarchal obsession hidden within the small community, a consciously oppositional (though not necessarily progressive) discourse that might have helped make

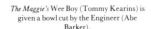

The Maggie's Wee Boy (Tommy Kearins) is given a bowl cut by the Engineer (Abe Barker).

The Gorbals Story. Peter Reilly (Jack Stewart) threatens to beat up Johnnie Martin (Russell Hunter) as Mrs Reilly (Eveline Garratt) intervenes and Nora (Isabel Campbell) looks on. A theatrical hit in 1946 in Scotland for the Glasgow Unity Theatre, *The Gorbals Story* transferred woodenly to the screen and was a critical and commercial flop. It was filmed at Morton Park Studios during an attempt to have Scottish theatre play London's West End.

sense of the *Trilogy*. It is this reductiveness, more than anything else, that makes the analysis inadequate to the more diverse representational context of the nineties.

The analysis also inherited a belief in an almost inalienable affinity between modernist, self-reflexive form and progressive representation; the converse being a suspicion of realism as a compromised, bourgeois form (and the *Trilogy* would have been identified – wrongly, I now think – as realist). The result was a formalistic, and curiously moralistic, strain in the analysis. It lacked a sense of an avant-garde or progressive practice which was determined by conditions and context and history. It also lacked a sense of the historical resonances which the myths still contained, and the quite ambivalent feelings which they could evoke:

20

it was insensitive, that is, to the implications for the experience of nationality identity of 'incorrect' pleasures – the catch in the throat when Bill Travers wins in *Geordie*; the feeling for the land; or the chauvinistic pride in *Tutti Frutti* as something which is ours, and whose important jokes are private to us.

The excitement of 'Scoth Reels' was partly to do with engaging with the local and the immediate, partly to do with film theory 'coming out' as Scottish, and partly, at the simplest level, to do with hearing Scottish accents debating the national culture in a Festival event which over the years had become a summer colony for London theory. Something of that excitement carried into the wider context of media culture, and put the representation of Scotland firmly and quite positively onto the educational and critical agenda.

The Channel Four Effect

If Scottish film and programme production seems more diverse than it did in 1982, and, as a consequence, if the question of representations seems more complex, the explanation is almost suspiciously simple: Channel Four. In 1990, it is still easy to be critical of Channel Four, and it is very easy to be wary of the direction of its development into its second decade; but, looking back over the last eight years, it would be hard to overestimate the extent of the transformation it has brought about in Scottish and British film and programme production. At the most obvious level, it has created the conditions for an expanding independent production sector. This in turn has created not only more, but more diverse films and programmes and representations. Perhaps even more importantly for the development of a film culture, it has allowed the work of the independent sector, and of a whole range of cinematic forms and national cinemas, to be seen. In the national peripheries, in Scotland and its peripheries, it is now possible to see work that ten years ago would not have been seen outside London, the major cities, or the occasional festival. Whatever the affection we may have for cinema, the capacity of television now to create not only representations but audiences for representations, is crucial to the development of a diverse culture: a national or regional culture as much as a film and television culture.

Perhaps most important of all for the future of an indigenous film industry Channel Four, perhaps for the first time in British film history, has caused an infrastructure to be born. More important than the immediate expansion of production, such an infrastructure includes, as well as production companies, the professional associations, the development funding, the training initiatives and legislation, which allow production to develop with some kind of continuity. Or at least, to be more cautious, Channel Four has caused such an infrastructure to begin to be born – as an aspiration, if not as an achieved reality, and in some places in a more developed way than in others. If British film history has been a lumpy narrative of heroic producers

B A Robertson in *Living Apart Together*. A pop singer, Robertson successfully sang his way through the movie. He went on to score *Heavenly Pursuits* for director Charlie Gormley.

21

Bill Travers' performance in *Geordie* was charmingly honest although the film was marred by false sentiment. Norah Gorsen mishandled her accent and performance as Geordie's girl, Jean. *Geordie* was produced by the English comedy team of Sidney Gilliat and Frank Launder who also made the inferior *Bridal Path* with Bill Travers.

staggering from surprised renaissance to familiar despair – from 'The Brits are coming' to 'There they went' – it is exactly because there has never been a stable industrial infrastructure (such as Hollywood provided for the American cinema) or consistent public support (such as cultural ministries encourage, sometimes uncertainly, for some European cinemas) to even out the course of development. Each producer has had to re-invent the wheel for each new legislative and commercial environment. Hence the centrality of producers to British cinema – Dean, Korda, Balcon, Grierson, Puttnam – and the importance for Scotland of a producer like Paddy Higson. Channel Four, by creating the conditions in which independent production could become viable as something more than a cottage industry or an individual obsession, offers the beginnings of a rational mode of production for low- to medium-budget films and programmes. Not yet a fully-fledged Fordist industry like Hollywood, more a kind of guild level, the independent sector nevertheless provides a structure for development. It is stable at least in comparison to anything that has gone before while still retaining creative flexibility (with all the nuances which that term may contain), and its viability as an economic proposition and as a potentially expanding area of employment calls into being support mechanisms of services and facilities. At the very least, perhaps, the question of that support environment begins to be raised as a material question of industrial support rather than as a question for the worthy but less dependable 'encouragement of the arts' – a question, that is, for the Scottish Development Agency or, more excitingly, for a properly-financed and re-organised Scottish Film Council.

There is, of course, an embarrassment in all this. It is that the Channel Four structure, however unruly it may occasionally have seemed, is in fact a continuously visible advertisement for the Thatcherite dream of a return to an economy driven by small businesses: self-reliant, lean, flexible, and, above all, entrepreneurial. Far from making the producer less central, the Channel Four system makes the producer the driving force of the economy, developing projects, seeking out gaps in the market, negotiating contracts, adjusting budgets and staffing levels. Without the fixed plant of the monolithic broadcasting institutions, the independent production companies reduce overheads and create their own service and facilities sector; without fixed staff, they rely on a freelance pool of skills, expanding and contracting as the broadcasting economy rises and falls. Such flexibility is the hallmark of the enterprise culture.

In practice, of course, the model works less smoothly than it does in the dreams of ideology. The commissioning process is frequently wayward, contracts are unduly complex, rights are disputed, lines of communication are uncertain, and, most disturbing of all, entry is less open (it is easier to stay in than to get in) and competition less intense than the dream would have it. But the commissioning system works well enough to be used by a Conservative government as a model for the wider ecology of broadcasting. And so we find the wonderfully paradoxical situation in which Channel Four – the minority Channel for minority interests, the Channel that brought us *The Bandung File*, *Out on Tuesday*, *The Eleventh Hour* and red triangle films, and brought calls from *The Daily Mail* for the hanging of the Chief Executive – becomes an exemplary model for the economic structure of British broadcasting as a whole. Following this model, the Broadcasting Act of 1990 introduces, by legislation for Channels Three, Four and Five and by implication for the BBC, a quota of twenty-five per cent of total broadcasting time to be allocated to independent production.

However suspicious those of us may feel who fear this government even when it is bearing gifts, there can be no doubt that this transforms British film and programme production. The infrastructure is clearly not yet capable of supporting a substantial industry, and there is still immense frustration in funding projects, or in allowing internationally recognized directors like Bill Douglas or Bill Forsyth to make the films they want to make in Scotland. Deep pessimism is just a hair's breadth away from guarded optimism. But, at least in the short run, before success breeds mergers, take-overs and centralisation, the advent of the fourth Channel does seem to have introduced a diversity to British broadcasting and British film and video production which it has never had before, a diversity not only in the forms of representation and in what, and who, can be represented, but also in the forms of production, and in the geographical and social locations from which it can come. While, in Scotland particularly, we still have to argue quite intensely over the limits of that diversity, and the mounting pressures on it, we also have to recognise that, relative to only eight years ago, it does exist.

George MacInnes as the young boy in *Ill Fares the Land* whose last lingering look at the sea personifies the sense of loss of community and the unified self. On a lighter note, the film was nicknamed 'Where Seagulls Dare' because of the difficulty of getting the birds out of shot and 'Ill Fares the Budget' by the industry generally because of rumours of over-spending.

In the early eighties, there is evidence that the Scottish filmmakers themselves were not quite sure how to relate to the new Channel. In 1981, Jeremy Isaacs attended a meeting in Edinburgh of prospective providers of films and programmes, and held out the possibility of a Scottish office which would act as a line of communication for the Scottish producers in their dealings with the commissioning officers in London. The producers rejected the offer, preferring to deal directly with the centre. While some producers now think that may have been a mistake, it is not hard to see why it seemed a good idea at the time. There is a long enough history of ghettoisation to justify suspicion of what looked like a potential core/periphery structure, and the new Channel was after all tied in to a commercial ITV structure which had never been particularly kind to its peripheries. And, in the event, as long as the structure was still settling down and while the Channel was establishing its identity and its practices under the personal authority of Jeremy Isaacs, it probably did the Scottish producers no harm to have direct access to an ear – and a purse – at the centre: 'Uncle Jeremy's backpocket' bailed out more than one production which ran over-budget. Under a tighter managerial structure, however, as Channel Four becomes increasingly bureaucratised, and particularly as it enters a looser and less protective relationship with Channel Three and starts to sell its own advertising, the uncertainty within an increasingly commercial national Channel around the relationship of nation, region and 'national region' remains uncertain. Without necessarily playing the Welsh card, the Scottish producers may have to seek ways of securing and extending their lines of supply and demand. Whatever else may happen, though, even in a seller's market, with BBC, Channels Three and Five also bidding for independent product, it still seems desirable to have a special relationship with the only Channel which is enjoined by act of parliament to be 'innovative and experimental' and to cater for minority audiences.

It was also in the early eighties that the Independent Filmmakers Association (IFA), which mainly from a London base had developed an oppositional and political film practice in the seventies, were lobbying and canvassing very hard, and, in the event, very successfully, to secure access to the Channel. Out of that lobbying came a remarkable informal coalition between the ACTT (the main union in broadcasting and film production), the British Film Institute, the IFA and Channel Four which resulted in a Workshop Declaration (and subsequently an agreement) giving union recognition to limited number of franchised workshops. Under the terms of the agreement, the workshops were allowed a lower than minimum level of staffing and salary in recognition of the collective nature of their organisation. As a condition of the agreement, they were to be regionally based. They would receive initial capital funding from Channel Four and could expect subsequent revenue funding in the form of commissions, and they would produce broadcast material, mainly for *The Eleventh Hour*, rooted in the region in which the Workshop was based. The effect was to create a Workshop movement with a specific commitment to develop film production and film culture in the regions, and, subsequently, in ethnic communities.

There is a separate history to be written about the Workshop Movement. The only point I want to make here is that Scotland was not represented in the activity which established the workshops, and the support within Scotland has never allowed the workshop movement to develop the level of activity which has characterised many of the English workshops. When one looks at Birmingham, and the educational and cultural work which the Birmingham Film and Video Workshop has done in the city; or at Sheffield, where the women's film cooperative is a key component in the city's bid for Channel Five; or, most of all, at Tyneside where the North-East Media Training Centre, inspired and staffed by local Workshops, provides a training model for the rest of the country, one begins to recognize that what was lost in the early eighties in Scotland was something more than the opportunity for some low-budget, avant-garde political films to be shown on television late on Monday nights. Where it has flourished, the Workshop Movement has been an important, innovative and committed component within the infrastructure and has given the lie to the early snobbery of 'real' independent producers.

So how does this expanded production base materialise in films and programmes and what are its implications for a cultural analysis of the representations of Scotland?

Seen from a distance, the continuities in representation are apparent. In global terms, Scottish film is still a periphery on the edge of a periphery and, in national terms, the core of production funding is still based in the south. In consequence, there is still an expectation of what a 'Scottish film' can be about and a calculation of which images are most readily marketable. Scotland is still more readily imagined, and the imaginings are more easily sold, along the predictable lines of the scenery, the small community, and the post-industrial male angst. Most debilitating of all, loss still pervades Scottish feature films, still appearing as the characteristic mark of really serious Scottishness: the loss of the natural community in *Ill Fares the Land* or *Venus Peter*, of innocence in *Another Time, Another Place*, of manhood in *Living Apart Together*, of the family in *Silent Scream*. The backward look, epitomized by the final shot of *Ill Fares the Land* of the boy's last longing look out of the back window of the taxi which is carrying him away from the natural but impossible community into the modern world, still seems a characteristic trope of 'serious' Scottish film narrative. It hardly needs saying that it is almost invariably the menfolk who bear the responsibility for this look.

At the same time, while such a satellite view may be necessary to establish the climate, it no longer seems adequate in describing how it feels on the ground. In its generality, it focuses the repetitions and misses the differences and the small surprises. It misses, for example, a certain heightened self-consciousness of the Scottish imaginary which

25

appears as an ironic distance from the familiar discourses: Charlie Gormley's *Heavenly Pursuits*, for example, as a replay of the feyness of Barrie's kailyard in the urban enlightenment of contemporary Glasgow; or Bill Forsyth's *Comfort and Joy* as a 'mild revolution' (the phrase is Michael Balcon's in the context of Ealing comedy) in the representation of urban violence. The knowingness of this irony can be fairly innocuous, but it also extends to *Tutti Frutti*, where, ticking away within the comedy, lies an ironic savagery which lays waste to whole areas of monstrous Scottishness.

The generality of the cultural overview, in its almost exclusive concern with the narrative feature film, also misses the particularity of the small surprises. More characteristic of television than of cinema, I am thinking here of a documentary like Rosie Gibson's *The Work They Say is Mine*, about women's work in Shetland, or like Timothy Neat's *Tree of Liberty* about Serge Hovey's musicological and creative work on Burns' songs, a documentary which treated Burns as something more than a bit of lad born in Kyle, and used Scottish landscape as something more than a romantic backdrop – transmitted on Burns' Night, the documentary injected a new discourse into an old and very tired broadcasting tradition, in the same way that Doug Eadie's and Mike Alexander's *Aly Meets the Cajuns* finally managed to find something to celebrate in Hogmanay television. For television also, it is worth signalling *Halfway to Paradise*, a series by Big Star in a Wee Picture which not only managed to make sense of youth programming, but also quite successfully straddled the gap between the local and the regional: on the one hand, in its accents and style, it seemed intensely particular to the west of Scotland; on the other, in its cultural eclecticism, it wore its Scottishness lightly and seemed only to happen to be from Glasgow.

This is not intended as a personal credit list of the best in Scottish film and television. All I am trying to point to are some of the possibilities which seem to come out of an expanded and more diversified production sector. While I would by no means argue that Scotland, in less than a decade of Channel Four, has miraculously surfaced from the sedimentation of centuries of tradition, I do want to argue that the accumulated small surprises of a diversified film culture begin to produce the feeling of something moving both within the traditions, and around them. Much of this movement, it seems to me, has to do with a new sense of locality and particularity. To return again to *Tutti Frutti* – which, with all the dangers attached, will have to serve as the touchstone for the possibilities of a new Scottish visual culture until something better comes along – it may be as important to recall the catch of recognition of verbal nuance, of local style, and, simply, of location, as it is to celebrate its withering irony. Irony on its own, after all, always risks reviving the tired old representations it is negating; it was the complexity of the recognitions which *Tutti Frutti* offered which seemed to take identities by surprise, opening them up to their uncertainties and uncomfortable contradictions rather than

A sea-death as the women carry the body of their man back from the water. In depictions such as *Ill Fares the Land*, it is the women's role to suffer and understand. As Neil Gunn said of their part in traditional communities, they are the black knots that bind history together.

sliding the easy images back in to their familiar routines.

This complex recognition, local and particular, is the possibility offered by a national culture or a national cinema which is neither parochial in its concerns, nor monolithic in the identities it projects. It seems to me that, at the beginning of the nineties, there are on offer in Scottish cinema and television more complex ways of 'being Scottish' than there were at the beginnings of the eighties. There are, of course, still some pretty banal and/or oppressive ways of 'being Scottish' too, but one of the effects of the relative proliferation of representations is to take the edge off the demand that each representation meet the requirements of 'correct Scottishness'. While, negatively, this may present a more difficult target to cultural criticism, positively, it opens production to the possibility of greater diversity and experiment, and gives it the right to be modestly successful, successful in parts, or even to die in the attempt at something interestingly new.

Scottish rock band Del Amitri in Big Star in a Wee Picture's *Halfway to Paradise*. Taking its name from its proximity to Celtic's football ground, *Halfway to Paradise* is a mixture of music, comedy and popular culture. It prides itself on being 'a kick up the arse for southern smugness'.

This means giving up the prescriptive certainties of a reductive political culture, and demands more complex ways of thinking about Scottish cinema and television, and about representations. The analysis of mythologies of national identity seems caught up in a self-validating cycle. Clearly, there is still a need for the negative critique of the routine representations of Scottishness, and, more simply, for straightforward anger at the continuing romance with loss and lost pasts. But as representations proliferate and diversify the focus seems to shift away from the content and structure of the representations towards the conditions in which they exist, and the pressures and limits which determine how they are produced and how they circulate.

Clearly all of the above cannot be laid directly at the door of Channel Four. By no means all the films made in Scotland over the last decade, nor even all of the most innovative programmes, were made for Channel Four. There is in fact a substantial argument which says that Channel Four has not done particularly well by Scotland, and has taken more revenue and more ratings out of Scotland than it has put productions back in. All I am suggesting is that it was Channel Four which first created the conditions in which independent production could develop a relatively stable production base, and become viable enough to attract other forms of support and compete in other markets. It was also Channel Four which made accessible to a national audience a wider range of visual and narrative forms and images and discourses and representations than had ever been seen before on British television. In those senses, Channel Four has to be given credit for extending the horizons of both the possible and the expected.

Widening the Aperture

The questions of selective representation and limited diversity need a wider frame of reference than they have usually had in Scottish film culture; that representation is a question of structures as well as of the imagination, and that Scottish film culture refers to more than

Tutti Frutti was a enormous success in Scotland, less so in England. The ways it examined and played with stereotypes, gender relationships and popular culture gave Scots a sense of the high standards which were possible in local production. The still shows the Majestics in all their glory: Vincent Diver (Maurice Roeves), Fud O'Donnel (Jake D'Arcy), Dennis Sproul (Ron Donachie), Bomba MacAteer (Stuart McGugan), Suzi Kettles (Emma Thompson) and Danny McGlone (Robbie Coltrane).

the production of Scottish films.

To take the last point first. There is a kind of fetishisation of production in many professional discussions of Scottish film culture which seems to assume without question an identity between film culture and film production: a revival in the former can only be achieved by a renaissance in the latter, and if you don't have the latter you can't have the former. The paradox is that when one listens to many of the established Scottish filmmakers talking you hear the authentic tones of a fascination with cinema (hence the hierarchical order to the fetishism of production: real production means shooting celluloid) and a saturation in film culture which was gained in various misspent youths in Saturday cinemas when production was still a cottage industry in Scotland. While it would probably be self-defeating to argue that there could be a national film culture without film production, it seems quite reasonable to argue that without a coherent system of exhibition, and without forms of critical and educational engagement production remains production and doesn't easily constitute a culture.

At a quite material level, what is true of Britain is also true of Scotland: the ups and downs of renaissance and despair in film production have taken place against a background of steady decline in cinema attendance since 1946. While this may have been arrested by the proliferation of screens and the dawning of the multiplex in the past few years, it seems unrealistic to believe that it will ever be reversed. And from the point of view of a Scottish cinema, while the multiplexes may have successfully drawn new audiences into the cinema, they seem to have drawn them in to see the same ten box-office movies in more seductive surroundings. The collapse of the commercial art cinema almost everywhere outside London has meant that for many of the regional film theatres the remit to promote film culture means keeping up with the latest releases which are not picked up by the commercial cinema. Only in the few cinemas where there is more than one screen (in Scotland, Edinburgh Filmhouse and Glasgow Film Theatre) is it possible to engage in any critical and historical way with the diverse practices of cinema, and it is still rare to find that engagement with Scottish cinema. Scottish films are not 'box office' in a culture which is, in any case, increasingly turning away from cinema, or in which, increasingly, cinema is simply not geographically available. It's in this context that the fascination with the glamour of production seems limiting. If Scottish film culture is to have any base at all in the cinema – which may already be a utopian fantasy – cultural institutions like the Scottish Film Council and the Film Theatres will need a more coherent and continuous policy of support with regard to the sensible exhibition and distribution of Scottish films in the same way that there is a policy with regard to Scottish film production.

This is to say that audiences do not simply exist, they are created. If one way of creating audiences is by exhibition policy, another is by critical engagement – witness the international success of French

New Wave or Italian Neorealism. But if the Scottish Regional Film Theatres have not yet found a way of creating audiences for Scottish films, Scottish film criticism has not been of much help either. A brief flurry of interest in the cultural journal *Cencrastus* following 'Scotch Reels' in the early eighties could not be sustained, and there is now nowhere that Scottish films can be discussed or that the issues confronting Scottish cinema can be debated with any continuity.

In this context there may be something a little chilling about the appearance of film and media in the Scottish Higher English exams in a section which includes specific reference to Scottish film. Many people fought quite hard for this kind of recognition, but for those of us who went through the Scottish secondary school system there must be a slight chill of ambivalence: if Scottish film has reached the point of appearing in the Highers then it must really have given up any pretensions to popularity or pleasure. In a depressingly familiar pattern, at the point at which cinema ceases to be a mass entertainment it becomes available as an educational study. In fact, however, education is the cultural sphere in which the idea of a Scottish film culture seems most credible. In both secondary and higher education there is a quite substantial engagement with film and media studies, and in secondary education particularly there is a developed concern with representations of Scotland. It is worth making the point that secondary education is the area where a coherent policy on the part of the cultural institutions – the Scottish Film Council, with support from the Scottish Education Department – successfully linked up with the commitment of individual teachers and the teachers' organization, AMES (Association for Media Education in Scotland) to produce real initiatives which make the Scottish secondary sector probably the most advanced in Europe in terms of media education.

I am sketching in this context because it is so frequently missing in discussions of Scottish cinema or Scottish film where the overwhelming tendency is to section each area of activity into separate compartments from which each pursues its own interests blissfully unaware of what is happening in the other. There is a sense, for instance, that film or media education has nothing to do with 'the film industry', one of the more grotesque results of which has been the all too predictable separation of education from questions of training. And there is a remarkable lack of interest by film-makers in fighting for appropriate forms of cinema exhibition for their work. While it would be naive to think that everyone should join hands together and form a culture by committee, it does seem important to establish that representations happen in a context, and that in Scotland that context is an area of quite uneven development. In a small country, it does seem possible to conceive of a film culture which is more than simply part of the rhetoric of academic discourse, a culture which has an institutional rather than simply an imaginary structure, and which is defined by something more than the current turn over of productions.

But even assuming that culture is quite a good thing, and a film culture is as good as any other, do we need a Scottish one? And what do we mean by 'Scottish'? This, finally, gets me back to the double sense of the term 'representation'. The argument for a Scottish cinema is the same as the argument for a cinema of diversity and of a multiplicity of representations which disperse monolithic, received identities. It is not, by its nature, a nationalistic argument, anticipating, in a sense, the break-up of the imaginary Scotland into its actual, experienced complexity of geography, class, race, sexuality, gender, rather than simply seeking to replace an old, obsolete imaginary identity with a new and positive one. While it assumes that it is as easy or as difficult to make films about individual feelings or social existence in Scottish accents or in Gaelic as it is to make them in English or American accents or in French, it is emphatically not an argument for a bland international style. This is the importance of the local and the particular – local contexts, particular histories – in which questions of accent, language and landscape take on significance as the signs of difference. In a period when the market is, at one and the same time, both increasingly international and increasingly centralised, difference seems like an increasingly important cultural commodity.

In one sense, then, the question of cultural representations in film is one of cultivating difference. But in that other sense of representation, in the sense of representative participation, there is a problem in representing real difference if the participants always remain the same. This returns representation to very material industrial and structural questions of access, training and funding, questions which can be quite uncomfortable in their immediacy. While it is relatively easy to get well-intentioned agreement that women or ethnic minorities should be properly represented in films, how do you get agreement on how they should be properly represented in the film or television industries? Given the significance of the workshops for the development of film culture, in its broadest sense, in the English regions and in Wales, how, at this stage, do you give them proper support in Scotland? What is the relationship of central belt independent producers to Gaelic production now that it has become economically attractive? What is the relationship to Europe? Who funds training and who has access to it? These are difficult and immediate questions of participation and diversity, yet it is hard to see where new and diverse representations are to come from if they are not to come from new and diverse participants.

The new questions for representing Scotland in the nineties are questions born of a measure of success and a recognition of potential. They are not simply critical and theoretical questions of the new forms and new discourses, though these remain important, but are also material and practical questions of the structures from which new forms and discourses will emerge, and of the ways in which they will find new audiences. Perhaps the real interest of the current moment for Scottish film culture is that it is increasingly difficult to ask one set of questions without also asking all the others.

30

Flickering Light: Some Scottish Silent Films

David Hutchison

cotland is not noted for its cinematic achievements. But it is not
the intention of this essay to argue that the absence of recognition is
a major injustice which needs to be rectified, particularly with reference
to the silent period. Although the Scots took to 'the pictures' with great
enthusiasm, there has never been in Scotland, until very recently,
anything which could possibly be described as a film *industry*, and
even now the industry which we have, dependent as it is on television
commissions and the vagaries of investment decisions made largely
elsewhere, ekes out a precarious existence. The situation of the Scottish
film industry might be compared to that of the Scottish theatre: both
have had to struggle in unfavourable circumstances, and both, however
buoyed up they might be by this or that temporary success at home
and/or abroad, face uncertain futures. Although it should be added that
there is one clear distinction between cinema and theatre in Scotland:
the mass enthusiasm for cinema has never been parallelled by a similar
popular commitment to the theatre.

The Lumiere brothers gave their famous first public performance in
Paris in December 1895, and in February 1896 they brought their show
to London. Not long after that their work was being seen in Glasgow
as Janet McBain shows in her 1985 book *Pictures Past*. English and
Scottish entrepreneurs did not waste time in exploiting the potential
of the new vehicle for mass entertainment and short programmes
of films were soon being given in halls throughout both countries.
Sometimes film was inserted into music hall performances, in a vain
attempt by that most solidly established form of working class culture
to reach an accommodation with its new rival. But it was not long
before music halls were being converted into cinemas – fifty or so
years later many of these same auditoria were to be transformed into
bingo halls, as television displaced cinema as the pre-eminent medium
of mass entertainment. Not all early cinemas were as well suited to
the purpose as converted music halls, and many were small, rickety,
unpleasant and even dangerous places, but by the end of the First
World War the age of the 'dream palace' was dawning, as Odeons,
La Scalas and Alhambras – or even less grandiose Picture Houses –

The Harp King 1919 (Ace Film Producing
Co.) Ace Films proudly announced the
opening of their new studio premises in
Rouken Glen park on the southern fringes
of Glasgow in October 1919. Production of
a five-reel Scottish romance had already
started. *The Harp King* was released in
December that year having enjoyed record
attendance at the Scottish Trade Show in
the *Cinema House*, Renfield Street; one of
only a handful of Scottish made features. 'It
exceeded all expectations' trumpeted *The
Scottish Cinema*, despite 'a slight fog that
filled the hall.' Sadly the studios were not to
survive long into the twenties with
bankruptcy cutting short ambitious plans
for a cinema acting college and a vigorous
programme of features.

David Watt as Leo Grant, the 'harp king', tackles villain Stephen Graham played by J C Baker. No known copies of *The Harp King* have survived as a testament to a still-born Scottish feature film industry.

sprang up throughout the land. The expansion of cinema exhibition in Scotland, where it is generally reckoned going to the pictures was more popular than anywhere else in Britain, was spectacular. By 1920 there were 557 cinemas in the country, by 1930, 634. Of these, 127 were in Glasgow, 39 in Edinburgh, 27 in Dundee and 15 in Aberdeen.

The apparent paradox of an enthusiasm for cinema being unaccompanied by the development of a cinematic industry is not difficult to explain. The key is the word 'industry'. At its peak the Hollywood industry was one of the largest employers in the USA, giving work to not only thousands of actors, writers and other creative personnel, but also to renters, exhibitors, box office staff and popcorn sellers. By 1920 this industry was well on the way to establishing itself as the dominant source of film entertainment for the world. Other countries, particularly in continental Europe, were able to fight back to some degree and often with the help of protectionist policies, develop their own film industries, but it was not easy. The experience of the British film industry is a case in point. Even if allowance is made for the difficulties the British (or English) have had with cinema – 'I do not think the British are temperamentally equipped to make the best use of the movie camera', said Satyajit Ray in his book *Our Films, Their Films* – the problems the industry faced in dealing with the cultural and economic power of Hollywood have never been satisfactorily overcome. How much more difficult it would have been for a small country like Scotland, even if it had had a government of its own committed to the development of indigenous culture, to compete with America.

But Scotland *was* represented on the screen in both fiction and actuality. However, virtually all of the fictions were created elsewhere, some in England and rather more in America. The discourses of 'tartanry' and 'the kailyard' are discussed elsewhere in this book, discourses in which Scotland is talked about as if it were either a country in which a wild and romantic landscape was peopled by kilted Celts, given to poetic musings, hot blooded outbursts and the frequent imbibing of whisky, or one whose couthy inhabitants lived in small inward looking towns, untouched by the forces which have shaped the modern world. These discourses have contaminated Scottish culture, and although their impact is much diluted today, early fictional representations of Scotland on the screen show their baleful influence. *Auld Robin Gray*, for example, made by Vitagraph in America in 1910, uses the poem of that name to tell a sentimental little story about a young girl forced to marry an old man for economic reasons. Fortunately he is a decent old chap and the film ends reasonably happily. It is pure kailyard. In Vitagraph's 1911 production of *Auld Lang Syne* elements of kailyard and tartanry are mixed in an eternal triangle narrative, at the end of which all three characters are reconciled. Both films use Scots subtitles in an idiom which would have been familiar to readers of the Scottish novelist S R Crockett in Britain and the USA.

The Romantic image of Scotland is well to the fore in the British production by Will Kellino in 1923 of *Young Lochinvar*, although technically this tale of passion is set in the Borders of Sir Walter Scott's imagining and not the Highlands, a distinction that is unlikely to have troubled its audiences. The film is enlivened by some comedy from Lochinvar's servant.

The kailyard view surfaces again in Paramount's 1921 adaptation of Barrie's *The Little Minister*. The film – one of several versions from Hollywood – was shot in what appears to be a very solid reconstruction

Auld Robin Gray 1910 (Vitagraph). Florence Turner as a young girl forced into marriage with older man for financial reasons.

Young Lochinvar 1923 (Stoll Films). Owen Nares as the hero resplendent in tartan trews, saves his beloved Helen (Gladys Jennings) from being forced to marry another.

of an Angus village, and the gossiping 'bodies' of the village are vividly realised by the actors who play them. But the connection between the events of the film and life in nineteenth-century Scotland is no stronger than the connection between Barrie's original novel and play and the real nature of industrial conflict.

One curiosity which is to be found in the National Film Archive, where copies of the titles discussed above are stored, is a very short 1905 film made in Britain by the Alpha Trading Company, and directed by Arthur Cooper, *McNab's Visit to London*. In it a Highlander visits his cousin in London, wrecks her drawing room by playing golf in it, loses his kilt, descends via the chimney to the maid's quarters, causes the poor girl to faint in horror, and is then chased from the house. The Scottish hooligan was obviously a metropolitan concern even at the beginning of the century.

All of this work emanated from outside of Scotland. If we search in the Scottish Film Archive, we will not find a lot of indigenous fiction. The little which exists is not very impressive. *Mairi, Romance of a Highland Maiden*, for example, was shot by an Inverness photographer, Andrew Paterson in 1912. The film catches well the beaches and cliffs of North Kessock where the film was made, but its story of smuggling and romance is insubstantial.

If fiction about Scotland emanated almost entirely from abroad, a large quantity of actuality film was made in the country itself. Actuality is much cheaper than fiction, since lavish sets do not have to be constructed, nor do actors have to be paid, so it is not surprising that there is a lot of Scottish material extant. Furthermore, the documentary movement in Britain and elsewhere had a number of Scots in prominent positions, most notably John Grierson, who worked with the Empire Marketing Board and GPO film units in the UK and then, having been invited to Canada by that country's federal government, was in 1939 given the job of setting up and running the National Film Board. And indeed it can be argued that the Presbyterian tradition encourages a didacticism which is much more appropriate in documentary than in fiction. Grierson's work has been thoroughly discussed elsewhere, particularly in Forsyth Hardy's *John Grierson – a Documentary Biography*, and will not therefore be considered here. It is worth stressing, however, that Grierson and others like him, had to leave Scotland in order to pursue their careers. Documentary in Scotland did not develop before the first Films of Scotland period, to the extent that it did elsewhere, but nonetheless there is a lot of fascinating material in the archives, whose interest stems as much, if not more, from the insights it offers into social circumstances as from its cinematic qualities. There is very little in the way of 'the creative treatment of actuality', but there is much which offers a record, admittedly of a selective kind, of Scottish life in the early part of the twentieth century.

A fair amount of this film has been widely seen in recent years through such television programmes as *Attic Archives* (BBC Scotland) and *The Way It Was* (Grampian). Both these programmes have drawn on the resources of the Scottish Film Archive, which since 1976, under the umbrella of the Scottish Film Council, has been amassing a collection of non-fiction film from all over the country (as well as some fiction film and television material). It is not surprising this collection has been utilised by television companies to create programmes which satisfy genuine curiosity about the past and also, it has to be said, indulge their audiences' nostalgia for days that are long gone. It is one of the curious side effects of television's constant use of actuality film from the past that almost unconsciously, we find ourselves thinking that the past depicted on film actually happened in black and white, because it is through black and white film – and photographs – that we have come to know it. This effect – which often works to distance, sometimes to render dull – is only one of the barriers between the modern audience and the actuality which is represented in the film.

Mairi – the Romance of a Highland Maiden 1912. One of only a handful of indigenously produced Scottish feature films in the silent era. Written, produced and shot by local photographer Andrew Paterson it used the scenery of the Moray Firth as a backdrop to a tale of romance and smuggling. It was premiered at the *Central Hall Picture House*, Inverness 20th May, 1912 and was to be Paterson's only venture into feature film.

The film record is not one which would be regarded as comprehensive by social historians. Too many of the films were made for celebratory purposes – pageants, gala days, the nature of an industrial process – for that, but even in the most tedious film of parades and welcomes to visiting dignitaries, there are sudden glimpses of everyday life, which contrast sharply with the main body of the film. For example, in a 1916 film which shows Sir Douglas Haig, the British commander in the First World War, at a graduation at St Andrews, after shots of the ceremony and the local fire brigade, we cut to shots of rather poor looking fisher folk, only to cut back to the future King George the Sixth teeing off on the Royal and Ancient.

Of course the people who made these films did not do so with the kind of serious purpose which was later to characterise the documentary movement. They were, for the most part amateurs or, at best, semi-professionals. Their principal aim was to record important events and show the resultant films, usually to local audiences. Often cinema proprietors made or commissioned such films for the simple purpose of attracting audiences to their halls. In a few instances major proprietors, such as Green's of Glasgow, put this kind of activity on a more systematic basis – Green's Film Service produced local topicals before the First World War, and during the war began issuing their Scottish Moving Picture news, which continued into the twenties, but it was never an operation to be compared with those of the London-based cinema news companies like Pathe and British Movietone. A couple of professional companies which relied for their livelihoods mainly on sponsored films did, however, manage to establish themselves north of the border, Scottish Films, which was started in Glasgow in 1928 by Malcolm Irvine, and Campbell Harper Films, established by the gentleman of that name and his son in 1930. In the thirties Scottish Films produced *Things That Happen*, a compilation of topical material reminiscent of Rank's post-war *Look At Life*.

McNab's Visit to London 1905 (Alpha Films). Our other national game? Arthur Cooper's McNab relentlessly pursues a lost golf ball in his English cousin's living room.

'Important' occasions figure largely in the film which has survived. So, we can watch a royal visit to Aberdeen in 1906 to celebrate the quatercentenary of the university – and see ladies in their finery

Great Western Road 1914. The ubiquitous promenade after church in the fashionable West End on an autumn Sunday. Local topical made by James Hart, projectionist and later manager of Glasgow's *Grosvenor Cinema.*

36

picking their way delicately across the street and trying to dodge the piles of dung deposited by the horses which have just been on parade, a reminder of an older form of urban pollution. We can participate vicariously in innumerable gala days and common riding ceremonies. But we can also reflect on the social circumstances which necessitated the kind of philanthropy recorded in the Paddy Black Memorial Mission District Trip of 1922. Two and a half thousand poor children from Kingston have a day out in Bellahouston Park in Glasgow as a result of the efforts initiated by Superintendent Black. A 1928 film, *Sadness and Gladness*, is on a similar topic. It was made for the Children's Holiday Camp Fund, and unlike most archive material has an element of dramatisation in its account of the happiness poor children dream of – and if they are lucky, attain – at one of the Fund's seaside camps.

There are films recording Glasgwegians on church parade in Great Western Road before and after the First World War, and film of citizens of that city paddling in the Clyde at Dunoon in 1910. On a more poignant note, there is a film shot in Hawick in 1914 in which troops destined for the front grin at the camera and indulge in a little horseplay for its benefit. By way of contrast in *Scottish Women's Hospitals* there are shots of field hospitals in France and Salonika. This film was made for the National Union of Women's Suffrage Societies in 1917, presumably as part of its campaign for the extension of the franchise. It is rather different from many other early films in that, like *Sadness and Gladness*, it was produced for a specific propaganda purpose, rather than as a record of events. It would be interesting to know how it was used, where it was shown and what impact it had on its audiences.

Labour history is not as well represented in what has come down to us as might be wished, and, as indicated earlier, recording the living conditions of working class people tends to be incidental to the recording of public events. But there is some film in this area. For example a cinema in Dundee in 1911 made a film of a carters' strike in the city which shows a large crowd of pickets 'persuading' blacklegs to join the strike. A film shot the following year by John Noble, the proprietor of the Oxford Picture House in the city, offers a glimpse of the Cox Brothers' Camperdown jute works, with Lumiere-like scenes of hundreds of workers leaving the factory as a train shunts its wagons on a bridge behind them.

Yet another Dundee film was commissioned by D C Thompson in 1911 to be shown locally. It lays before its audience the production process which gives rise to the *Courier* newspaper, and ends with a shot of one of its delivery boys, aged about thirteen, puffing contentedly on a cigarette as he peruses the paper.

Several industrial concerns used film in this promotional fashion. The Borders firm of Peter Scott had a film company, probably Pathe, make *From Wool to Wearer* in 1913, specifically to be used at the Ghent Exhibition that year. The film begins with shots of sheep in Australia, from whose wool the firm's Pesco underwear was made, and then shows the production process through to the dispatch of orders and the (obligatory) workers' exit from the factory. The film ends with a croquet on the lawn fashion parade, in which the ladies model, not underwear, but knitted coats. There is an unwitting contrast between the Edwardian elegance of this scene and the hard toil depicted in the factory scenes.

The Scottish Co-operative Wholesale Society was – and remains even in its revamped modern form – a major force in the retail trade. In 1927 it commissioned *How Bluebell Margarine is Made* which appears to have been aimed at audiences in Co-op halls, and designed to emphasise the purity and modernity of its production process. A didactic tone is also evident in *The Scottish Shale Industry* produced in 1930 for the Scottish Oil Agency. The viewer is taken through the various stages of the production process and then shown for approbation the housing

Dundee Courier – the Making of a Great Daily Newspaper 1911. Final scene from an ambitious promotional film made by a Gaumont News 'stringer' for publishing house D C Thomson. The youthful newsvendor enjoys an illicit puff whilst the train carries him and his bundle of *Couriers* across the Tay.

Greens changed the title of their *Moving Picture News* from *Scottish* to *British* as they entered the twenties and opened a London office. Sadly this attempt to move into the heartland of British film-making failed to secure the future of the newsreel which was to fold a few years later. It is for their activities in film exhibition that they are now best remembered.

and recreational facilities available to the workers.

Away from the urban areas of the country, the islands of Scotland attracted a fair amount of attention. As early as 1908 Oliver Pike, the wildlife cinematographer, made a short film on St Kilda, with shots of fishing and bird snaring, and then in 1930 John Ritchie, an amateur ornithologist from Paisley, made a film of the preparations for the evacuation of the island – there are, for example, shots of sheep being loaded. The film was kept secret until 1979, as no visual record of the evacuation was supposed to have been made at the time. Watching the film sixty years later, the viewer is struck by the frightened way in which several women react to Ritchie's camera – they put up their hands and flee in the opposite direction. Whether it was the sense of violation which filming can produce in people who are not used to it, or the stress of the coming evacuation which caused the reaction is not clear.

A more anthropological kind of film was made in the thirties by Jenny Gilbertson, some of whose work was bought by John Grierson when he was with the GPO Film Unit. *Scenes From a Shetland Croft Life* and *Da Makkin o' a Keshie* (both 1932) depict peat cutting, and a crofter weaving a basket to carry the peat, respectively. Neither has any real cinematic distinction, which is probably generally true of films of this period.

The obvious exception to this generalisation is work by Norman McLaren, who was later to pursue a distinguished career, mainly in animated films, under the aegis of the National Film Board in Canada. *Seven Till Five* was made by McLaren in 1933 when he was at Glasgow School of Art, and depicts a day in the life of the college. There are some

A Glimpse of the Camperdown Works 1912. Re-released twenty years later this local topical was to be screened to an audience captivated by the experience of seeing themselves, friends and family on screen at Jack Noble's *Oxford Picture House*. Resplendent in Sunday best hat Noble's wife positioned herself in the vanguard of the mill workers as they poured out of the gates to be captured on film by her husband and his colleague.

fast cutting, and unusual camera angles and close ups, which indicate that a creative mind is at work. A more substantial film is *Hell Unltd* which McLaren made with Helen Biggar in 1936. This was produced for the Glasgow Kino group, an organisation concerned with exhibiting and making films of interest to the working class. Douglas Allen's article in *Scotch Reels* deals in some detail with the hidden working class film tradition. *Hell Unltd* is an anti-war film which unashamedly uses stills, scenes with actors, animation and slogans to ram its message home. There are several striking images in the film including one where the head of an arms manufacturer is metamorphosed into a grenade. Question might be raised about the politics of the film – made at a time when the intentions of Nazi Germany were already clear – but not about the feel for cinematic technique of its creators.

For McLaren to bring his talent to fruition he had to leave his own country, as had other would-be film makers. There is little to be gained by speculating as to how a film industry might have been fostered in the early part of this century in Scotland. It did not happen, and it is

Hell Unltd 1936. Using a mixture of live action, diagrams and animation Norman McLaren and Helen Biggar's powerful anti-war propaganda film was instrumental in raising money for refugees from the Spanish Civil War.

39

The cutting room at Scottish Films India Street studios, Glasgow, scene of great excitement on the day Malcolm Irvine and cameraman Graham Thomson arrived fresh from Loch Ness with footage of the monster. Developing, printing and editing were all done on the premises and the third issue of their monthly cine magazine *Things That Happen* (1936) revealed all to an eager public.

highly unlikely that it could have happened. The film which has been discussed in this essay which was made in Scotland holds all kinds of interest but it does not represent the beginnings of a Scottish cinematic tradition. Perhaps such a foundation is now in the process of being laid down, but it certainly cannot be discerned in the holdings of the Scottish Film Archive.

I must record my gratitude to Janet McBain and her staff at the Scottish Film Archive for their untiring assistance in the preparation of this essay.

Screening the Heyday: Scottish cinema in the 1930s

Adrienne Clare Scullion

At the beginning of this century, in Scotland as elsewhere, cinemas quickly became a revolutionary force in entertainment and in popular culture. Many more people went more often to the cinema than had ever gone to the music hall or theatre – women and children would often go independently to the cinema in way that had been socially unacceptable in relation to theatres. However, it was really after the First World War that cinema became *the* entertainment of the people – in spite of, or because of, the fact that by the end of the war American films dominated the market place.

The inter-war period was one of intense media activity in Scotland. Newspapers, magazines and journals debated issues of socialism, fascism, nationalism, unemployment, public health, housing as well as having an involvement with critical and literary developments. The 'Scottish Literary Renaissance' sprang into life, only to fail within the space of a few years. During that time, however, it did produce an unprecedented number of artists and texts able to command respect and interest on an international level. Theatre began to establish itself more securely as part of the cultural scene – in particular developments amongst amateur groups encouraged participation in production and also engendered, if not the habit, then at least the experience of visits to the theatre.

Radio broadcasting began in Scotland on 26 March 1923 and by the early years of the next decade the BBC was reaching more than forty per cent of Scottish homes in an unprecedented manner. Radio at that time had unique powers for the dissemination of news, comment, music and entertainments. Like no medium before, radio could unite the nation. News events could be reported across the country instantaneously, listeners could hear a host of musical performances as well as a cross section of drama and fiction readings; at a different, but no less revolutionary level, everyone everywhere knew the exact time. However, radio was fundamentally a domestic medium. The real advantage cinema still had was that of escapism. One had to leave the home in order to see a film. Not only was this in itself attractive to those living through the worst of the Depression, but the world which

The manager surveys the queue for the regular children's Mickey Mouse club at the *New Tivoli*, Edinburgh, 1936. The Saturday matinee was to become a regular feature of adolescent life for several generations.

they entered was really *different*, more than the fantastic one of the film narrative itself but the stories were shown within a *Picture Palace*.

For a shilling or less, ordinary people could enter a richly decorated milieu that had little or nothing in common with their own domestic environment. It was full of ushers and attendants each dressed in uniforms and often supervised to military levels of precision. It was a world full of indulgent distractions – marbled foyers filled with plants, plush carpeted walkways and staircases leading to grand auditoria. Even if the local cinema was on a more modest level, it was still a place of escape, of warmth, a place to meet friends, take children and even the ideal place for courting in the days of overcrowded living conditions. The screening of newsreels, shorts and feature films on top of all this was a treat that few were able to resist.

Within this busy scene of cultural activity and financial hardship the cinema as economic phenomenon was flourishing. From being a popular activity immediately after the war, by the 1930s cinemagoing was something of a way of life – for many, at least a weekly activity. Certainly in Glasgow there was no shortage of opportunites to visit the cinema. There were ninety-eight cinemas in Glasgow in 1937, with a seating capacity of 133,659, as well as twelve theatres and three music halls.

The cinema habit affected almost all of Scotland – even in smaller towns cinemas were springing up. From the Borders to the Highlands another trend was developing: theatres were either converting into cinemas or just closing down completely. Dundee's two theatres became cinemas leaving Aberdeen's *His Majesty's Theatre* the only live theatre north of the Forth. Indeed it was Aberdeen that saw intense and long-lived rivalry between two local chains – *Donalds'*, run by James Donald and family, and *Aberdeen Picture Palaces* run by Bert Gates. This battle continued from about the time of the First World War until 1941 when *Donalds'* finally bought out their rival.

Under the managership of Jimmy Nairn in the 30's, *The Regal*, Stirling, became the focus of community activity during the town's annual Infirmary Week. After the regular film screening patrons could enjoy the best of local talent performing to Jimmy's direction in *The Regal's* 'Midnight Show', all in aid of charity.

In 1929, just before the introduction of sound, Glasgow alone had 127 cinemas. Dundee as many as twenty-eight in the 1930s serving a population of under 20,000. One name which unites both these cities is that of Green: their chain of cinemas expanded to include *Green's Playhouse* in Glasgow (the site until recently of the *Apollo*) and the *Playhouse* in Nethergate Dundee (which opened on 4 March 1936): the biggest cinemas outwith North America at the time. The name, *Playhouse*, is obviously a Green's favourite as it was also used for their Ayr cinema. The opening of *Green's Playhouse* in Glasgow, in 1927, is an indication not only of the exhibiting success of the Greens but also of the dominance – financial and cultural – of cinema over other media of entertainment by that time. It had a reported capacity of between 4,200 and 4,400, a full orchestra pit and was luxuriously appointed in reds and golds, down to and including the carpet – a specially woven Templeton's carpet declaring 'It's Good. It's Green's'. *The Playhouse* also had its idiosyncracies; in addition to the tastefully appointed *Geneva Tearooms*, above the cinema auditorium was a ballroom – two of Glasgow's favourite activities catered for under one roof.

The first full length talking picture in Scotland was shown at the *Coliseum*, Eglington Street, Glasgow – a venue owned from 1905 until around 1929 by Moss Empires Ltd. and then by Scottish Cine and Variety Theatres. It was first screened on 7 January 1929. This is an important date for the *Coliseum* - the first screening of a talkie and the first day that the *Coliseum* became a full-time cinema. Previously it had balanced both theatre and variety bills but really it was too large to remain a theatre (it was licensed for a capacity of 2,225) and was too far from the city centre. A Scottish Film Council history describes the scene:

Green's Playhouse, Renfield Street, Glasgow shortly after opening in 1927. Designed by John Fairweather with interior furnishings by Guthrie and Wells it represented the apogee of the 'picture palace'. Cinema orchestras, so crucial to the art of the silent film, were soon to disappear as the 'talking picture' erupted onto the screen.

> At the opening it was accompanied by a second feature, but the advertisements next day apologised to the hundreds who had been turned away, announced that the second feature had been dropped, and that *The Singing Fool* would be shown at 1, 3, 5, 7 and 9. The film's run, which continued until 9th February, was perhaps the most hectic in the history of Scottish cinema, and at its end the cinema's staff were given special recognition by the proprietors for the considerate way they had handled the hundreds of thousands who had queued up during those remarkable weeks. An amusing story has survived about the length of the queues. A passenger boarded a Langside tram at the Central Station and asked if it would take him to the Coliseum. The conductor replied, 'Aye, but if its the queue you want , you'd better take the Kirklee caur. The end of the queue's now at Charing Cross.'

Across the country, however, it wasn't just the grand picture palaces that attracted patrons, the smaller suburban and small town cinemas also proved popular. Small chains of cinemas, sometimes family run, could be found across the country. Most were to be found within the central belt but they are to be traced from Ayr to Aberdeen and in the Borders. In the north the smaller and more remote communities were better served than might be expected. Under the auspices of the Highlands and Islands Film Service travelling projectors and films toured to parts of the country not served by a local cinema but able to find a village hall or any large room able to serve the purpose. On a slightly larger scale, Inverness was to become an important link in Scottish film history as Caledonian Associated Cinemas was based in the town. The company was founded in 1935 operating nine cinemas all in the north-east – by 1950 the chain could boast forty-nine cinemas.

Despite the huge popularity of talking pictures and the rise and rise of the picture palaces, 1929 did have its victims. In just the immediate aftermath around fifteen cinemas in Glasgow alone closed – in the main unable to afford the vast cost of equipping their auditoria with sound. However, the cinema going habit was as strong as ever in Scotland and although audiences still preferred the American product, British studios did produce some popular favourites although this is not at

The Capital, Union Street, Aberdeen. Designed by AGR Mackenzie for Aberdeen Picture Palaces. The splendour of the art deco design could be enjoyed whilst taking afternoon tea in the cinema's restaurant. Opened in 1932 it remains one of the few picture palaces of the 30's to retain its cinema organ.

all clear in a letter published in *Kine Weekly* on 3 November 1932. Richard Williamson of the *New Savoy Theatre* at 203 Hope Street saw Scots reception of English accents as a problem and wrote:

> Film producers and renters in London are all racking their brains to discover why it is that 90% of British pictures flop in Scotland. The reason should be obvious to anyone with a grain of intelligence: the filthy language is one. Another reason is the majority of British talkies are devoid of entertainment.

British cinema was, however, at least beginning to depict real and working-class life in Britain – encouraged to some extent by the ramifications of the 1929 Quota Act. This was a fundamentally protectionist strategy that necessitated that distributors rent and exhibitors screen a proportion, a quota (up to twenty per cent) of British films. The Act was generally viewed as unsuccessful, however, as there were too many loopholes. What exactly constituted a 'British' film? It did little, as was the intention, to divert money towards indigenous production and what it did encourage came, rather dismissively, to be referred to as 'Quota Quickies' – a film made in Britain cheaply and quickly in order to bolster that proportion of screen time which was British. This is not to suggest that there were no productions of quality and distinction during the period. British cinema did produce, for example, a number of dramas during the 1930s some of which even worked around notions of social realism. Towards the end of the decade, for example, a number of challenging films were released – *Edge Of The World* a 1937 Michael Powell film and two Victor Saville productions, in 1937 *South Riding* and in 1938 *The Citadel*. Along with another British film, *The Lion Has Wings*, this latter production was, according to figures published in *Kine Weekly* (on 11 November 1940), cinema's biggest money maker of 1939 in Britain. Indeed production had developed rather successfully during this period; an article in the *Evening News* of 5 August 1935 notes that, 'In all some 200 pictures will be made [in Britain] this year – equalling nearly half of Hollywood's output'. No Government legislation, however, was going to enable Britain to compete successfully with the industrial model and products of Hollywood.

Exhibition skills were still high, however. With actual cinema attendances boosted by the arrival of sound and then colour the business community rushed to capitalise. New cinemas were built. New industry leaders came to the fore. In a BBC radio talk of 31 March 1938 John Grierson, while celebrating a flurry of (documentary) film making, comments that, 'Down in London the most powerful single figure in the film world is John Maxwell, a Scotsman. . . .' That this most important figure was the head of the *ABC* chain of cinemas perhaps points to the exhibition skills developing in Scotland.

ABC was a company that could trace its roots back to Glasgow in 1916 and a company called Scottish Cine and Variety Theatres, formed by lawyer John Maxwell. The company owned a number of theatres, including as has been mentioned, the Eglington Street *Coliseum*. The success of the group was unparalleled and expansion across Scotland (to include a subsidiary company, Kirkcaldy Entertainments Company, with five cinemas in that one town) was equalled only by the acquiring of an equivalent company – Associated British Cinemas – in England. ABC Limited was registered as a subsidiary of British International Pictures on 26 November 1928 (with initial capital of £1 million). It was a company with its own links back to the distribution network of the French company Pathe. The two companies merged in 1932 forming one of the biggest exhibition circuits in the country, equalling *Gaumont-British* owned by J Arthur Rank (who had, incidentally, acquired Moss Theatres in November of the same year). This company itself would merge with *ABC's* main rival, the *Odeon* circuit under the leadership of Oscar Deutsch. *Odeon* quickly expanded into Scotland – building new cinemas and converting old ones to the signature art deco house style (complete with faience tiling). Famous *Odeons* in Scotland include the Glasgow *Odeon*, formerly the *Paramount*

Opulence for Dundonians. *Green's Playhouse* in the Nethergate was opened in March 1936. 'We want U in' ran the slogans. Designed, as its sister cinema in Glasgow, by John Fairweather its 4126 seats in gold and burnt orange, red, flame and pink were to serve cinemagoers for 35 years.

The Edge of the World 1937 (Rock). Director Michael Powell's dramatisation of life on the remote island of Foula, inspired by the real life drama of the evacuation of St Kilda in 1930.

Port Brae Cinema, 1930. Cinema going in Kirkcaldy was dominated by John Maxwell's ABC Circuit. By acquiring the Kirkcaldy Entertainments Co in the twenties they effectively controlled all five cinemas in the town.

and purpose-built as a cinema in 1934, opening in January 1935, and the *Odeon* in Edinburgh (formerly the *New Victoria*).

Despite the political debates that were involved with the Scottish Literary Renaissance and the politics implicit within such groups as the Glasgow Workers' Theatre Group (GWTG), for instance, active political protest during the 1930s was a much more marginalised business than it had been immediately after the war and in the 1920s. The General Strike had been defeated, the Labour movement split, the Depression really biting. While small sections of society still debated issues of nationalism, for instance, the dominant ideology of the time was of consensus; a particularly strong desire in the face of the ongoing threat of war in this period. The British cinema of the time seemed to produce films signalling this feeling. However, it did so with such determination, consistency and singlemindedness that one might rather suggest that instead of reflecting a reality it was actually trying to produce such a feeling in what was actually a split and divided community.

The desire to create consensus and community in contemporary British society also has its uneasy parallel in Scottish culture. One of the major concerns of the contemporary literary debate was around the distinctiveness (distinctive, that is, to British culture) of Scottish culture and in particular of Scottish popular culture. Now, while this is a repeated and current debate, it was thrown into marked focus from the late 1920s by the Scottish Renaissance. Work emerging from this group was very much concerned with Scotland in the twentieth century; re-examining the cliches of the traditional depictions of Scotland's cultural and social life with a crucially contemporary spirit. Yet the bourgeois elements of twentieth-century Scotland were little changed from their nineteenth century predecessors. Values were of thrift, Sabbatarianism, diligence and forebearance, and this was continually recreated in representations of a 'pawkish' and 'couthy' society – the essential view of Scotland, or so it seemed. Even images of industrial and urban Scotland seemed to petrify on the easy recognition of a distinctive set of stereotypes. Popular culture refers to one set as 'hardmen and mammies' boys'.

These images were the mainstay of much of Scottish popular culture and certainly may be traced in the popular novels (for example, those of J M Barrie) and in the drama of the period; in texts performed by the Scottish National Players (although their repertory contains notable exceptions to this, including as it does the successful use of verse drama in Gordon Bottomley's *Gruach*, which they first performed in 1923 and the performance of Neil Gunn's first play *The Ancient Fire*, premiered in 1929) and in at least some of the texts performed within the Scottish Community Drama Association (SCDA). Joe Corrie's work, for instance, offers an interesting point of reference. While offering a contemporary view of current problems he reuses the narrative cliches that dominate Scottish literature – and whilst these were certainly hugely popular (especially amongst SCDA groups) they

The Citadel 1938 (MGM). Robert Donat as
a conscientious young GP thrust into the
unfamiliar world of the Welsh mining
valleys.

do not provide a progressive vocabulary for drama. The image of
Scotland portrayed in texts like George Blake's *The Mother* and even
the ubiquitous *Campbell of Kilmhor* by J A Fergusson were increasingly
perceived as producing a reductive and reactionary set of images for
Scots. These representations were increasingly at odds with the actual
lived experience of most Scots.

It was important that Scots increasingly found themselves represented in empathetic and recognisable ways across the media, but
images are only important, useful and affective if supported by a
framework of cultural and social dimensions. Certainly the publication
of *A Drunk Man Looks at the Thistle*, *A Scots Quair*, *The Silver Darlings*
and *Scott and Scotland*, as well as the staging of the plays of James
Bridie, are important – particularly in terms of literary prestige and
the nation's cultural capital – but there are problems. To find a
distinctive national voice is simply not enough; that it can be found
in a loosely united grouping (the 'Scottish Renaissance') may allow a
degree of experimentation unavailable to the individual, the lone voice,
but as the disintegration of that loosest of movements shows, without
domestic economic support and critical involvement it is all too easy
to let this energy dissipate. There came to be no focus (politically or
aesthetically) and no point of social or literary reference.

But Scotland does have its unique institutions – those of the Law,
the Church, education and culture. The Saltire Society was founded
in 1935, ironically too late to be part of the energy and political
force of and behind the Renaissance writers: but perhaps that was
as much an advantage as a disadvantage. In any event, the Saltire

47

Society is the ultimate cultural representative of the Scottish Civil Society, and as such really came to be more interested in ensuring that it did not become the agency that will affect cultural and social change but maintain the 'traditional' role of Scottish culture – as backwardlooking, as upholding the accepted and acceptable social order and as being a culture ratified by the structures and codes of another's cultural policy, at best a north British version of Scottish history, literature and society. That the Scottish Civil Society would have a commitment to the living culture of the nation has come to be inconceivable. Its function goes little beyond the mythologising of past cultural products or the mercenary use of particular sections of the cultural scene as a means of establishing and reaffirming the elite nature of the bourgeois.

The only bourgeois response to the alienation of Scottish culture from institutional ratification was one of retreat – either the actual or the intellectual relocation in the South, or the emotional return to an increasingly mythologised past with the coincident celebration of the Makars that came to signify some lost Golden Age: this being more akin to the role taken on by the Saltire Society. Certainly the role of the bourgeoisie was not that of the rising middle class in other countries emerging from the industrialising process of the nineteenth century – one of leading the nation towards the modern.

In terms of a film culture that would re-examine the organisation, the form and the content of that medium in a similar way to that undertaken by those involved with theatre and the written word, participation in production and the discovery of relevant images of Scotland and Scots proved to be even more difficult than in the drama. The Scottish Film Council (of the British Film Institute) was established in 1934. Its remit was both cultural and educational and yet it had no staff, no premises and an annual grant from the BFI of only £100. SFC had four committees: Education, Entertainment, Amateur Cinematography and Social Service. Aside from the crippling staffing and financial difficulties (which gradually eased), SFC found that most developed sector of the cinema industry – the exhibitors – tended to either ignore it or view it with some suspicion. The exhibitors in the thirties felt that the Social Services Panel had a covert (and commercially distasteful) interest in censorship. According to the account given in *21 Years of the Scottish Film Council*, John Grierson suggested to the SFC that it form the first Films of Scotland committee. The Council declined the move into production and, tragically as far as SFC's effective involvement in the fullness of film culture is concerned, the matter passed to the Empire Exhibition General Council and on to the Scottish Home Department. SFC's educational and cultural provision grew with the development of the film societies (discussed below) and the establishment of the Scottish Central Film Library. However, it did not relate in its early years to the whole spectrum of cinema in Scotland, professional production was eschewed and mainstream exhibition was so popular that it was difficult for the tiny agency to find a role.

In spite of the institutional difficulties of developing an integrated film culture (the legacy of which continues today), SFC was active in the support of an alternative movement which began in the late twenties: the Scottish film societies.

Scottish inter-war film culture has now come to be closely associated with the development of the documentary form and the figure of John Grierson in particular. Certainly Grierson and many of those he brought to work with him at first the Empire Marketing Board and then the GPO Film Unit were Scots and many of the films they made were of Scottish subjects, but this is only one, well documented, element in the story of film in Scotland. Where Grierson's documentaries pushed the notion of film-as-public service, as educator and film-as-weapon, other groups were equally examining film-as-art. Scotland was at the forefront of this remarkably popular movement. 1925 saw the founding of the London Film Society. On 22 November 1929 the Glasgow Film Society was founded with an initial membership of 80 (but rising to over 400 by 1932-1933). In the following year the Edinburgh Film Guild was formed. While these groups were primarily interested in the screening of films (the first season of the Glasgow group included *The Cabinet of Dr Caligari*, *Drifters*, *The Girl With the Hat Box* and *The End of St Petersberg*) each group attracted a number of amateur cinematographers and then a number of small groups interested in actual film making; for instance the Meteor ('Shooting Star') Film Society, which in 1934 organised the first Scottish Amateur Film Festival(SAFF). The Film Societies remain important, however, as they were able, often with much complicated manoeuvrings, to screen films banned by the censors. The 1909 Cinematographic Act conferred upon local authorities the right of inspection of cinemas (and other venues used to screen film) to ensure that fire precautions had been made. From 1912 the British Board of Film Censors (BBFC) could advise the local authorities as to the content of any film but it was the decision of each local authority whether to grant a licence of the exhibition of the film. It was this, rather unco-ordinated, form of censorship that shaped part of the history of inter-war film culture. In 1926 Eisenstein's *Battleship Potemkin* was censored, in 1928 Pudovkin's *The Mother* and by the beginning of World War Two the BBFC had censored eight early Soviet productions. But as the final implementation of censorship was up to the local authorities differences occurred across the country, from authority to authority and from election to election.

As private clubs, however, the Film Societies were able to screen not just non-commercial productions but banned films as well: the 1930-1932 season of the Glasgow Film Society included the first Glasgow screenings of *Battleship Potemkin*, *Storm Over Asia* and *The Passion of Joan Of Arc*.

The problem for the film societies was that they essentially fostered bourgeois notions of art and culture – effectively splitting art from politics, a division quite untenable for many of the amateur film makers of the time. So there was a space in the film scene for a

49

Drifters 1929. John Grierson's first film for the Empire Marketing Board. Assisted by cameraman Basil Emmott, he commenced shooting in July 1928 in Lerwick. By the end of November after filming in various ports country wide, Grierson was back in London ready to edit the footage, which was premiered at the London Film Society, 10 November 1929 to a rapturous reception.

more explicitly political use of medium, and further to allow workers to view this same type of film for less than it would cost to join one of the Film Societies. This became possible under the auspices of the Workers' Film Societies, established in London from 1929. In the early 1930s a number of Workers' Film Societies opened up across Scotland – Glasgow's and the Edinburgh Workers' Progressive Film Society both were founded in 1930 and other branches soon followed in St Andrews and in Dundee: to join the Edinburgh branch cost annually just 6/- for the unemployed and 12/- for those in work. While the Workers' Film Societies did encourage actual film making the most important function was that of screening and discussion. Only in Glasgow, however, did some kind of workers' film group survive beyond around 1933 (and only there because on the failing of one version of the Film Society another would be established in its place). Both the Film Societies and the Workers' Film Societies survived at the whim of the local authorities who could refuse to license the screening of any film. To help combat the vagaries of the licencing process exceptionally strict membership rules were enforced. In Glasgow, for instance, to introduce a non-member or guest to any screening (up to a maximum of 100 at any one meeting) a ticket had to be bought a minimum of two days in advance from a specified agent's shop. The ticket had to be bought by a full member of the society, who could only buy two such tickets for any performance. Authorities were not slow to seek out any irregularities and so stop the Sunday screenings.

While the Film Society movement – concentrating on viewing film-as-art – continued throughout the 1930s and beyond, the more politicised, Left film groups had a particularly difficult time only improving to any degree towards the latter part of the decade. Technical improvements (the development of 16 mm film stock) and the hardening of political attitudes, particularly affected by the outbreak of the Spanish Civil War, combined to make Left films a point of unification for many.

Kino was founded in 1933 by, among others, Ivor Montagu, as a section of the Workers' Theatre Movement. From 1936, however, *Kino* was less a distribution and administrative group and more and explicitly an agitational and educational force within the Left political scene. The central company of Kino Films Ltd was certainly the largest distributor of working class films between the wars. It has been noted that the group distributed 158 different films in the 1930s. Based at Collets' Bookshop, *Glasgow Kino* (also formed in 1933) were very much involved in the active and agitational use of film. Their progressive booking policy ensured that any trade union or workers' group could have relatively easy access to a wide range of political films – from Soviet dramas to contemporary reports and newsreels from Spain. While the screening of Soviet, American, Spanish, Irish and Czech material was certainly an important and useful agit-prop tool *Glasgow Kino* were also involved in the filmmaking side of things. It was they who distributed *Hell Unltd*, a powerful anti-war 16 mm short made in 1936 by Helen Biggar and Norman McLaren at the Glasgow School of Art, as an attack on armaments manufacturers. It won a prize at the 1937 SAFF.

Both Biggar and McLaren are important figures in the development of Left and of film culture. McLaren had already established something of a reputation as an amateur film maker. A McLaren film, *Seven Till Five*, won the first prize at the second SAFF in 1935. In 1936 his abstract film *Colour Cocktail* shared the honours in the category 'Interest Films By Individuals' with a film called *Happy Day* made by T Lawrence, a Dundee based amateur film maker. After completing *Hell Unltd*, McLaren went with Ivor Montagu to film in Spain before returning to work under Grierson at the GPO Film Unit and then finally making his reputation international through his work at the National Film Board of Canada.

Helen Biggar, meanwhile was to have a much closer relationship to the development of a Left culture in Scotland. She was a member of the Communist Party and to the forefront of the Kino Group. Her father, Hugh Biggar, was a founder member of the Independent Labour Party, a Councillor and then Lord Provost of Glasgow. Her political commitment combined profitably with her Art School training to lead her into design work with the GWTG. She worked with artist Tom Macdonald on the design for the famous GWTG project *On Guard For Spain*. This was a poem, written by Jack Lindsay in 1936 and staged

Hell Unltd 1936. A protest against the arms race and the greed of armaments manufacturers, which found a sympathetic audience in the period leading up to the Second World War.

Concern for republican Spain featured strongly in the slogans and floats parading through Glasgow on May Day 1937. Made by the Clarion Scouts film society *Glasgow, May Day 1937* was widely shown in the late summer and autumn of that year.

as a mass declamation by the GWTG from 1937. It was one of their most popular and challenging productions. *On Guard For Spain* was directed by Lawrence Lawson for both outdoors at rallies and indoors at concerts and meetings. Eight actors, dressed in the uniforms of the International Brigade share the speaking of the verse while arranged around the flag of the Spanish Republic, which was waved by a flag bearer to reflect the pace of the action depicted in the poem. At indoor rallies the emotional effect was said to be considerably heightened by the dramatic use of lighting effects.

Helen Biggar's contribution to Left theatre in Glasgow also continued beyond the demise of the GWTG in 1940 as she and many of that group's members became involved with the development of Glasgow Unity.

Biggar also directed Glasgow Kino's own production – *May Day 1938 – Challenge To Fascism* – a film perhaps following the example of a Clarion Film Society depiction of the 1937 May Day celebrations in Glasgow. This film made frequent appearances at the Clarion Scouts' regular Sunday film shows. Biggar's film had a semi-newsreel style and was intended to set the Glasgow Green rally in some kind of wider political context. Made with money raised by the local Labour movement the film mixes scenes of the actual gathering with dramatised scenes of a Glasgow family's day out to the rally and extracts depicting contemporary world events. It is not wholly unexpected to find that the members of the family are played by actors from the GWTG.

The film, however, was less than successful, failing as an agit-prop piece. *Kino* itself was in something of a decline. It was still possible to see Left film in Scotland but it was distributed and supported on a much smaller scale than had been the case in the few years at the end of the 1930s.

Film going – to a picture palace, a small local cinema, a touring projector or a film society meeting – retained and built upon its popularity throughout the 1930s. The film culture of the inter-war years was ultimately a successful one. It was able to maintain (with varying degrees of success) a mix of film screening of both mainstream, commercial products and of alternative and political films, and some actual indigenous production – although this predominantly centred on small politically motivated productions but with an important input into the documentary movement.

What is, perhaps, of particular interest is the ease with which a film culture was integrated into the wider social, political and artistic life of Scotland by the 1930s. It was this free mix of interests, of skills, of resources and of personnel that ensured, on the one hand, the huge popular appeal of cinema going and, on the other, the equally important artistic and critical success of the parallel development of a counter cinema. That these different kinds of cinema could co-exist in a society that was certainly in social and economic crisis is a clear indication of the vitality of film culture in the early decades of this century.

A Scotland as Good as Any Other? Documentary Film 1937–82

Neil Blain

The Boundaries of Civilisation

I used to think civilisation stopped north of London.
Have you been to – East Kilbride – before? (Pronounced as one attempts the name of a hamlet in the Balkans.)
I haven't even been to Scotland.
I don't believe it. Aw, it's not in America the Scots need to publicise themselves: it's in London.

Two initially unseen explorers, the first English and his American companion, thus begin Charles Gormley's script for the well-constructed *Why Scotland, Why East Kilbride?* (1970), over symbolic aerial shots of the Clyde estuary. An empty, timeless landscape gives way to the cultural sophistication and economic attractions of west central Scotland at the end of the sixties: and preconceptions are duly overturned. Meanwhile the more prosaic *Cumbernauld, Town for Tomorrow* (1970) offers some raunchy disco shots and a miniskirted girl in a sports car to compensate for the relentlessly responsible commentary.

A number of Scotlands make a variety of cases for themselves on the screen between the late thirties and, in the main, the mid-seventies, since thereafter the documentary for the cinema screen becomes an ever more rare phenomenon. There is a Scotland of landscape, seascape, quaint small towns, rugged timeless faces and cities steeped in the past – at least on celluloid there is – and there is also a swinging Scotland, groovy East Kilbride and fab Cumbernauld, full of futuristic technology, electric guitars and passionate affirmations of modernity. *A Plan for Living* (1976) on the new town of Livingston, featured a life before AIDS but seemingly so long after the epoch of *Freedom of Aberfeldy* (1943) and *Waverley Steps* (1948) that surely the difference wasn't wholly explained by the changes in the culture, but of necessity also by even

53

Glasgow 1980. The approach to the new Kingston Bridge scything through the old burgh of Anderston to traverse the river Clyde. Made in 1974 by Ogam Films for Films of Scotland this was intended as the first of a pair of films looking at the ambitious twenty year plan for the regeneration of the city. Oscar Mazaroli's shooting for the sequel, with a working title of *Glasgow's Progress*, was abandoned about 1978 when it was becoming apparent that the target completion date of 1980 was not going to be met.

greater changes in its representation. 'Maybe there is something in the old ways,' says a Dominion soldier in the Aberfeldy of 1943, but tell that to East Kilbride Development Corporation.

There are yet other visions of Scotland: municipalist, formalist, romantic, visionary, facetious, cynical, lazy, innovative, confident, apologetic, realist, reactionary, informative, propagandist, cannibalistic and even, later, ironical, about films about Scotland. But not the predictive *Glasgow 1980*, made in 1974 with Bill Forsyth as editor. Cheerful music underscores nightmare shots from under the Kingston Bridge, and, as tenements crash down under the demolition men, 'it had to change' we're informed, to give birth to 'a planned and integrated community'. The old ways were not forgotten in this planner's apologia: 'the best of the old keeps its place in the new Glasgow'. Civilisation doesn't stop north of East Kilbride, either.

The American who makes rigorous demands of East Kilbride is played by Bruce Boa, who later gave Basil Fawlty a much harder time over the ingredients of a Waldorf Salad, though he was a lot nicer in EK than in Torquay. The role of judgement by outsiders – 'how ithers see us' – is as prominent in Scottish documentary film over this long period as in other cultural forms.

In the impossibly contrived but likeable *By Lochaber I Will Go* (1960), a hymn of praise to mobile banking, the stereotypical Englishman who is the narrator tells the story of his first astonishing encounter on Lewis with a bank on wheels: 'fancy coming across the most advanced development in modern banking in one of the most remote areas of the British Isles!' But this is a man who realises that civilisation doesn't stop at Inverness. Singing the praises of Lewis's seascapes, he proceeds to judge the Callanish stones: 'the finest in Britain – after Stonehenge'. Lewis is older than Aberfeldy and even more modern than Glenrothes – 'there you have it: the very ancient and the very modern'. His face falls when he realises that the 'typically dour Scot' with whom he has been conducting a one-sided conversation in a bus-shelter is a bank inspector and knew of these marvels all the time.

Other English visitors are having an even better time. In *Busman's Holiday* (1959), wherein the bus-driver/narrator takes a coach tour of the Highlands, two London typists, one impressively underwired beneath a cerise sweater and central to the interests of the cameraman, pose smilingly and alluringly in the doorway of the bus. In fact the strawberry blonde in question is for an important cinematic moment poised gymnastically in the opening with a hand on either side of the doorway, leaning out of the bus as though auditioning for a German mountain film. The typists also pose on rocks, and against landscapes; the prominent blonde, now in short sleeves, even undertaking an impromptu and revealing dance during a halt for a musical interlude with a harmonica, in the way coach trips do. This rather leering approach to women in tourism films recurs even in the sober *Holiday Scotland* (1966), where the cameraman seems fascinated by the contours of one of the lady lunchers at a Dirleton hotel as she sways to the table.

But *Busman's Holiday* manages another electric moment, a metonym for Scottish cultural history. As the busman/narrator and his wife enjoy their quiet contemplation of the landscape, a bored lad tucked in behind his mother at the window opposite menacingly fingers his harmonica. The busman and his wife look concerned, though the husband smiles bravely. Gordon raises the instrument to his lips: but his mother, with a glance at her fellow-passengers, brusquely removes it from Gordon's custody. 'His mother soon changed his tune', says the narrator, Knox-like, with satisfaction. He and his wife smile at each other. Cultural imperatives have triumphed. 'Never mind, perhaps some other time', says the narrator without much sympathy. It is a brutal judgement. But this is nearly the 1960s, and Gordon has the last laugh as the typist dances to his tune at the end of the film.

A Mission to Project Scotland

Almost all post-war Scottish documentary films intended for the cinema were made for the Films of Scotland Committee, set up in 1954 under the umbrella of the Scottish Council Development and Industry, and disbanded in 1982. But, as the moving spirit behind it and (with Grierson), behind much of Scottish film culture, Forsyth Hardy, said in an interview in that year (an edited version appears in Colin McArthur's *Scotch Reels*), 'it was always just on the edge of that umbrella': in other words, Hardy had to go about persuading a variety of sponsors into putting up money for films, with, as the main

By Lochaber I Will Go 1960. Anglo-Scottish Pictures for Films of Scotland. 'A hymn of praise to mobile banking'.

lure, the guarantee that they would be distributed. That promise was possible because of the influence in the film industry of the Committee's chairman, Sir Alexander King.

The sponsors ranged from a variety of industries to banks and public and governmental institutions. As far as possible, a 'hands-off' agreement was reached whereby the visibility of the product or services and the influence of the sponsor might be kept minimal. One hundred and fifty films emerged from Hardy's twenty years as Director of Films of Scotland. Sponsors' influence is variably evident and the publicity often surprisingly indirect or discreet (though by no means always). Yet the agenda for films produced on such a basis was of necessity bound to be circumscribed. Where the films demonstrate only a superficial concern with the realities of industry or take a romantic approach to Scottish history or construct a hackneyed and disappointing view of Scottish culture, the needs of the sponsor are sometimes a part of the explanation.

But sometimes we may need to account for these things in other ways: early on, London units made the films; later, when production

Busman's Holiday 1959. Anglo-Scottish Pictures for Films of Scotland. Visitors against the grandeur of the Scottish landscape.

took place mainly and then exclusively in Scotland, there are questions about the predilections of the filmmakers, as well as wider questions about the attitude of Scots generally to their own culture. No one answer accounts for the nature of the Films of Scotland output and generalisations are better avoided.

There had been a Films of Scotland Committee before, too, in 1938, set up to make seven films for the Glasgow Empire Exhibition. These were *The Face of Scotland, Wealth of a Nation, The Children's Story, Sea Food, They Made the Land, Scotland For Fitness,* and *Sport in Scotland.* The impulse behind this, and the formation of the later committee, and underpinning discussion of the Scottish film scene in various publications of these periods, was to make Scotland visible to the world, and not just visible in any terms. In his editorial in the *Educational Film Bulletin*, no 28, March 1944, T A Blake speaks of the need for films which 'give a true picture of Scotland' and which 'portray the spirit, culture and enterprise of a people the world knows as Scottish'. And he knows what he doesn't want: 'the bonnie bonnie banks of Loch Lomon' in a tartan border is not Scotland':

> A panning shot of Braemar needs something more than a High-lander in the foreground to distinguish it from Jyvaskyla or the High Tatra. The incense trail from Hadramut to the Aegean pulsated because life vibrated through its world of storm and strife and adventure. But the road to the isles or from them to mid-Atlantic or Nova Scotia, shorn of sentimentality, could be no less tremblingly alive.

In the programme for the *Scotland on the Screen* event in the Regal Cinema, Edinburgh, on 25 August 1957, the same impulse is put thus:

> Scotland is a country rich in subjects for films. Her industries have a great range, her scenery has a beauty which lingers in the senses. She has a long tradition and a thousand institutions with a proper pride in their record. The material is there; and Films of Scotland offers the means by which it can be brought to the screen and projected before the eyes of the world.

Yet both these and other statements of these periods have a marked ambivalence about them. What sort of Scotland, which of a number of potential Scotlands, will emerge from such intentions?

In fact the 1957 programme consists of *Life in the Orkneys, Scotland Dances, The Silver City,* in which a number of different visitors including a Scandinavian sailor explore Aberdeen, *Tam O'Shanter,* a recitation against suitable drawings, *Enchanted Isles, Festival in Edinburgh,* and the Disney short *People and Places – Scotland.* The programme notes contain what is perhaps an apologia: Disney's aim is to project 'not the contemporary life of the country his unit visits, but the traditional

Busman's Holiday 1959. The bus driver joins an appreciative audience as the scene is set for an impromptu dance display.

and timeless elements which form its fabric'. This includes fishing, weaving, curling, Hallowe'en and 'the simple trust behind a cross-road cattle deal'. The programme demonstrates far from the only mismatch one finds, in the progress of Scottish documentary, between declared intention and corresponding achievement.

Festival in Edinburgh, however, is nothing if not cosmopolitan in its opening. By happy coincidence, the director finds, in the same crowded medium shot, on the battlements of the castle, all at once, and looking smilingly over Princes Street and the city, an African girl in national dress and four other visitors from distant parts, another two of whom, from the Far East, are by fortunate chance also wearing their national garb. And when he investigates the other side of the battlements there, too, are further representatives of distant continents. Not to be outdone, the Scots wear their kilts. Edinburgh's a colourful place in 1954.

A Selective Vision

It is worth considering, too, the matter of how the documentary film itself as a form was understood in Scotland by those producing it. It was inevitable that the powerful presence of John Grierson would make itself felt with particular force in his native land, for although working

58

elsewhere, his interest in the representation of Scotland and his role in making the country visible continued. The contradictions in Grierson's aspirations for documentary film have been much discussed. Although starting out with a strong declared intention to put working people and everyday life on the screen, his concern with 'shape' and 'beauty', and the influence of these preoccupations on other filmmakers, have clear results for parts of the Films of Scotland output.

Speaking in the autobiographical film *I Remember, I Remember* (1968), he proposes a view of documentary as 'a visual art which can convey a sense of beauty, and a sense of beauty about the ordinary world'. But if the ordinary world isn't 'beautiful', will there be a place for it as it is? 'We live by putting things into orders and patterns,' he says. He cites Picasso with admiration: but perhaps Picasso's main contribution was to disorder and depattern, to subvert, reformulate, reframe. How about documentary?

It is this sort of debate about Grierson which enlivens discussion of the work he influenced as well as his own early film *Drifters* (1929). It was Grierson himself, whose views on documentary underwent a complex evolution, who had said in 1942 that 'the penalty of realism is that it is about reality, and has to bother forever, not about being *beautiful* but about being *right*'. But in the set of films produced by Grierson for the first Committee in 1938, the tension between realist commitment and poeticism of style is already apparent. It isn't that realism was or is incompatible with certain kinds of rhetoric. But – and this may be seen as much as a trait of documentary films of the period as it is of those which were specifically Scottish and Griersonian – there is a danger that the poetry can actually replace the life which it started to depict. This very self-conscious poeticism, which was to persist as a characteristic of a significant element of the Films of Scotland output in a fashion which rapidly became anachronistic, was evident in the 1938 *They Made the Land*, and is discernible thirty and forty years on in some of the later films.

But not all the Empire Exhibition films were in this vein. There was, for example, the astounding *Scotland for Fitness*, presented by Sir Iain Colquhoun, then Chairman of the Fitness Council, who addresses the camera with an aristocratic suavity in itself fascinating as a socio-historical fact. He interviews several active people, including a mountaineer who appears as though by good fortune on the set on his way to the hill, and on location a certain Mrs Brown, an instructress with RP tones which prove a nice middle-class match to his own upper-class drawl.

A formal interest in the shape of things and an at times irritating and disabling poeticism or lyricism is not the only persistent tendency of the continuing output of Films of Scotland. The same group of 1938 films included *Face of Scotland*, which, like the later *Heart of Scotland* (1962), begins with a fragment of Latin, a Roman invader's view of Scotland, another instance of the Scottish preoccupation with external judgement, and more importantly, a reference, of which there are so many in the films over the years, to myths minted by others of the emptiness, desolation, and later the violence and turbulence of the country. And another characteristic of this sort of film is to try to reassert as far as possible some often mystic continuity between this past and the Scottish present.

Shots of cloud, moor, hill, stones, burns, cloud, rain, and then – historiographical conventions well to the fore – 'racked with war, across its landscapes rose many castles and keeps'. And: 'as times passed these people of this land,' poeticising convention dictates the need to say 'these people of this land', though plainly they aren't these people of, say, Abyssinia – 'made for themselves a simple but individual civilisation'. But the cut almost immediately after this is to a contemporary farm and two farmers. Thus is a certain spurious continuity established.

The film's struggle to reassert continually notions of the continuity of what is in fact a wholly mythic Scottish history takes many forms. The dead of Bannockburn are at one with those of Lucknow and beyond. There are reluctant glimpses of cities into which four out of five Scots, as the film admits, are 'crowded' in the Central Belt. But the words are hardly uttered when the view returns to the stones of the ruined crofts: the nostalgic music which accompanies the ruins is held into shots of urban Scots in the pub: 'behind every Glasgow family, they say, you will find a croft, a farm, or a fishing village'.

Further montages seek to establish the reality of a desolate rural Scotland to be discovered under the surface which is modern industrial society. This tension will play itself out in many Films of Scotland releases in later years. In this film, most startlingly, a big Glasgow football crowd is enlisted as evidence not of radical and vast historic change, but rather of continuity. Its faces express the 'givens' of the Scottish character, like ambition and determination.

There is not just one sort of problem with these films when we place them beside what we objectively know about the history, the culture and the society of the country which they are supposed to be representing. There are many tensions and contradictions in their different ways of talking about Scotland. We should not, for example, imagine that the especial problem with the Films of Scotland output is its fondness for a particular kind of tartan past. That is only one of many elements in the versions of Scotland which this body of work produces: some familiar and verifiable, some enlightening and instructive, some risible and harmless, and some irritating because of the wider political significance of their failures.

An Optical Illusion

A Touch of Scotland (1964) is the surreal masterpiece of post-war Scottish documentary. Having decided to be ahistorical, asocial, acultural and amoral, it does so with splendid consistency, making hardly the slightest concession to material fact. Glasgow, for example, is represented, at the

close of the film, by a lengthy sequence involving a Highland Ball at the
City Chambers. The astounding script reaches Whitmanesque levels in
the celebration of contradiction though it is at its best, as we shall see,
when it gives up the process of signification altogether.

The script is determined to establish the illusoriness of the present. A
young couple play football with their infant daughter under Edinburgh's
Castle Rock: 'everywhere in Scotland, today marches and interlocks
with yesterday and many yesterdays past', says the narrator in a rather
pastward manner. We move, to no avail, to Stirling: 'the twentieth
century busies itself with its brief occasions in the lee of something
(sic): a fortress crown on a city hill called Stirling Castle that was
already old when Alexander 1st died within its walls in 1124.' The
Highlands are pleasingly empty, 'here, if you like, even a driver can
be alone'.

Cut to an Edinburgh full of ghosts which are 'many and potent',
but which fortunately don't 'readily intrude into the busy values of
today'. The past is noisily obliterated in an early form of disco, just
after the narrator quite self-contradictorily claims that one can never
escape from the past in Edinburgh. This dialectic of the occult is
wonderfully crystalised in a shot of Edinburgh castle from inside a

The Heart of Scotland 1962. Templar Films
for Films of Scotland. The stark contrast of
the bounty of the land against the
technological modernity of Grangemouth's
refineries.

A Touch of Scotland 1964. Glaswegians display their dancing talents amidst the setting of the City Chambers.

Princes Street fashion store. The castle looms potently behind shoppers while a mannequin in foreground silhouette makes a sinister gesture over the top of a bus advertising McEwan's Export. Meanwhile the modern chaps drinking in a hotel wear kilts anyway.

A Touch of Scotland peaks in a sequence of shots in the Clyde estuary, and off Oban. Here, the commentary becomes sublime. Shots of seascapes: the narrator takes a deep breath, and begins to intone with energy, as though determined to persuade us, quite against his sense of the possible, that the script has a meaning. 'In the sea one has many neighbours. For some the sea unites us, and divides us, and our relations remain, as they say, most amicable. The seals off Oban ask nothing of us but tolerance' – shots of seals – 'and a certain tact. We ask little of the seals but trust and good manners'.

Hardly daring to investigate what this film might mean, the commentator may nonetheless note how its view of Scotland obliterates not only the whole of Scotland's existence right back to the middle ages. However, its implication that Scotland has a 'darker' or more 'turbulent' past than any other European nation is a mistaken commonplace in documentaries.

The Creative Hand of Government

There was another tradition, less value-loaded and milder and subtler in rhetorical intent, corresponding to a purer, 'factual' sort of documentary conception, which might in some cases use actors and reconstructions and other fiction devices, but was concerned with 'information', albeit often in someone's interest. This is true of some of the Films of Scotland output. But for a period before the establishment of the second Committee in 1954, a number of films had been produced in connection with various activities of the Scottish Office, under the energetic Forsyth Hardy's overall supervision. These included propaganda films made in Scotland during the war, and public relations' information films for departments such as Health, Education, and Agriculture, in the war years and just after. It was indeed the cessation of such government filmmaking activity which would lead to the setting up of the 1954 Committee.

Some of the films, such as the likeable *Freedom of Aberfeldy*, mentioned above, had a clear agenda, in this instance, the insertion of Scotland into a particular kind of national/rural myth with the diaspora in mind. There is a splendid montage of Scottish names spelled out tribally on Aberfeldy's shop signs: MacNaughton, McGregor, McLeish, McInnes, Haggart, McKercher, McGrouther, and a Mrs McRitchie. 'A fine collection of Scots names the shopkeepers had', says one of the New World soldiers, admiringly, though alas one or two not especially Scottish names stray into the corners of a couple of later shots. A certain version of ethnicity suits the film's purpose. And indeed the Scots are a nice decent hospitable lot in this film, produced by Campbell Harper Films who at this time were effectively alone in being a Scottish company able to produce films on this scale.

Waverley Steps is another film for the Scottish Home Department, a charming enough introduction to the amenities of Edinburgh, though a little prone to oddities such as the gratuitous piper in full highland dress mysteriously playing *The Rowan Tree* outside a bar late at night. The Danish sailor who provides the film's narrative continuity will not, presumably, notice the overwhelming preponderance of RP accents on Edinburgh's streets. There is a Scottish surgeon, and a Scottish banker, but the dominance of what otherwise sound like English voices makes this smack almost of tokenism. Only the working classes are allowed to sound Scottish in this film and some of those, such as Mrs Linklater, sound a bit alarming. The romantic life of a railwayman provides a moment or two of strong, albeit veiled, eroticism, which is hard to connect with the Scottish Home Department in 1948.

The austere and strongly informational *Children of the City* (1944), which was produced by Paul Rotha, and had some fine camerawork and sensitive direction is a naturalistically dramatised case-study of juvenile crime in the context both of a variety of forms of deprivation, and the various stages at which the state intervenes to regulate and rehabilitate. If the film is not entirely disinterested, that is only partly

Budge Cooper's sensitive direction of *Children of the City* (1944) reveals the considerable personal commitment she brought to the film. Her research over a period of months resulted in this study of juvenile delinquency which could have been made in any of the urban centres in Scotland. That it was principally shot in Dundee was due to a large degree to the film-makers appreciation of the quality of the light over the city.

because it is made to promote a certain kind of state and municipal patriarchy: for also strongly to the fore is a keen realist interest in the social disadvantages of city life.

Shot mainly in Dundee, this surprisingly densely-textured film makes much of its cityscapes, its social purposes emerging satisfyingly from the severity of its mis-en-scene, with its feel of enclosure, its high walls, tenements, blocked sun, claustrophobic terraces and stark urban long-shots all appropriately rendered in its black and white cinematography (films referred to from the fifties onwards are almost invariably in colour). These are contrasted with interpersonal sequences in which there are some thoughtful and adventurous close-ups. The narrator reassures us that it's only a small percentage of children criminally disposed after exposure to such an environment: 'but what about the other three-quarters of a million children in the cities and towns of Scotland', he says, as a small girl walks symbolically along the margin of a triangle of shadow cast on a street imprisoned by tall tenements, and the prognosis seems gloomy despite the initial promise.

This was, in a sense, a high order of sponsorship as well as a high order of filmmaking. In its cinematic quality and in its realism, this film is closer, ironically, to what Grierson seemed at periods in his career to want than much of what actually appeared under his influence.

Scotland's Campbell Harper company produced, in 1947, a film of equally fine cinematic moments in *Caller Herrin'*, whose generous multiplicity of camera positions, fine composition and streamlined montage results in exhilarating passages of space and movement as a hundred steam drifters an afternoon leave to feed on the then limitless supplies: 'the herring must be moved quickly while they're

Waverley Steps 1947. Greenpark for the COI/Scottish Home Dept. The Scottish Office initiated a series of sponsored documentary films during and after the war. The last of these, and arguably the finest, *Waverley Steps*, looked at the lives of a number of Edinburgh's citizens over a 24 hour period. Here the coalman has finished his rounds for the day and is giving the bookie's runner his line for the afternoon's race.

still bright in the eye and the sea-tang is still on them', says the narrator in resonant RP tones, giving 'tang' something more than a mere diphthong which makes the phrase sound doubly inappropriate on his lips. *Caller Herrin'* has striking and dramatic shots of steam drifters ploughing through a heavy swell and some especially hypnotic shots of scores of steam drifters in procession entering and leaving the Scottish port of Fraserburgh. One shot from a camera in the boat at the tail of such a departure to sea has a long column of these photogenic old ships snaking smokily past the lighthouse, the frame packed with masts, funnels, gulls, and ships, the viewer's eye led compulsively out of the harbour by the furthest boat.

Other films from this context of production might be less ambitious, and satisfactorily matter of fact, like the 1947 *Ayrshire Cattle*, a lucid, businesslike and economical film full of pasteurised and digestible technical detail.

Of Giant Infants and Forlorn Imps

In the 1959 *Bonnets Over the Border*, a car-rally film made in the interests of an oil company, there is a poignant moment when we get a glimpse of a Scottish car, a 1913 Glasgow-built Argyle tourer. 'It should know the way', the narrator in his RP accent says wittily, over a vibraphone version of *Will Ye No Come Back Again*: there are some truly horrible things done with Scottish airs on the musical scores of the fifties and sixties. Scotland was briefly to get a car industry again.

Often in the Films of Scotland output the interest in industry is rather formalist, with an emphasis on the 'dramatic' shapes of containers and cooling towers, or, a favourite documentary discourse familiar from all over the world, but worked especially hard in Scotland, the montage of semi-abstract shots of mass-production lines, of automated processes, or of skilled work filmed from unusual angles to turn it into 'art' rather than work.

Colin McArthur has commented (in *Scotch Reels*) on the way in which *Seawards the Great Ships*, the Oscar-winning short directed by the American Hilary Harris 'from an outline treatment by John Grierson', renders invisible the actual social and historical circumstances of shipbuilding. The limitations of a concern with the visual properties of industrial process as form are repeatedly evident. A number of art forms have successfully treated work in its economic, social and political contexts, but this celebration of the Clyde seems little interested in them. An absorption with the shapes of materials, components and part-completed vessels, a general intention to eulogise and mysticise, and a script disposed to personification and hyperbole combine to emphasise tradition, timelessness and destiny over the specificities of work history and class structure.

'The men who build these monsters are like other men, hardier than some, tough in sinew, warm in spirit.' A group of these sinewy warm hard fellows are having some tea on an enchanting morning beside the

Caller Herrin. 1947 Campbell Harper for the COI/Scottish Home Dept. The fleet sets out in the early morning. A promotional film to stimulate consumption of herring. In general supply despite the rigours of food rationing, the public nevertheless needed encouragement to buy up the vast quantities of fish being landed at the Scottish ports.

river bank. The skies are sunny, there are strong morning shadows and screaming gulls. It looks very pleasant, and the men are photographed as an integral part of a workscape of ladders, tresses and plates. One of them is warmly sharing his provender with the gulls, and the viewer knows instinctively that this isn't the kind of fellow who will throw an unsuspecting gull a hot chip. 'Dwarfed by the steel giants they create, they live among ships, and remain themselves.' What it is which they thus avoid becoming remains a mystery.

The film's absorption with the visual intricacies of the industrial process is hard to resist, and technically there is much which is admirable about it. Yet its persistent note of transcendence grates increasingly as it progresses. Its insistence upon 'mighty pieces of steel', 'giant jigsaws', and a flanging machine which contrives at once to be 'brutal', 'loving' and 'uncompromising', leads to rapidly diminishing returns. As 'the ship's form becomes clear', the tempo of shipbuilding quickens into a 'great thundering symphony'. The following montage intercuts a number of shots of hands, legs, drills and other isolated fragments with shots at variable distances of enthusiastic, responsible working-class experts plainly relishing their subordination to the mystic pattern. The humorous, at moments rather contrived-looking shots of witty workers' graffiti, which are all visual jokes of an unchallenging variety, only bolster the impression of men at home in a deeply natural process.

The launch and post-launch sequences are notable for the script's contraction of *Touch of Scotland* syndrome: 'here is a feat both splendid and improbable: a mountain of steel that has never before moved as one will be flung downhill into a strip of water to become alive'. Emboldened by this flourish, the script now breaks completely free of its strait-jacket.

In a dramatic low angle shot, a hawser descends in slow motion from the deck, to be grasped expertly by a pair of warm sinewy hands: 'a rope to tether a live thing: the giant infant of the shipyard, floating free, feels her first curb, the first of many moorings, in the first rope, that ties her to her first tug'. The giant infant departs to the sound of tugs. 'Of her own strength at last she moves', intones the script, with an invertedness which would have graced the March of Time.

These characteristics are widely evident. In *The Heart of Scotland* to another Grierson outline and directed and photographed by the impressive team of Laurence Henson and Eddie McConnell, the conversion of known social values and historical facts to components of some timeless and transcendent dimension seems especially laboured. We begin with the usual attributions to Scotland of vastness, emptiness, turbulence and bloodiness. The script has much of the contrivance and poeticising so familiar from elsewhere, despite the inventiveness and assuredness of the shooting and cutting.

Like the much earlier *Face of Scotland*, the film is deeply concerned to establish a continuity between the medieval past and the technological present. A scientific investigation of moss-land becomes an act of timeless heroism: 'to win back land from such a long stagnation,

Seawards the Great Ships 1961. Templar Films for Films of Scotland. Half of the necessary finance for this film came from the Clyde Shipbuilders Association with the stipulation that it was to be a tribute to the Clyde and to its shipbuilding greatness.

some man must say, this is my land under me, I give myself to it and here I will live with it'. All the man is doing, actually, is testing the depth of the bog and getting earth samples.

Even as late as *A9: Highland Highway* (1982), the historical synthesizing, and the motion from the material to the timeless and mythic, still intermittently appears. The road represents the latest in engineering skill and technology, but the historic nature of the route is heavily emphasised. Despite the strongly informational tendency of the film – and there are some good road-based travelling shots as well as some exhilarating aerial work to accompany a discussion of landscape architecture – the actual process of work, when we see it at the end of the film, is familiar. To Oldfield-influenced synthesizer music we are treated to some more timeless teamwork by 'these twentieth-century Highlanders'.

But the material nature of Scottish life will out, anyway, sometimes when it's least expected. The uninvitingly titled *Holiday Scotland* in fact opens with promise. Despite the mandatory castle, this one is at least placed, rather spikily, in history: 'many an Englishman bled his fingers on it'. The film soon becomes rather prosaic ('you'll find several golf courses – this is one of them'). But it has a moment to relish.

On the ferry *The Maid of Kylesku* is a little, very bright red car in a huge gloomy landscape. The music is mournful and the ferry is dark green and its paint is peeling against a background of empty mountains.

The little car is moved slowly on the turntable and shot from a variety of distances and camera positions as it circles. Are we looking, suddenly, at a car-industry marketing film? Yes, since *Holiday Scotland* is mainly a compilation of footage from other Films of Scotland movies. After a moment or two the shot is chiefly about the car rather than the place, and the music is mournful on its behalf. It is a sad sequence because it represents, out of place, out of context, out of time, and like a predictive intrusion from the collective Scottish unconscious, a vision of further industrial death. The car is a Hillman Imp. Unlike the Argyle, it looks lost.

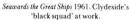

Seawards the Great Ships 1961. Clydeside's 'black squad' at work.

Scotland in the Material World

The work of Murray Grigor has suggested how to open up other documentary discourses about Scotland.

Prospect of Scotland (1975) has a sort of polemical strength. Opening on a reference to Scotland as 'the country with a rich romantic past' and shots of a traveller browsing through postcards of Nessie, Highland cattle and pipers, and of duty-free shop fare of whisky, and packaged grouse and salmon, the film quickly subverts viewer expectations. Scotland, we discover, is 'the second most industrialised nation in Europe: only Germany has a higher percentage of her population engaged in industry'. It is thereafter chiefly to matters such as nuclear power, petrochemicals, oil production and other industrial activities,

Clydescope 1974. Viz for Films of Scotland.
John Byrne and Donald Holwill's
animated Billy Connolly off 'doon the
watter' with banjo and bicycle.

as well as transportation, that the film addresses itself.

Other documentaries, such as the rather mannered 1966 *County on the Move*, about West Lothian, had sought, as did the later East Kilbride and other new town films, to modernise Scotland in representation: in *County on the Move*, the metaphors are often aggressively industrial ('six small towns are the ball-bearings of West Lothian') but despite its new schools 'filled with the techniques for teaching far and beyond the three Rs' and its motorways and the general air of contemporary hustle and mobility which the film conjures, it retains a number of the formal interests and historical attachments of *Heart of Scotland* and others of that ilk.

Grigor's film is more ruthless in its subversion of established myths about Scotland, eschews elements of these previous discourses, and ends with a flourish in which, again browsing through a postcard rack, the

69

traveller finds Scotland represented by petrochemical plants, aircraft, oil platforms and reactors.

The earlier and particularly interesting 1974 *Clydescope*'s lightness of touch and ironical approach to the representation of Scotland provide a refreshing demonstration of how lyricism and sonority can be avoided with profit. The film deploys visual jokes, an ironical narration, animated sequences and the emphatically contemporary presence of Billy Connolly, along with a general air of playfulness, which could hardly be more different from the approach of *Seawards the Great Ships*. It is therefore more satisfactorily about its subject than many a previous attempt and despite its ironies, begins its project with a relish to discuss the country in its recognisable contemporary form, inasmuch as its purpose allows it.

Avoiding cliche with determination, it begins with Biggar Folk Museum. History there is a material history, political and military, with never a ghost in sight. This approach is maintained throughout. The authorial stance is in fact rather detached, not so much by irony as jokiness. This, and the device of using Billy Connolly's mad tramp on a bicycle as a narrative link, mean that the film isn't without weakness. It hovers rather confusingly on the edge of being a sort of star vehicle for Connolly. Yet at the same time it becomes sufficiently absorbed in its location material intermittently to forget his role. There is some skilful intercutting of 1909 travelogue footage and a periodically bizarre score featuring Connolly's musical talents. (In the Arran sequence this inaugurates a certain sentimentalism.)

But the film's wobbly moments are only the results of its adventurousness, though there were other instances – notably the same director's *Scotch Myths* (1982) – where jokiness so supplanted irony that a worthwhile project was in danger of foundering. But here, nothing could be a more welcome change from sonorous reassurances about the ghosts of the Scottish past, than the shots of a German family enjoying the bears in the park on Loch Lomond. As they pull away in their VW, we see a Swedish car parked in the layby, and moments later, two French girls from a 2CV shouting encouragement to a compatriot in a cosmopolitan cycle race: Scotland in Europe (prophetic stuff). There's bluegrass on the soundtrack: music from the diaspora. And Glasgow, rather slighted by a certain sort of tourism film, is back where it should be, at the centre of things.

Best of all, perhaps, is the sense of a view of Scotland from Scotland, not that distant interest of a *Crofter Boy* (1955) or *Introducing Scotland*, (1958) a view from the south, where local names and terms are pronounced with a fastidious detached care. And not the sort of hybrid consciousness found in *Seawards*, where Glasgow is a British river in the British shipbuilding tradition: or in a number of the travelogues, and other films, in which a seeming sympathy for Scotland barely disguises an attitude to her which is, if thought through, politically very hostile indeed. And if Grigor is not fully sure what to substitute for what is deconstructed: well, who is?

Hollywood Comes to the Highlands

David Bruce

It was John Grierson, inevitably, who put it in a way that allowed no answer. In 1960 David Cleghorn Thomson, the editor of the Saltire Review, asked Grierson if there could be a Scottish film industry. Grierson's answer came as a letter for publication.

> Sir, – You ask me: is a Scottish film industry possible? My own answer is No. You remember the burghers of Calais who, poor souls, failed to fire a salute for the English king and were up, hats off, on the royal mat. They said they had seven good reasons to advance. They duly advanced them cogently and in great detail, one by one. The seventh was that they had no guns. Don't let us fool ourselves. It is not in the Scottish mind or heart these days to risk the necessary dough.

Grierson reckoned that even without the problem of the guns, there were plenty of other lesser reasons for the impossibility of it all. There wasn't the talent. There wasn't the special need that existed in small countries with their own language to protect but, above all, there was no real interest on the part of public authorities in the making of film. Only when public interest and those of the filmmakers coincided, as they did briefly in the Films of Scotland documentaries, could there be any chance of even modest success. As for feature film studios with all their paraphernalia that was quite another matter.

Grierson was correct, as usual. At least he was at the time. The problem of the public dimension certainly was there. But even in 1960 there were those who couldn't rest easy with what Grierson and others said because, surely the logic against a film industry in Scotland was based on experience which was passed and surely times had changed, and if other small countries could do it why not us?

Of course there were problems of definition. To most people, and the press, 'film industry' meant 'Hollywood', which meant stars and studios and hundreds, maybe thousands, of jobs. Despite that, surely the popularity of film was such, and the potential rewards so great, that even we must be able to make something come about? It seems that the dream refused to go away.

Certainly the continuing mass appeal of the movies was never really in doubt. Even in the days of the steepest decline in audiences, when

" We've signed him up; his grand-father posed for Landseer."

Glasgow Evening News, 28th May 1946

cinema closures were at their most frequent and migration by the millions to bingo seemed to signal the end of movie-going as a popular form of entertainment, the appetite for films never really waned; it was only the means of transmission that changed.

Even now, after the recent upturn in attendances, the number of people seeing films in the circumstances for which they were originally intended – projected on 35 mm in a dark auditorium – is small in comparison with the total of those seeing them on television. The fact that cinema and television need each other has not always been evident to those who run the industries but it is clear enough now. No new satellite or terrestrial network is likely to eschew feature films if it can get them and new films, or the lack of them, can be a determining element in the attractiveness of every broadcasting package. The audience figures for film still count in millions and tens of millions.

Although the financial importance of film to broadcasting is not in doubt, the contemporary social importance of cinema-going as a habit is less clear. Cinema may be one of the best formats for creating audiences on a recurring basis but it is not unique in that respect. What's much more interesting, particularly in a small and, maybe, developing culture such as our own, is the cultural significance of cinema and the status we should allow or give to film as a means of expression. If cinema mattered in Scotland, does that become an argument for a full-scale industry? Should we still bother whether or not we have a cinema business or filmmaking studios and would we be any less ourselves if we do not make and show film in this country?

Cinema has a tremendous capacity to sell itself by its glamour. It might be thought that after all these years we would know enough about the movies and their ways of working (and not least their track record in dealing with Scotland) to have developed some sort of defence against the hype, but not so. 'The Highlands could become a new Hollywood,' said the Aberdeen *Press and Journal* on 23 May 1990. It was referring to the rather provisional award of modest development grants to two Scottish film projects which would be based in the Highlands.

Small though they may have been, they were indicative of a new kind of thinking about film. The important thing about those awards was that they were based on an assessment of the potential economic impact of location shooting by film companies. This new, realistic, awareness stemmed from the success of Orkney Islands Council's decision to back *Venus Peter* with a £60,000 grant, an investment which was rewarded with a local spend of several times that amount. The notion of 'glamour' was less important than that of economics. How much cultural factors played a role in the decision is an interesting question but does not provide the whole answer. The thought that there can at last be a positive and progressive realism to filmmaking in Scotland, based on cultural *and* economic returns, is very encouraging. Realism has not always been conspicuous in Scotland's ambitions to become a filmmaking nation.

Any discussion of Scotland's cultural experience and aspirations has to begin with a recognition of its political circumstances. Whatever the rights or wrongs of the situation, Scotland, since 1707, is a component of the United Kingdom, a country ninety percent of whose population do not live in Scotland. In making comparisons with 'other small countries' we have to acknowledge that we are not usually measuring like against like politically but, at best, culturally. Even culturally Scotland is not in a very strong position to determine its own priorities. Culture often depends on economics, and in no form of expression do money and art come closer than in cinema.

There was always another kind of obstacle to a feature industry in Scotland. Because we suffered the double burden of being a part of a larger economy which was in turn dominated by American cinema and because we spoke a form of English, filmmaking never seemed to 'belong' to us as a potential means of expression. We were always avid consumers but making movies was something that went on elsewhere – mainly in Hollywood – and the idea that we would go to the pictures to see ourselves as we would represent ourselves did not seem much of a possibility until Bill Forsyth took us by surprise.

Many of the contemporary Scottish filmmakers are the product of a 'school' of high grade documentary film-making, mostly on 35 mm, for the Films of Scotland Committee. Forsyth Hardy, the committee's director, pursued the idea that the creation of a skilled workforce in documentary was the precondition for more advanced forms of filmmaking and his line of pursuit was vindicated to some extent when the Children's Film Foundation commissioned story films – in effect low-budget features – from the talents which Films of Scotland had nurtured. Although there was no breakthrough into mainstream feature filmmaking there was some sense of direction, and the necessary elements were certainly taking shape before *That Sinking Feeling* was made.

The conceptual step, to make us believe that films by us about us could possibly be of interest to anyone other than us, was quite hard to grasp. However, long before Bill Forsyth took the first steps to capture film as a credible medium for our use, and well before Grierson's bucket of cold water in 1960 there had been at least one serious attempt to create a 'Scottish film industry' which had it succeeded would have dramatically changed our perception of film. That attempt may have been largely forgotten but apart from being an interesting tale in its own right it illustrates the whole problem of equating 'film industry' with 'film studios'. It is a story of raised expectations and of misdirected sentiment.

In 1946 a sense of direction was rather absent in the attempt to create a Scottish film industry. The scheme owed almost nothing to careful preparation and everything to a romantic idealism which derived its energies partly from nationalism and partly from the glamour of films. This was the time when Hollywood was at its most powerful, before television, and while the audiences were at their all-time high peak.

Joseph MacLeod was the prime mover in the attempt to establish the Scottish National Film Studios. During the Second World War, he was famous as the first personality news broadcaster. His 'acceptable' Scottish accent and the catchphrase 'and this is Joseph MacLeod reading it' endeared him to many listeners. Too radical for the BBC, he resigned in 1945 in opposition to its 'unrealistic attitude towards post-war broadcasting'.

Although there are not many people today with first-hand accounts of the story, and the documentation is sparse, it seems that the initial idea was proposed by Mr T G Wolk who was described in the *Scots Independent* as a 'Russian expert' and his plan as 'this important undertaking for civilisation'. Apparently there had been serious discussion of the scheme immediately before the war but it was two short essays by Wolk that eventually triggered the project. No Scottish enterprise can proceed without a committee and on 3 November 1945 a group of 'interested persons' met in Glasgow to set up the initial machinery for launching the project. The Chairman was Sir Hugh S Roberton whose prominence and public acceptability would have been beyond doubt through his conductorship of the Glasgow Orpheus Choir. The rest of the membership was less famous but included several distinguished Scots such as Moultrie Kelsall, William McLellan and William Montgomerie, but perhaps just as significantly it lacked any representation from the established film people or from government.

The key figure, however, was the managing director who was appointed at the outset. Joseph Macleod was at least as famous as Hugh S Roberton, possibly more so. During the war, Macleod was one of the select band of radio news readers known by name. It was a practice adopted by the BBC for the duration as a help to insure listeners against deception by enemy imitators and then abandoned for many years until television determined that news-readers, like other people, had identities which could not be ignored. Macleod was therefore associated in the public mind with both the most seriously threatening, and the most encouraging aspects of the war and was consequently a national figure and certainly one of the best known Scots of the time. His voice was deep and distinctive and, in his broadcasting, demonstrated just enough of his native origins without damaging his acceptability elsewhere.

His qualifications for the job of Managing Director of Scottish National Film Studios were less impressive. As a poet (in his own name, and as 'Adam Drinan') he had a good reputation but beyond that he brought less practical experience than idealism. Indeed he had a poet's vision but also a training in law, and eight years experience with the BBC. His parting from the Corporation was by way of resignation but it seems to have been less than amicable. He was thought to be too radical for the spirit of the times and a Scottish national cause would have fitted in well with his ambition. Apart from some documentary commentaries, it was to be his first and last experience of film.

The initiators' vision was of a scale of filmmaking which makes today's modest achievements look like an apology, and there are elements of it which are embarrassingly familiar given the lack of progress of the intervening four decades. The best sense of what Macleod and his colleagues were after is to be found in a small twelve page booklet which they produced as a fund-raising and consciousness-raising device. It is called *Scotland on the Screen* – a title adopted later by the second Films of Scotland Committee for its public shows more

Someone Wasn't Thinking 1946. Scottish National Film Studios. Setting up a shot. The camera is hidden by road menders' hut to encourage natural behaviour by those pedestrians not aware that they were being filmed.

than ten years later. Its cover design shows a rather distorted outline of Scotland projected on to a screen in a shade of lilac. If its content sometimes seems also somewhat removed from reality, there is no question of where its heart is.

It is written in a slightly elevated tone characteristic of the times. It is full of generalities about film, but more obviously about Scotland, its heritage, its abuse by London, its unique people. It is about patriotism and how if the reader is a good Scot it is inevitable that *he* (no suggestion of otherwise) must support the initiative which will redress the imbalance of all previous representation and give us back national pride, by way of the silver screen.

The 'Introduction' deals with the 'goodness' of film. It deplores the representation of Scotland on the screen.

> Hollywood and London, with few exceptions, have presented the Scot as a bibulous comic in small parts. In fact, however, no country produces human individuals with sharp characteristics more naturally or more abundantly than Scotland. This is indeed a feature of the Scottish nation!

Scotland's history and Scotland's scenery provide it with 'unbeatable' film material, 'true instruction or rich entertainment'. There is a demand for such films and only the Scots, not Americans or English, can interpret Scotland. Scottish National Film Studios have been organised and planned with these facts in mind.

Hope Street, Glasgow. Preparing to shoot
scenes in the dramatised instructional film
on road safety.

In the main section of the pamphlet 'The Purpose', audiences are identified at home and abroad where:

> the loyal and maintained interest in Scotland shown by people of Scottish parentage or connection in the Dominions or in the United States of America is well known.

The Gaelic-speaking communities of 'Canada and Newfoundland' are cited as potential recipients for a:

> supply of films of Scottish scenery and beauty spots, films of historic places and incidents accurately and brilliantly made . . . A regular but not rushed Scottish News Reel will not only describe current events, but explain them.

One of the most important functions of a new Scottish Film Industry will be the 'spreading of knowledge of Scottish industry and culture in foreign countries' but 'in this delicate matter', the policy of the Scottish National Film Studios will not be 'indiscriminately commercial'. The film industry will 'play a not unimportant part in the coming revival of Scottish prosperity'. There will be specially dubbed versions for foreign countries.

> Real international knowledge of the way other peoples live, eat, buy, relax, play, work and travel is the only sure guarantee of

76

world peace; and the screen is the easiest international method of distributing such knowledge and understanding.

Positioning extras ready to start shooting a scene.

The scale of the promoters' ambition becomes fully evident on page seven. Under a sub-heading 'Other activities', the potential subscriber learns that, 'As soon as practicable, a site in suitable climatic conditions will be chosen, in the northern half of the country where a model community' will be formed. 'Here the Scottish National Film Industry will take root.'

> Young talent will be trained in the technical aspects of filmmaking and equipped to take their place later *as creative artists and good Scots* (my italics) . . . Film archives, a reference library, and other amenities for the serious study of the art of the cinema will be initiated in conjunction, perhaps, with a Chair of Cinematography at one of the Scottish Universities or Technical Colleges . . . It is essential that brains, skill and equipment shall be of the very highest quality. Scottish film must be an example to the world.

All this and a great deal more was to be brought about by a financial package which included foundation credits from the North of Scotland Bank and a combination of loans and donations from the people and institutions of Scotland. Staffing would be no great problem as 'English and American film studios contain a large number of skilled Scottish artists and craftsmen, who can earn large rewards there, but

77

would rather return to Scotland if they could be assured of equally good rewards.' The most up-to-date equipment would be installed. Constant research would be undertaken 'so that the latest discoveries can be explored at once'. Temporary offices 'pending the move to the Highlands' were taken at 121 St Vincent Street, Glasgow, C2.

At this distance the impossibility of it all seems clear almost to the point of absurdity. The 'model community' has echoes of New Lanark, but also the Darien Scheme in it and the idea of finding somewhere with a suitable climate seems as likely as that of hundreds of exiled Scottish film technicians flooding back from across the world; but we must remember the context. The war had only just ended; the cold version not yet begun. If ever there was a time for idealism it was surely then.

Inevitably reality prevailed, and fairly quickly. The attempt to lease a redundant airfield in the north-east came to nothing. The financial target of £60-100,000 got about a tenth of the way to success and only one film, a road safety documentary called with no irony intended *Someone Wasn't Thinking* (produced by 'Scotsmen in Scotland') was made. Even it, sadly, has vanished without trace, save for a few production stills.

By mid-1946 the company was already in difficulties; a restructured Council, including writer and political activist, Naomi Mitchison, couldn't help, and although the final winding up meeting didn't take place until December 1954 the effective end came on 16 January 1947. Sir Hugh Roberton, in the Chair, had no doubt that Joseph Macleod had done his best. It had been 'an economic failure', 'a failure of Scotsmen' and 'films are chancy, anyway'.

The films Joseph Macleod had in mind to make included a biography of Mary MacArthur, the trade union pioneer, and a Scottish-Spanish co-production on an original story *The Young Brother*. A story of 'Lowland industrial life' was promised 'true, exciting, funny and moving . . . which may well be a model of what an authentic film on a Scottish theme should be', but perhaps the most remarkable aspect to the whole enterprise lies not in it itself and its ambitions but the enthusiasm it aroused in others at the time.

It was a key element of the scheme that it should involve and have the backing of the Scottish people. Perhaps the appeal to nationalism was a little crude at times but there was also a very strong democratic imperative present. At the first statutory meeting of Scottish National Film Studios in April 1946 Roberton referred to 'local representation in each town'. Fund-raising was conducted on a basis of loans and donations, £10 being the standard amount for a loan. The list of donors and investors contains not only the expected well-known individuals but a range of organisations including several local co-operatives. The SCWS itself lent £2,000 for four years, Greenock East Co-op £100. The Lanarkshire, Dumfriesshire, and Greenock Central Co-ops lent £500 each. Lord Glentanner lent £100, Gordon Jackson £10 as did the Glasgow Skye Association. There were donations from the

South Shields Caledonian Society, the Glasgow Orpheus Choir, the Rev Selby Wright, the Kilmarnock Burns Club and individuals from New Zealand, Canada, and Malaya, but the plain fact was that the amounts were generally small and there were far too few of them.

On 21 March 1947 the Glasgow *Evening Times* carried a regretful piece to the effect that 'Joseph Macleod's patriotic return to Scotland has not yielded the results he had hoped for – he has resigned from Scottish National Film Studios Ltd and this morning entrained for the south'. He had returned from exile, full of enthusiasm for the 'brave new Scotland' only to find that 'the going is still sticky'. He had gone with a policy of 'no recriminations'.

In fact there had been a certain amount of nastiness in parts of the press centring on Wolk's origins and Macleod's politics and lack of experience and certainly there was no denying that the whole affair could have been better handled. Macleod was utterly sincere but he and his colleagues failed to make any significant connections with Government in Scotland or with the major businesses and financial institutions. The list of investors is remarkable for those it leaves out as much as for those it includes.

A private letter to Macleod, written in 1946 suggests clearly what was wrong. He had failed to approach the Scottish Office on the grounds that he did not wish to approach them for work until he was able to carry it out. He, or rather those who had employed him, had also failed to make early connections with those who were already involved in film in Scotland, and who were probably already considering other initiatives. Whether offence was taken and co-operation withheld is not clear but Macleod writes 'I find my native race as touchy as ever'. The moral of the story was evident enough: however good the intentions and worthy the project, it is essential to remember that Scotland is a small country and you must make all the right connections first.

The whole episode seems to confirm Grierson's dictum that it was simply not in the Scottish psyche to make feature movies and particularly not in the psychological make-up of public authorities in Scotland to become involved. (Incidentally, Grierson himself was almost entirely absent from this affair, other than to recommend Harry Watt to Macleod as a possible director.) At least Grierson did concede that the public authorities were the key and if there is one crucial distinction to make between the time of Macleod and Grierson and the present it is in the attitude of public agencies in Scotland to film.

Gradually cinema has become an issue for local government. The establishing of Regional Film Theatres, the growth of media studies, and the recognition of the potential economic impact of filmmaking, leading to the formation of Scottish Screen Locations (an organisation formed specifically to promote Scotland as a venue for filmmaking) have encouraged local authorities to consider film and all the media industries as potentially important to them.

Another equally important change has been within the film industry itself. To the promoters of Scottish National Film Studios with their strong nationalist inclinations, the need for Scotland to have a film industry of its own was partly symbolic, a sign of virility, like the national football team at the World Cup, and the possibility would not have occurred to them of having a film industry without the full cost and complexity of film studios in the Hollywood sense. In fact, as we have found, it is possible to have good filmmaking without studios at all.

Even so, the equation of industry with studios remains strong in the public mind and it is possible to find very similar press headlines in 1946 in relation to Scottish National Film Studios and in 1984 with reference to a proposal to establish a state-of-the-art film studio in Clydebank. *The Scotsman* headlines of 7 February 1984 would have done just as well thirty-eight years earlier; 'Clydebank reaches for the stars'. There is a similar feel to a report in the *Sunday Standard* on 15 May 'Hollywood touch to old shipyard'.

As promoted in 1984, the Clydebank scheme has parallels with Scottish National Film Studios but is very different in most respects and the differences illuminate shifts in the perception of film as well as advances in technology. Like Scottish National Film Studios, it was on a grand scale, both physically and financially. The idea was to convert a 60,000 square foot factory in Clydebank at a reported cost of over £10m in order to produce spectacular films using a 'revolutionary' system called 'Futuronics' which, in effect, disposed of the conventional need for massive sets to create large-scale effects. A combination of computer technology with a front projection system created the illusion that actors are working within the most elaborate and spectacular settings while in fact operating on a bare floor.

Scottish National Film Studios had depended for its appeal on pride in Scotland's place in this world – whatever that might be. Clydebank represented the very opposite. Its rationale was that film was so universal not only from a consumer perspective but in its manufacture that it didn't matter in the least what national context it operated in. 'Futuronics' would even bring its own scenery with it and the choice of Clydebank was a device used by international business largely for financial reasons. Certainly those reasons included benefit to the local community but only because the community could supply people with skills as joiners and electricians – the skills no longer required by a shrinking shipbuilding industry. The decision to come to Clydebank had nothing to do with Scotland in any cultural sense and everything to do with the economic development status of the area.

The other significant difference was the involvement of public authorities in the project. The possibility of public investment in a film project on such a scale was never even contemplated by the promoters of Scottish National Film Studios. Considering the state of the immediate post-war economy in Scotland such a thing would have been certainly remote but in any case it was not in the mood of the times. Public investment was expressed in the nationalisation of heavy industry, not the entertainment business.

It would be too easy to characterise the difference between Scottish National Film Studios and the Clydebank project as being noble cultural aspiration versus market economy. For one thing, Clydebank would have ended up as more of an expression of public confidence in filmmaking than Scottish National Film Studios through public financial investment. It is only in their scale, and what they were seen to represent (a Hollywood of our very own) they are very similar.

It would also be easy to forget that in the meantime Scotland has in any case acquired film studios which though admittedly of more modest proportions than the proposition we have been examining have still managed to fulfil the function of allowing studio-based filmmaking to occur here. Setting aside television studios in the broadcasting and educational sectors there has been filmmaking at Edinburgh Film Productions' studio near Penicuik since the sixties which may not have encompassed full scale feature work but deserves to be recognised as the first successful venture of the kind.

In 1985 a former cinema in Springfield Road, Glasgow, which had been used at one stage by the BBC as its first television studio in the city, was leased by Antonine Productions Ltd and became the base and studio for *The Girl in the Picture*. The premises, Blackcat Studios, were purchased the following year and have since been used very successfully for feature production and, more recently, for independent studio-based television. Blackcat has also been successful in attracting a limited amount of public funding albeit only as loans and it, too, may well benefit from the evolution of positive public authority thinking towards filmmaking in Scotland.

Any attempt at reaching conclusions, or forecasting developments on the basis of our limited experience in trying to create a studio-based film industry in Scotland, must be tentative but at least some matters are reasonably clear. For instance we can be fairly sure that the sudden arrival of a ready-made, studio-based industry of the 1946 model is liable to remain as improbable as it was then. Neither local nor international economics will allow us the satisfaction of a studio-led industry resembling those of the Scandinavian countries. Their films and national languages and other cultural issues are close to their governments' hearts; and the public is ready to pay the subsidising price.

Norway is frequently quoted as a model for Scotland but that country is only partly in parallel with us. Their six to ten features a year may provide us with a desirable target and their public authorities' attitude to film is enviable but their politics and their cultural pre-occupations are different from ours.

The English-speaking Commonwealth nations provide better parallels. Even they however have more favourable circumstances for filmmaking both politically and climatically. At any rate, a simple single-stroke solution does not seem available to us.

Far more likely as a way ahead is a combination of self help and a

81

winning of public authority support. Scotland's first truly indigenous feature films were made by Bill Forsyth by making rather than by agonising about film. The moral is plain enough. If we do need studios – and there are those in the business who are not convinced that we do – we will achieve them incrementally, brick by brick, as we have made whatever progress we have to date.

The public perception about the movies may not change greatly. Hollywood will still be coming to the Highlands, or Harthill for that matter, every time there is talk of feature filmmaking in Scotland but maybe we shouldn't complain too much. It may be that the glamour and the hype are inimical to the presbyterian soul but, like the movies themselves, we will go on loving them just the same.

Family Pictures

Andrew Young

In the pioneering days of Scottish cinema, two families were to make a significant contribution to the industry. They were the Singletons in Glasgow and the Pooles in Edinburgh. Their influence was to cover many decades and was to bring a richness to the lives of the cinema-going public. Their success over the years was because of a love of what they were doing rather than an ambition to make a lot of money. They were the right people in the right place at the right time and they had the foresight and flexibility to adjust to changing trends.

The Singleton dynasty was launched in 1908 by Richard Vincent Singleton, whose sons George and Vincent were to create a Glasgow institution, the *Cosmo*. This was the first custom-built cinema outside of London for the showing of quality films, irrespective of where they came from. It was a far-sighted piece of initiative that added greatly to the range of films that could be seen in the most film-conscious city in Britain, possibly Europe.

Self-improvement and education were ideals among the working class in the late Victorian and Edwardian eras, a fact that did not go unnoticed by the Singletons or the Pooles who had a natural instinct for knowing what the public wanted and they were showmen who knew how to make the most of what was available.

George Singleton is a man of the century, which was only five hours and forty minutes old when he arrived, born in a tenement at 92 Main Street, Bridgeton, in Glasgow's east end.

The fact that George celebrated his 90th birthday on 1 January, the day Glasgow started its year as European City of Culture, seemed appropriate, as, in his own quiet way, he contributed a great deal to the cultural regeneration of his city. To the public he was for long *Mr Cosmo*, as represented by the drawing of the little bowler-hatted gentleman used on the logo for the cinema advertising. It was not just in the cinema business that he made his contribution. He was a founder member of the Citizens' Theatre, eventually becoming its chairman. For twenty years he was director of the Scottish Orchestra which he saw develop into the Scottish National Orchestra of today, and he was on the Board of the Scottish Film Council

George always knows exactly what age he was in any year of the century and he has no doubt that he was eight when his father first entered the cinema business in 1908. And, to a lesser degree, that was when George made his entry, too, going round with a tray, shouting; 'Car-a-mels, toffee, choc-o-late!'

'Mr Cosmo' the dapper bowler hatted figure who appeared on programmes and in the press inviting patrons to sample the delights of the latest offering at the *Cosmo*.

83

The world in which the young George Singleton was growing up was an exciting place, full of new ideas waiting to be grasped. Shortly after he was born the family moved to Rutherglen just over the city boundary. His father was a socialist of high ideals who believed in the improvement of the working class, by reading and self-education. His mother was a supporter of the suffragette cause and he had an aunt who was a militant suffragette. One of his earliest memories are of two ladies coming to the house in Rutherglen and staying for a couple of nights. At the time he thought this strange as it was a small house and normally they would not have had room to accommodate visitors. It was not until years later that he was told they were suffragettes on the run, staying in safe houses, after having set fire to the stand at Ayr race course.

There was always music in the household, together with the interest in politics and thoughts of a better life. George's father was a pioneer of the Independent Labour Party. His parents were modern-thinking people, quite advanced in their ideas, yet they never thought of sending him to university. Nor did the idea occur to him, although there was nothing to prevent it. He was happy to leave school, aged 15, and go into the family business.

His father had started up a small printing business but was a hopeless businessman, more interested in new ideas. He produced a lot of political pamphlets, and, because he was also printing posters and programmes, showmen started coming to see him. This was when he was introduced to the earliest film shows, and then, because of his interest in music, he started playing the piano for silent films in his spare time. Eventually he decided to have a go at presenting film shows himself. George said, 'This was on a part-time basis at first but after a while my father decided he would just sell the printing business. That suited me fine because I loved the cinema. He sold it to another politically-daft person and when the 1914 war came along he was arrested and served a term in prison for printing seditious anti-war propaganda.'

His father started running cinema shows in odd halls, like the town hall at Motherwell, on Saturday nights and in the public hall in Larkhall. George said: 'I was just thinking about some of the risks we took without realising it. These were public halls with loose forms for seating. There were a lot of political meetings in them in those days and they just pushed the forms back when there was a dance or concert. When we moved in we made a space, tied up a screen at one end of the hall, then planked a projector down in the middle and there was nothing between the projector and the audience. They were sitting there, smoking their cigarettes and pipes. In the winter they would gather round a fireplace at one end of the hall, and here we were with these highly inflammable films lying around. It terrifies me just to think of it now. We were quite unaware of what we were doing. There were no safety regulations in those days.'

'There must have been a few mishaps. I think we were pretty lucky.

84

We did have a fire in a place that my father had in Blantyre. It was a hall above a pub and there was only one stairway up to it. The only heating in the hall was an open fire. But in this case we had a proper projection room on another floor higher up. As a result of the fire we had to build another exit.'

They used to run two shows a night, at 6.30 p.m. and 8.30 p.m. The timings were decided to some extent by the transport that was available. In those days when his father was in Lanarkshire they were dependent on the Lanarkshire tramways which ran to Cambuslang. Having got to Cambuslang, they changed over to the Glasgow tramcars to get home.

One of the difficulties he remembers acutely was that on a Friday night they also ran go-as-you please competitions and it was more difficult to regulate the times. Almost invariably on a Friday they had to walk home with the drawings in their pockets, seven, eight or nine pounds in coppers. 'To walk from Burnbank to our house we had to cover a distance of about ten miles, carrying whatever we had to carry, and there was always plenty. We always had to divide it up between us. Because we changed the films every night in those days, fortunately we didn't have to carry them home with us. They came up each morning.'

He remembered there had been a whole lot of film renters in Glasgow, all sorts of little places where they had films, single reel in the main. A feature film would be two reels. The running time of a feature then would be round about twenty minutes. That would be two reels. A reel took eleven minutes to be projected. Admission prices were tuppence and fourpence. The dear seats were at the back.

The Singletons had two cinemas in Bridgeton, the *Paragon* and *Premier Pictures*. With boys running the reels of films between the two cinemas, the family would make a profit of fifteen pounds on a good week. *Premier Pictures* had belonged to one of the real founders of the cinema business in Glasgow, a Mr Bennell who ran *BB Pictures*. He had the *Wellington Palace* on the south side and in the basement he ran a film rental business, too. His son took over and became an important man in the cinema business. Sir A B King was to become one of the major renters, not to mention a friend of all the Hollywood stars who came to Scotland.

In the very early days they had films from all over the world. They had French and German films. The language didn't matter as they were all silent, although they did have sub-titles. At that stage his father only played the piano occasionally, such as when they were running the variety competitions and he would go and help out. That was what he was good at – accompanying singers.

In the early days there was a system of grading films according to their age. They were not exclusive. It was known as the open market. It was 7s 6d a reel, roughly, and that was for three nights. Of course it went up from that if you were in the centre of Glasgow and you wanted to run the new films. But the Singletons were not doing that then. The

Paragon Cinema in Glasgow's Gorbals 1926. Converted from a United Free Church the wooden pews that it was furnished with proved economical when it came to squeezing in all the children in the queue for the Saturday matinees. Some proprietors with an eye to maximising their profits would keep the fatter children to the end.

George Singleton's *Commodore Cinema* in Scotstoun. Opened in 1932 the name was chosen to reflect the area's maritime connection although the *Odeon* circuit were subsequently to change this to suit their house style. The splendid design by cinema architect John McKissack survived until demolition in the 60's.

films were about three months old when they got them. If they broke down, they had to repair them. A programme usually lasted a little less than two hours.

In 1910 when, of course, George would be ten, his father got the hall in Burnbank, Hamilton, and started his first six-nights-a-week cinema, calling it *Premier Pictures*. By the time George was fourteen, he was going to Burnbank regularly at nights. Gradually, they got some other halls. He was called up at the end of the First World War and served in the air force but was never involved in any of the hostilities.

As George got older he became more responsible for running the business. When he was twenty he felt that they were in a rut, so he formed a company to take over his first cinema, an old church in the Gorbals that had been converted by a bookie known as Little Titch, a well-known character on the south side of the river. George thinks they paid about eight thousand pounds for it, a great deal of money in those days and an indication of how the cinema business was beginning to grow. The pews were still there and they kept them as it made it easier to pack more people in. This was also to be called the *Paragon* and the prices were more or less the same as in the other places – tuppence, fourpence and sixpence.

He appointed his chum, George Archibald – 'a very able fellow' – as manager of this new *Paragon*. Then, after a while, Little Titch decided he would open another cinema. He got another old church in Eglinton Street and called it the *Bedford*. He needed someone who knew about booking the films and running the place so George Archibald became his manager. Archibald, who had made his name at the *Paragon*, was a very active socialist and became the youngest-ever town councillor in Glasgow. He stood for Parliament two or three times in Aberdeen South but did not get elected.

From the *Bedford*, Archibald went to London to take up an appointment within the cinema trade association. And from there he became secretary of United Artists in London. When United Artists took an interest in Odeon Films he became a director of that organisation, which brought him back to George Singleton. (Later he was to become Lord Archibald.) Odeon Films did not have any cinemas in Scotland and he asked George to sell the ones he had, which he did in 1935. 'At that time I still had the *Paragon*, so Lord Rank who subsequently became head of the Odeon chain, got the pews as well. He was a very religious man, a Methodist,' said George. 'Sir Alex King used to say there was a Methodism in his madness. I read in Jimmy Boyle's book of how he and his gang used to get into the *Paragon*. One of them would buy a ticket, then open a side door to let the rest in. But that was when Rank owned it. There were about eight cinemas in the deal that covered Glasgow, Falkirk, Hawick, Dundee. I was in the process of building a beautiful cinema in Dundee and they got that as well. That left me out on my own with no cinemas at all.'

The first cinema George built when he went out on his own was the *Broadway* at Shettleston in 1930. It cost about thirty thousand pounds and seated about 1,650 people. He then built *Rutherglen*, another fine cinema, which was recently sold by Rank, who had been running it as a bingo hall, to Mecca. And in that transaction Mecca also got the old *Broadway* at Shettleston. Rank did very well, selling Mecca six places for about three million pounds. When George sold out to Rank in the mid-thirties, he got something like 400,000 pounds and said that he got nearly as much as that for his house in Helensburgh when he sold it towards the end of the eighties.

After selling out, he and his brother Vincent took over the old *Boulevard* cinema in Knightswood and called it the *Vogue*. He had started to call all his cinemas the *Vogue* after building one in Rutherglen. The next major project was the *Cosmo*.

He and his brother Vincent built the 800 seat *Cosmo* in Rose Street at 'a quite substantial cost' and it was opened in May 1939, just before the outbreak of war. The first film shown in the *Cosmo* was a French dance film, *Carnet de Bal*. A lot of people might have regarded it as a gamble, others as a piece of inspiration for *Mr Cosmo* to bring in foreign films from anywhere, good as they were. 'The thing was that my brother and I had been involved in the building of this project and we thought we knew a good film when we saw it. The advent of sound had deprived the people of Glasgow from seeing all the good films that were then being produced all over Europe,' said George. 'I was in London a lot at that time and we knew that many wonderful films were being produced in France, Italy and Germany, also in Norway and Sweden, and they were not being seen. There was no reason why the people who had any taste at all should be deprived of these films because they had their distinctive contributions to make. Each country had its own distinctive contribution to make. Each country had its own approach to films. And it was a pity that these were being lost. I thought there must be an audience in the west of Scotland. I wasn't any highbrow but my brother and I decided there must be lots of people like ourselves in the west of Scotland who would appreciate good films from all over the world.'

'Here we had this fine city with all these people, university and art school, and all the professional people that were here and I knew perfectly well too, that working class folk had taste about films, too. I could see that from our other places. So we thought we would make a special thing. This was going to be our contribution. But we also tackled it as a strictly commercial thing. We were not doing it just to pander to a few intellectuals. We would go into it and try to make it as popular as possible.'

'We did so and we had a definite policy when we started and which we maintained for many, many years – we would only run one feature film and we would run short films and try to select interesting short films because they were a lot of interesting short films being made. And short films were how the men and women engaged in production learned how to make films. And it was important that they should be encouraged, too.'

The Vogue Cinema Riddrie, one of a chain of cinemas of the same name built in the late 30's for George Singleton. Once again architect John McKissack created a classic thirties look to the sumptuous 1800 seat hall which was opened in March 1938.

Queuing for the British premiere of *Jazz on a Summer's Day* at the *Cosmo*, 1960. A stylish building in keeping with the type of programming that was intended for the city's art house. 'Entertainment for the discriminating' became the trade mark of the *Cosmo*.

Right from the beginning the idea of 'entertainment for the discriminating' took off. It wasn't a slow business either. It was the biggest specialist cinema in Britain and it was the second cinema that had been built in Britain specially for the showing of good films. The *Curzon* in London had been the first. The *Cosmo* became the *Glasgow Film Theatre* (GFT) in the mid-seventies when it was bought by the Scottish Film Council.

A lot of people probably never thought how the *Cosmo* got its name. The word is short for *Cosmopolitan*. George Singleton, brought up in the business, knew that a short name of about five letters would look better on the front of the building and in the adverts.

The Poole Family came to the *Synod Hall*, Edinburgh from Gloucester for the first time in 1896 with Charles W Poole's *Myriorama* or *Panorama*. It was a travelling show but it was normally presented at town halls up and down the country. The shows consisted of paintings on canvasses on giant rollers that came across the proscenium. It gave an in-depth impression. There were three paintings so that you could see the action in perspective. These canvasses were about 28 feet wide by about 12 to 14 feet high and there was a lecturer who, as the pictures were hand-pulled across slowly, would discuss them. There were static types of shows such as St Peter's, Rome. But on the other hand there were presentations such as the Battle of Trafalgar in which all three paintings were of ships with masts coming down. That was when the Poole family became masters of the sound effects that were to be used when the silent films came in.

There was the gunfire from the ships. There were battles of the Boer War. It was moving pictures, in the original use of the term with effects. 'It was really, if you like, the newsreel of the day, because every time there was a disaster my father immediately got our artists together to prepare a presentation,' said Jim Poole. 'Unlike in the case of Lord Grade, our most successful presentation was the Titanic. We had the whole thing . . . the Titanic leaving Liverpool, striking the iceberg and all the essential action, with the lecturer, the sound effects and an orchestra. It was very realistic . . .'

Interspersed with all this they would have a break from the canvas pictures, and had variety turns, usually about four or five. And in order to set the stage for the variety turn they had to clear the canvasses off. This was when the early silent films were coming in and they had a cinema screen which was merely a linen sheet which they pulled across the proscenium and pegged down, and then they would have a *Felix the Cat* film or something of that nature. Then a whistle would blow, a person would run across and take the screen off and there was the stage set for the variety turn. The variety turn finished and then, bang, the screen was pulled across again, and then after the rest of the short films were finished, another whistle, and bang, the sheet was pulled back and there was the panorama or *Myriorama* for the *The Dark Durbar at Delhi*. It was real showmanship.

These kind of shows travelled all over the country and were the reason for the Pooles first coming to Edinburgh in 1896. They had earlier been to Dundee and Aberdeen. Jim Poole says that the word 'myriorama' was just a word invented by his grandfather to mystify and impress. He had decided that 'panorama' was too simple a word and he wanted to capture the public's imagination. Grandfather Poole was born in Wiltshire and started his entertainment empire in Gloucester in 1850.

Jim Poole, aged 78 in 1990, said there was a big exhibition recalling the old panorama shows at the Barbican in the late eighties and the Poole family was represented. 'I was absolutely amazed at the numbers there were all those years ago, not all essentially commercial. Some were geographical and purely educational,' he said.

Myrioramas, or panoramas, were becoming increasingly uneconomic and as the films started to catch on more and more, the panorama tours started to grind to a halt. But such was their popularity in Edinburgh – not so much in Glasgow or Dundee – that when people heard that Poole's *Myriorama* wasn't going to come, there was quite a furore. His father, John R Poole, decided it would continue at the *Synod Hall* at Christmas time. So in Edinburgh for years there were the pantomimes at the *King's* and the *Royal* down Leith Walk, and the Pooles' *Myriorama*, essentially a family show, and then, of course, the circus. 'It continued incredibly for ten to fifteen years after all the other touring panoramas had finished,' said Jim. 'It only finished in 1928 and that was basically because the production costs for just a three-week season, with having to paint new pictures and up-date productions was just too much compared with the economics of putting on a suitable film. That really was the end of an era.'

Early silent films that proved very popular at the *Synod Hall* included the first big Western, *Covered Wagon*. Another hit was Rudolph Valentino in *The Four Horsemen of the Apocalypse*. Because of their interest in *Myriorama*, the Poole family were all geared up to provide more than just music for the silent films. 'We used to have effects for battle scenes and all kinds of things behind the screen,' said Jim Poole. 'We still had a couple of members of staff who were experts on effects. Not every telephone was heard to ring but for major scenes such as battles and chases there was a whole set of equipment, like drums, wind machines, giant wooden rattles which were used for masts of ships coming down . . . There were motor car horns and for one film, called *What Price Glory?*, which included a big chase, father arranged for a Harley Davidson motor cycle to be at the back of that stage. At the start of the chase he kick-started it and kept revving up the engine.'

'With *Four Horsemen of the Apocalypse*, there was supposed to be a big explosion and father didn't think our usual sound effects were good enough. He went to a quarry and got some electrically-activated detonators which he put in a rubbish bin at the end of the corridor in the *Synod Hall*. At rehearsal there was a bang but he didn't think much of it and said they would try it with two detonators. We ran

An advert from a trade journal, which possibly explains why Rudolph Valentino is not mentioned by name. *The Four Horsemen* was an immediate sensation and established Valentino as a star and Ingram as a director who had set new cinematic standards.

89

the reel again and there was a bigger bang and then a rather peculiar woomph! Father said: 'That's fine'. Then he went out to find that the corridor, 250 feet long was a foot deep in plaster. The first charge had loosened it; the second brought the whole bloody lot down.'

Coming into the period of the talkies, one of the hazards was that films like *The Singing Fool* and *The Jazz Singer* had the sound on disc. These were big discs on a turntable and they had to coincide with the action on screen. Jim remembers a nasty moment with the film *Madame X*, starring Ruth Chatterton. In one sequence she had to say: 'Well I know what I know and I'm just going.' The trouble was the needle stuck and long after she had left the room and was seen to get into a taxi she kept saying: 'Well, I know what I know and I'm just going.'

The *Cameo* became the Poole family's art cinema in Edinburgh, and, before *Filmhouse*, it was used to show entries for the Edinburgh International Film Festival. That continued under their ownership until 1982.

Jim Poole looks back with affection at the *Synod Hall*. It had originally been a theatre that had failed, then it became the headquarters of a church. It was going to be Edinburgh's central civic hall for the presentation of freedoms of the city and concerts. But the Usher family presented the *Usher Hall* and that was why the *Synod Hall* became available for the Pooles – 'It was an incredible place when you think of all the simultaneous activities that took place there. It was not just a cinema auditorium. There was an indoor rifle range, a bowling alley; it had the Royal Scottish Geographical Society offices; three dancing schools and about another three activities. Our cinema had about 1400 seats. Our connection with it ran from 1896 to 1965 – a fantastic span for any family to be associated with the one place.'

A family dynasty. Poole's Myriorama at the *Synod Hall* during the first Christmas season 1906–7. JKS Poole and his staff adopted similar pose on the last day of operation on 31st October 1965. The site, for so long synonymous with the best in entertainment, subsequently regained something of its former fame as the capital's celebrated 'hole in the ground'.

The Rises and Falls of the Edinburgh International Film Festival

Colin McArthur

In diplomatic circles it is said that a newly independent nation's first acquisition is an airline, its second a film festival. The popular idea of a film festival is a glittering period of two to three weeks of important films, important people in evening dress and important awards, a magical time when the cinema and its denizens come within hem-touching distance of ordinary mortals. A film playing to near-empty houses as part of a season on Yugoslav cinema can become within a film festival, a focus of adulation or condemnation, a source of journalistic copy, an event.

There are today in excess of 250 film festivals throughout the world, and the number is rising. Most function mainly or exclusively within the popular idea of a film festival and it is becoming yearly more difficult entirely to eschew this idea. More arguably, it may not be desirable for a festival to hold itself apart from the popular idea, but embracing it exacts a heavy price.

This has not always been so as the history of the Edinburgh International Film Festival demonstrates. The impetus for its being set up in 1947 – only Venice and Cannes predate it – was not, as the tendency is nowadays, to confer prestige on a locality and to attract tourists. The thrust behind Edinburgh's creation was a passion for cinema, and more, a politics of cinema, the wish to advance the interest of certain cinematic forms and institutions and to create knowledge and debate about them. The key figures in the group which set Edinburgh up were Norman Wilson and Forsyth Hardy both of whom had been active in Scottish film culture in the decade and a half prior to the festival as film journalists, as members of the Edinburgh Film Guild and, in Forsyth Hardy's case, as a wartime civil servant in charge of documentary film production in Scotland. Hardy's film column in *The Scotsman*, the journal *Cinema Quarterly* edited by Norman Wilson, and the exhibition activities of the Edinburgh Film Guild were important in raising film consciousness in quite diverse ways in Scotland in the

Roberto Rossellini's *Paisa* (1946) deals with isolation and community during the American liberation of Italy. Paisa is a dialect word meaning 'one belonging to a village'. The boy (Alfonsino Pasca) feels sorry for the GI MP (Dots M Johnson) and tries to keep him awake so that he doesn't have to steal the soldier's boots.

thirties. That generalised passion for cinema heated up into an active politics of cinema as the decade wore on, the cutting edge of that politics being the documentary idea. Hardy, in particular, was a close friend and associate (and was later to become the official biographer) of John Grierson who was at that time very effectively propagandising on behalf of the documentary idea in British government circles and realising the idea institutionally through official organizations like the Empire Marketing Board. The documentary idea was further institutionalized during the war at the end of which, as an idea and practice, it was riding high. Its practitioners had made a massive contribution to the war effort and British documentary had come to be perceived as a major movement in the development for initiatives in many other countries and arguably inflecting the aesthetics of narrative cinema in Italy, Poland and even the United States.

It is scarcely surprising, therefore, given the orientation of figures such as Forsyth Hardy and the demonstrable importance of the ideas and practices he had championed throughout the thirties and the war period, that the idea of documentary should underpin the emergence of the film festival in Edinburgh. It was indeed called the First International Festival of Documentary Films, its advisory committee included such stalwarts of the movement as Basil Wright and Paul Rotha, and its programme booklet was entitled *Documentary 47*. A key feature of any film festival emerging out of a passion for cinema rather than prestige and hype, is the quality of its accompanying documentation. The first Edinburgh programme booklet carried considered pieces by John Grierson and Forsyth Hardy and articles on documentary practice in Australia, Poland, Czechoslovakia, Denmark and Canada. There is even a piece by Norman Wilson on documentary in Scotland which is, in retrospect, hauntingly prophetic:

> There are no technical fireworks about Scottish documentary. The subject matter – the social problem, the question of ways and means, the organization of resources – is regarded as more important than surface brilliance. Beyond that it is difficult to say that Scotland has evolved any distinguishable quality in its films. Perhaps that in itself is characteristically Scottish.

It is clear, even at the start of the Edinburgh Film Festival, that the organisers were beginning to expand the idea of documentary beyond simple factual short films to embrace the notion of documentary/realist aesthetics although this was never worked out at a theoretical level. The first festival included feature films such as Roberto Rossellini's *Paisa* and George Rouquier's *Farrebique* and the 1948 festival opened with the world premiere of Robert Flaherty's *Louisiana Story* and included Rossellini's *Germany Year Zero*. The festival's continuing commitment to knowledge and debate about the cinema was evident not only in its programme booklet (which again included substantial essays and even more wide-ranging reports on the documentary scene throughout the world) but also in that other indicator of serious intent in a festival, a programme of public lectures and debate. The lecturers in 1948 included Basil Wright, Paul Rotha and Arthur Elton and the lectures dealt with 'the aims and principles of documentary'. By 1950, however, there were indications that the politics of documentary, at least as far as the festival was concerned, were running out of steam. It was already referring to itself as the Edinburgh International Film Festival, having dropped the word 'Documentary' from the title and, while it continued to produce a programme booklet structured round documentary and show films like Visconti's *La Terra Trema*, the opening film of the 1950 festival was *The Wooden Horse*, a problematic choice not only in terms of its quality but also in relation to questions of documentary even in its widest application.

Cultural operations rarely come to a sudden stop. The principle of uneven development applies, even in processes of decline. Thus, the Edinburgh International Film Festival maintained its attempt to generate debate about cinema in, for example, its 1952 conference 'New Directions in Documentary' and its 1953 conference 'Television, Film and Reality' while the films it showed and the critical documentation it produced moved ever further from the documentary idea. By 1954 even the booklet had shed the term 'documentary' and included an article on the American feature film producer Walter Wanger and one on John Huston and a piece on film in America begins by talking about documentary and ends up talking about *On the Waterfront*, *Riot in Cell Block 11* and *A Time Out of War*. Some of the feature films shown over this period indicate how far the festival had drifted from the discourse of documentary: *The Caine Mutiny*, *Gate of Hell*, *Ugetsu Monogatari*, *Doctor*

Sponsored by Standard Oil, *The Louisiana Story* is a drama-documentary which tells the story of a Cajun boy (played by Joseph Louis Boudreaux) and his 'natural' lifestyle in the bayou at a time of oil exploration. Flaherty's romanticism obscures the tensions between nature and industrial development. The world premiere of the film opened the 1948 Festival.

at Sea, East of Eden, The Lady and the Tramp. But perhaps the clearest signal that the end had come for a politics of cinema predicated on documentary is the title of a piece in the 1954 programme booklet by John Maddison entitled 'Documentary is NOT Dead'.

The decceleration of the Edinburgh documentary cinema policy was clearly bound up with the waning of the form in the wider cinema. Cinema audiences were in decline, television was rising, cinema was beginning to explore other systems such as colour and widescreen which, if not inherently hostile to documentary, were certainly not associated with the form, and many of documentary's ablest practitioners were moving elsewhere. John Grierson himself became involved in feature film production with the government-aided Group 3. Forsyth Hardy re-entered film production as Director of Films of Scotland in 1954, his considerable energy thereafter being directed primarily towards the raising of funds for sponsored documentary films in Scotland rather than towards festival affairs. The stagnation which is evident in the Edinburgh International Film Festival from the mid-fifties to the mid-sixties, though flowing primarily from the lack of a policy on cinema to replace the worn-out documentary policy, was undoubtedly exacerbated by the administrative arrangements for running the festival with a series of short-term appointees acting as director for a year apiece.

The tensions with regard to its own identity and function which afflicted the EIFF at this time are well described in the report of an officer of the US State Department who had attended the 1952 festival.

> The directors are under pressure to maintain the 'integrity', 'the character of the . . . Festival', that is, to keep it a 'producers' festival', an open forum for 'the loving makers of movies' . . . They are under no less pressure from public opinion (which) asks why the film has failed to take its proper place among the Popular and Cultural Arts in the Festival of Music and Drama, why its starry-eyed devotees flock by themselves in smaller theatres instead of filling large houses with people . . . In other words, there is pressure to turn the 'producers' festival' into a 'public's festival' on the order of what Venice and Cannes claim to be . . .

Another hauntingly prophetic formulation. There is a danger of erecting a folkloric account of the EIFF whereby, after the energetic commitment to the documentary idea of the early years everything simply switched off for a decade to be reborn phoenix-like with a passionate commitment to a new politics of film. Of course the actuality was much less clear-cut. Although, in 1955, Norman Wilson was still claiming that 'Edinburgh . . . will remain the centre for Films of Reality', the aesthetic strategies of films programmed at Edinburgh became ever more diverse: *Reach for the Sky, The King and I, Lust for Life, Eyes Without a Face, Virgin Spring, World of Apu, The Criminal*, plus scores of short films of every

The Wooden Horse is fairly standard POW material or, as the publicity said, 'The Most Sensational Escape of Our Time!' Have the stars tunnelled out already? Leo Genn, David Tomlinson and Anthony Steel are not here but David (Dan Cunningham), Panfret (Anthony Dawson) play chess and discuss Blighty and duty with Bennett (David Greene) and Robbie (Michael Goodcliffe).

conceivable aesthetic form. The EIFF over this period initiated and, it seems, discarded two awards which it presented each year. There are references in the mid-fifties to the Selznick Awards and to *Ugetsu Monogatari* receiving the Golden Laurel in 1955, the award to be given to 'a film-maker whose work through the years has contributed to international goodwill and understanding'. Such a formulation sounds the warning bells of decline. The cutting edge of a precise politics of cinema such as had characterised the documentary initiative, is replaced by a woolly gesture which could mean anything and which would not be out of place at the crassest of commercial film festivals. The Golden Thistle Award, sponsored by Films of Scotland, appeared in 1964 and was presented that year to King Vidor. Though less crass than the earlier award – for instance it involved the retrospective showing of six of the awardee's films with the implication that there might be a relationship among them – the terms of reference were worryingly vague, 'made annually in recognition of an outstanding contribution to the Art of the Cinema'. The crucial omission was any argument as to why King Vidor was important and what the purpose was in honouring him in 1964. Yet, to muddy the idea of a total shut-down of ideas and commitment over this period, the very notion of running a retrospective of filmmakers's work at a film festival was, in the 1960s, quite a progressive move. Further scrutiny of the period reveals other commitments to the idea of a serious film festival however half-baked they now seem. The 1962 press digest refers to the EIFF having instituted 'a five-year plan whose general aim is to demonstrate the links between the art of the film and the older arts'. Attempts included the programming of films round the themes of Film and Literature and Film and Drama but the process of decline is most marked in the thin and anecdotal documentation, symptomatically now called 'souvenir programme' which supported these initiatives. Supposed seriousness was evident on other fronts too. Conferences such as 'What is a Television Film?' continued as did some form of public lecture programme, though these came to be styled, chillingly, 'celebrity' lectures. The first of these was delivered in 1954 by Anthony Asquith on the theme of the relationship between actor and director and succeeding lectures included Roger Manvell on 'Shakespeare to Sillitoe' and Jerzy Toeplitz on 'The Creative Impulse in Film-Making'. Whatever the merits of what might have been said by particular lecturers, as a programme it was completely unfocussed and it comes as no surprise to find the 1966 lecture by Fons Rademaker untitled. Celebrity reigns: anything goes.

Thus, while it is correct to see the period in question as one of decline for the EIFF, it should not be thought that the Festival lost its seriousness of intent. Its institutional arrangement of short-term directorial appointments was not conducive to the continuity and development of policy and the full realisation of that policy in pro-gramming, documentation and events. But the crucial lack, following the withering of the documentary initiative, was the presence of a festival director who had a passion for cinema, a wish to advance the claims of certain cinematic forms over others, and the appetite to conduct this argument in public. It is to the credit of the EIFF that it was able to put its own house in order in precisely these terms.

Murray Grigor was appointed Director in 1967. Film festivals are complex mechanisms and (again the law of uneven development) we do not find a new politics of cinema emerging fully-formed, from the head of Zeus as it were, in the festival of that year. Carol Reed was awarded the Golden Thistle with no particular case being made for his receiving the award, the programme booklet contains a desultory discussion by Frederic Raphael on film censorship and little else by way of critical documentation. There is evidence of a greater attempt to impose order on the diversity of films shown by grouping them under headings such as 'A British Film School?', 'The American Eye', 'Experimental 67' and 'Film and the Arts', but perhaps the most resonant portent of things to come was the selection of Robert Aldrich's *The Dirty Dozen* for the opening gala performance that year. Although historically oriented to the documentary idea and to cinema as 'high art', the EIFF had not totally eschewed an interest in Hollywood. However, that interest tended to focus on the older, more 'respectable' aspects of Hollywood. What was scandalous about opening the 1967 EIFF with *The Dirty Dozen* was the suggestion, implicit at that stage, that the violent underbelly of Hollywood was a source of legitimate cinematic pleasure and critical interest. That portent was not realised in the 1968 EIFF which, in retrospect, has about it the feeling of an obituary for the documentary initiative of earlier years. The main organizing principle for the programme booklet is indeed 'The Documentary Idea' and John Grierson looms very large throughout. He delivered the celebrity lecture that year and the programme booklet contains a reprint of his 1933 essay 'Documentary Symphonies' and his outline treatment for *Seawards the Great Ships*, an Oscar-winning documentary about Clydeside shipbuilding which had been produced through Films of Scotland. Grierson's receiving the Golden Thistle award in 1968 further enhances the sense of closure on the principles and practices with which he was associated. The more extensive critical documentation of the 1968 booklet can be read retrospectively as one of the signs of the EIFF's return to a serious engagement with cinema.

1969 is the year in which the most decisive break with the past is evident. Murray Grigor had been joined at the EIFF by Lynda Myles and David Will and their collective orientation was towards a very different kind of cinema than had enthused the generation of Forsyth Hardy and Norman Wilson. The revaluation of Hollywood cinema became a central interest of younger critics at this time. Like all other cultural movements this was a complex and uneven phenomenon, but some of the strands which fed into it were dissatisfaction with the virtually blanket condemnation of Hollywood by film critics of the left (on account of its being a capitalist enterprise) and the right (on account of its catering for a mass market); the presence in the educational system of a new generation of teachers from working-class backgrounds who wished to validate rather than condemn the cultural choices of their students (Stuart Hall and Paddy Whannel's *The Popular Arts* is a key text here); and growing familiarity with French film criticism and

Major Reisman (Lee Marvin) measures up the disciples in Robert Aldrich's *The Dirty Dozen*. A box office smash, it spawned imitations and helped make stars. Hollywood was making its presence felt at EIFF.

97

the importation of its ideas into Britain through journals such as *Oxford Opinion* and *Movie*. It was within this movement, and with allies drawn from its cadres, that Grigor, Myles and Will were to re-energise the EIFF and give it once more that passion for cinema and commitment to a politics of cinema which had characterised its founding and its early years. At the particular moment when Grigor, Myles and Will connected institutionally with this movement two ideas about Hollywood cinema were central. Firstly that precisely because Hollywood was a highly 'compromised' milieu in terms of commercial demands, institutional interference, and the presence of powerful genre traditions such as the western and the gangster movie, it was fruitless to try to discern the art of the Hollywood director on the basis of looking at 'his' films piecemeal. Only on the basis of considering the whole or a substantial part of 'his' canon might the nature of 'his' recurring thematic and stylistic concerns be revealed. Formulated in French film criticism as the 'politique des auteurs', this approach was anglicized as 'the auteur theory'. The second idea which was current was that a film might be of interest as much for the way it was realised on the screen as for the ostensible seriousness of its subject matter. This opened the way for films previously dismissed or reviled to be looked at carefully. This interest in cinematic mise-en-scene was developed in Britain primarily by the journal *Movie*.

These two ideas came together triumphantly in the 1969 EIFF's retrospective of the films of Samuel Fuller with a supporting book of critical essays edited by David Will and Peter Wollen. The impact of the Fuller retrospective as an event, with the gregarious Fuller himself present throughout, the weighty historical presence of the book of essays, and the discernible influence of both book and event in the wider film culture (books and articles on Fuller proliferating, the season being taken up by the National Film Theatre in London and other film theatres elsewhere) tend to obliterate the memory of other strands within the EIFF that year: Student and Independent Films, AIP Thru Roger Corman, Kenneth Anger, Andy Warhol, a graphics season and a tribute to the recently deceased young British film-maker Michael Reeves. In fact the list connects well with the Fuller in its attention to the interstices of Hollywood and American independent cinema and the presence of its visceral qualities in Reeves' films. A powerful if uneven sense of identity is evident within the EIFF for the next decade or so with the most significant strands being its commitment to younger Hollywood directors such as Martin Scorsese, John Carpenter and Paul Schrader; its openness to avant-gardes; its early recognition of the significance of figures such as Werner Herzog, Ousmane Sembene and Hans-Jurgen Syberberg; and its close alliance with new thinking about the cinema among British critics, theoreticians and educationists. Over this period substantial seasons and publications were produced on Roger Corman, Douglas Sirk, Frank Tashlin, Raoul Walsh, Jacques Tourneur, Psychoanalysis and Cinema, and History/Popular memory. The productivity of this work was immense, in particular feeding into

Ai No Corrida or *In the Realm of the Senses*
(1976) was scripted and directed by Nagisa
Oshima to ask the audience to look at sex.
Shown at the 1984 EIFF, the film proved
too demanding for the censor and no
certificate was granted in spite of the film's
undoubted merit. Two lovers retreat from
the militarist Japan of 1936 into their own
violent sexual fantasies. Eiko Matsuda and
Tatsuya Fuji contemplate the ultimate.

the work of teachers of film and cultural studies, the activities of
regional arts associations and regional film theatres, and the practices
of the nascent British film workshop movement. The break in the
above list between posing questions round the work of particular
directors and round more theoretical questions indicates some degree
of divergence between the interests of the EIFF and its allies in film
theory and education although both remained mutually supportive.
To structure retrospectives and publications round the films of Sam
Fuller, Roger Corman, Douglas Sirk, Frank Tashlin, Raoul Walsh and
Jacques Tourneur, while scandalous to a certain kind of conservative
critical thinking about the cinema, nevertheless takes as given the un-
problematic nature of directorial authorship. It was precisely this idea
which became increasingly problematic in film theory and education
as it became more widely current in the journalistic film culture of the
'quality' press which is the main conduit of news and opinion about
film festivals.

It could be argued that the EIFF's identity was much less clear-cut
in the 1980s though, as previously, the decade is uneven. The strength
of Edinburgh in its earliest years and in the decade from about 1969
was its sense of purpose, its clear awareness of why it did what it
did, its commitment to an explicit politics of cinema and culturally
productive film work. While this did not wholly vanish in the eighties
(the 'Scotch Reels' season and book had discernible influence on
film studies within Scotland and beyond) it is difficult to guage the
rationale for certain decisions in the eighties. Why, for instance, was
it considered important to mount a Joseph H Lewis retrospective in
1980, or a retrospective of Japanese cinema in 1984, and where is

the evidence of either of these initiatives being culturally productive in terms of new ideas, new writing or new filmmaking practices? The EIFF was reorganised in 1989 with Jim Hickey (who had been with the festival since 1969 and had succeeded Lynda Myles as Director in 1981) relinquishing the Directorship to David Robinson, film critic of *The Times*. On the evidence of the official programme for 1989, Edinburgh's distinctiveness as a film festival with a specific politics of cinema is at an end. It reads:

> We have tried to create a festival which is not elitist or exclusive, but will offer something to every sector of the community. As always, the Festival aims primarily to bring to Edinburgh the best of the past year's international cinema . . . The main focus of the Festival this year however is on new talent. At least thirty films are by new directors. Fifteen of these have been selected for a special New Directors series; and these will compete for the Charles Chaplin New Directors' Award . . .
>
> Edinburgh is by tradition a non-competitive festival, but we are very proud to host not only this prestigious new award, but also three other prizes, destined for student film-makers, whose work is selected for the Young Film Maker of Year Competition . . . As well as (this) there are daily Lunchtime Animation shows, while documentary – always a special concern of Edinburgh – is highlighted in a new Eyes of the World series. A further innovation is the New British Cinema section. One of this year's two retrospectives is also British. Titled *1939 – Another Country*, it sets out to present a portrait of Britain on the eve of the Second World War . . . A second retrospective offers the complete works of Pier Paolo Pasolini.

At both the historical moments, the immediate post-war period and the decade or so from 1969, when Edinburgh's critical cutting edge was sharpest, there was the strongest possible sense of great issues being at stake (documentary/realist cinema versus more stylised, 'escapist' cinema; 'popular' versus 'high' art) with appropriately explicit critical discourses for advancing the arguments. All of this seems very far from the blandness of '. . . will offer something to every sector of the community' and the nebulousness of '. . . the best of the past year's international cinema' and '. . . the main focus . . . is on new talent'. Other questions suggest themselves. What is the rationale, other than the temporal one, of the retrospective *1939 – Another Country* and where is the documentation which explores the issues (both cinematic and historical) it poses? Why was Pasolini chosen as the subject of a retrospective at this particular moment and where is the documentation which explains the choice and confronts the issues it raises? Is it wise – given the repeated demonstration in recent years of the constructed nature of all cinema, including documentary – to entitle a documentary series 'Eyes of the World'? Who were the figures making up the group to choose the winner of the Charles Chaplin Award and what criteria governed their choice? There is no suggestion here of deliberate secrecy. A telephone call to David Robinson revealed that the group consisted of Krzysztof Zanussi, Percy Adlon, Susannah York, Jim Haynes, Forsyth Hardy and Janusz Rosza. What is at issue is the assumption that the criteria for choosing the members of the group and the winner of the award do not need to be spelled out. This is an assumption at one with a critical discourse which talks about '. . . the best of cinema' and '. . . new talent', a discourse which is slippery and elusive compared with the concrete and polemical analyses of earlier phases of the EIFF.

In fairness to David Robinson, it should be said that he took over the Directorship just about a hundred days before the EIFF was about to happen, but once again the issue lies elsewhere, specifically in conceptions of what a film festival should be and do. When EIFF reconstituted itself in 1989 it opted, in David Robinson, for a distinguished, well-informed and well-connected film journalist capable of delivery the kind of festival which offers 'something to everyone' and which would offer a critical discourse much closer to traditional public discourse about the cinema, a festival, in fact, like all the others. In making this choice the EIFF will certainly have created a responsible operation which, once a year, will bring considerable pleasure to Edinburgh. What is more doubtful, however, is the extent to which the EIFF recognises the fact that it has opted *not* to fashion for the 1990s a politics of cinema analogous to the documentary initiative of the forties and the auteurist and post-auteurist initiatives of the late sixties and seventies.

This chapter has been substantially concerned with the cultural policy of the EIFF. However, anyone with a passing knowledge of how film festivals operate will know the extent to which finance and administration impinge upon policy. This can be exemplified as a series of financial/administrative questions. Will the EIFF Director be given enough money to travel abroad and see what is actually being made in world cinema? Will individual filmmakers, film companies and, sometimes, national governments permit their films to come to Edinburgh? Will the chosen films arrive in time and in a form which is screenable? Will there be money available to repair the projectors if they fail? Is there enough money to cover the expenses of visiting filmmakers? Will they throw tantrums and make demands on the director's packed schedule? Will the programme booklet be ready on time? And from what sources will the money come to cover all these?

Such questions have impinged on policy right from the start of the EIFF, but as everyone knows they became acute in the 1980s as a result of central government policy towards arts bodies in receipt of public funding. It was Jim Hickey's unenviable lot to have to wrestle with these problems throughout the decade.

It makes no real sense therefore to write about cultural policy without assessing the importance, or perhaps even the determining nature, of finance and administration and it is to be hoped that future accounts of the EIFF can do this in more detail than is possible here.

At its founding in 1947, and for many years thereafter, the EIFF seems to have functioned largely on voluntary labour helped by temporary secondments from existing Scottish film cultural institutions such as the Scottish Film Council and Films of Scotland. From quite early on it did have a money-raising mechanism called the Edinburgh Film Festival Fund into which were paid small donations, mostly from film trade bodies which were recorded in the annual programme booklet. These donations tended, individually, to be under £30 and, even by 1962, the largest donations were £200 from the Scottish Film Council and £250 from Granada Theatres. The financing of the EIFF throughout the seventies is complicated due to its tie-up with the emergent film theatre, the Edinburgh Filmhouse, and their sharing of premises and personnel, but the festival entered the eighties with an income of over £50,000 about twenty per cent of which was trading income, the remainder being grants from the Scottish Film Council and the British Film Institute. Due to the peculiarities of arts funding in the United Kingdom the latter had for long been player on the film stage in Scotland at the level of capital funding (revenue funding being handled by the Scottish Film Council). At about the time of the EIFF's second great moment (the late sixties/early seventies) the BFI also became influential in revenue funding with regard to the EIFF, partly out of general recognition of its increasing excellence, but more particularly because a faction within the BFI valued the EIFF more highly than the BFI's own London Film Festival and sought to advance its interest accordingly.

But as well as entering the eighties with sharply increasing income, the EIFF also carried a substantial deficit. Its history over the decade from 1980 might be written as the struggle between cultural and financial considerations and the makeup and orientation of the EIFF in the nineties might be understood in part as the outcome of that struggle. At the end of the decade (1988) income had risen to over £100,000 and was showing a surplus of over £18,000. The proportion earned at the box office had risen to nearly forty per cent with grants from the SFC and BFI making up the same amount. The 1988 accounts record for the first time a figure (£6,700) described as 'sponsorship'.

It seems clear that in common with other arts bodies relying heavily on public funding the EIFF, in the chill Thatcherite wind of the eighties, sought (with some measure of success, it would seem) other sources of income and cost-saving. The crucial question is the extent to which the changed financial environment is connected with the EIFF's abandonment of the polemical stance which, in its two great historical moments, earned it the right to be called the best film festival in the world.

Whisky Galore!

Murray Grigor

I hope you realise it's a parody of a documentary.
Sandy Mackendrick, Director
(Press conference, Quimper Film Festival, France, 1990)

Well I think it has become a kind of folk tale . . . rather like Aladdin . . . because it goes on and on . . .
Compton MacKenzie, Author
(BBC radio interview 1966)

It's for real: it's not a satire: that's how it is in the Highlands.
Charles Crichton, cutting-room doctor
(Television interview, 1990)

The British film industry is in crisis (again). In 1990 production halved over the previous year. A delegation of film people meet Mrs Thatcher. Ex-Prime Minister Edward Heath, in a moment of inspired guidance, suggests to assembled producers that they should consider abandoning their current lust for exotic locations and overseas co-productions and make films as British and inexpensive as that classic *Whisky Galore!* 'Well said Ted,' said Mrs Thatcher (did she raise her glass?). From two who seldom agree on anything, could there be some sense in this?

Yet this most popular Scottish film (as most Scots would agree) was only made as a result of another British film crisis. But then it was a crisis of *over* production.

As film theories ebb and flow like the Solway, the stabilising fact remains; great films have great hands on the tiller, with great crews around them. How are we to explain otherwise when such all time favourites as *Casablanca* or *Whisky Galore!* were wrought out of such production despair. But if the turmoil of *Casablanca* was so confusing that the production team shot two endings, how are we to consider *Whisky Galore!* which stumbled back to Ealing with no ending at all? Or at least there was none apparent to Ealing's studio chief Michael Balcon, who advised chopping down what had then been assembled into a sixty minute second feature.

Both these movies have become classics of their kind. Both were the work of strong directors, Michael Curtiz and Alexander Mackendrick, each with his own cinematic style.

When Andrew Sarris wrote his now unfashionable wonder book of auteurs *The American Cinema* twenty years ago, he wriggled over

Sandy Mackendrick makes a directorial point while pipe-smoking Gerry Gibbs (director of photography), Marjorie Owens (continuity) and Chick Waterston (camera) look on. *Whisky Galore!* was the youthful-looking Mackendrick's directorial debut. He also made *The Man in the White Suit, Mandy, The Maggie, The Ladykillers, Sweet Smell of Success* and the under-rated *A High Wind in Jamaica.*

OPPOSITE
Turning things inside out. On a shoot which had to be entirely on location, some of the 'indoors' were outside. Through the 'house window' would be seen the village of Castlebay and Kisimul Castle.

the inclusion of Curtiz: 'The director's one enduring masterpiece is *Casablanca*, the happiest of happy accidents, and the most decisive exception to the auteur theory.' But as Sarris says later of Charles Laughton's brilliant one-off *The Night of the Hunter*, 'Directors, not writers, are the ultimate auteurs of the cinema that has any visual meaning and merit.' Sandy Mackendrick slips into the Sarris pantheon of lesser gods under the heading 'Expressive esoterica'. The fact remains that his first film contained the promise of an original artist. Perhaps because of the chaotic circumstances of his first production Mackendrick was able to learn so much, that the effortless control of his middle career (so clear in such masterpieces as *The Ladykillers* and *The Sweet Smell of Success*) was all laid down as he and his team fought the elements against impossible odds on that wet summer on Barra.

Whisky Galore! also resulted from the happiest of accidents. In 1948 Ealing studios were too full to allow the extra productions demanded by the sudden withdrawal of American pictures in protest at the British government's seventy-five per cent import tax. Ealing's press officer, the Russian-born Monja Danischewsky, saw his opportunity to get out of the publicity department and into production and persuaded Michael Balcon to let him develop *Whisky Galore*, Compton Mackenzie's hastily written novel, which the studio had optioned. Balcon agreed but made two strong stipulations. The film had to be made entirely on location (interiors and all) and the director had to be an experienced hand. In the end a persistent Ealing storyboard artist, whose only film experience had been in advertising shorts and (more significantly) in directing war time documentaries, kept pressuring Danischewsky.

104

It was Alexander Mackendrick, best known around the studio for his devastating cartoons. Years later he explained that since he had been conceived in Hollywood (his Scots parents had eloped) he had early warning of the perils of the place. Born in Boston he was quickly returned to the west end of Glasgow, where his family roots included close connections with the locally famous Annan photographers.

'Sandy chose Sandy,' Danischewsky would later say and Balcon relented. He was, after all, the man who had given even caption artists their chance at directing; Alfred Hitchcock for example. But he kept Mackendrick on his storyboard salary of £30 per week, half what the cameraman got and well short of his new producer's salary of £80; a rather imbalanced start for the two to set out in harmony. Perhaps Balcon saw from the start the creative possibilities inherent in the dynamic tension between two such radically different personalities; Danischewsky, the clubable warm-hearted Russian Jewish romantic and Mackendrick, unyielding, obsessive, driven by the Presbyterian work ethic. Certainly from what everyone who worked on the production has said since, the yoking together of these two irreconcilable opposites gave the film its thrust and extra nudge at every turn.

The only thing that the producer and director had in common was their inexperience. But it didn't stop there. Since nearly every British technician at the time was busy working, the inexperienced but enthusiastic would fill every technical grade. When the crew landed on the remote Hebridean island of Barra it became clear that this was to be everyone's first picture; the islanders included. 'On *Whisky Galore!* it was the blind leading the blind,' remembered the camera operator Chick Waterson.

Even the author got in on the act, making his first screen appearance at sixty-five as Captain Mackechnie; the skipper who ploughed the SS *Politician* with her cargo of gold onto the rocks off Todday amidst the swirling mists. Mackenzie's inexperience meant that his few lines of dialogue were to take up a night of valuable studio time around a wet studio tank. The crew admired his writing, but shouldn't he stick to that? Mackenzie himself had his own fears when he saw the first draft of the screenplay, 'There goes another of my books west.' Danischewsky remembers Balcon saying, 'All I can see is a lot of elderly Scotsmen sitting by the fire and saying "Och aye".' But in the end the screenplay, the work of Angus Macphail (Ealing's script editor) Danischewsky and Mackendrick, is a far tauter thing than Mackenzie's rambling book. Especially after Danischewsky had done a bargain with Mackenzie who threw in a couple of scenes from his earlier Todday novel *Keep the Home Guard Turning* for the cost of a box of cigars.

Mackenzie was chronically over-extended financially when he dashed off *Whisky Galore!* (his 64th novel in his 64th year). Its discursive style ambles on through an almost unedited meandering plot, peppered with Gaelicisms, *ochoin! ochoin!* The wreck of the boat, when the whisky tumbles in its hold, (the film's obligatory scene) happens more than half-way through the book. The novel might have sold just a few

Sandy Mackendrick exchanges opinion with producer Monja Danischewsky while Compton Mackenzie looks unsure of what is going on. Mackendrick and Danischewsky drifted further apart as the long location shoot on Barra continued.

thousand copies and, like the *Politician* whose fictional story it told, sunk without trace, had it not been for the young Ealing film team.

In Mackenzie's novel the plot pivots on the religious differences of the Todday islanders, just as the Outer Hebrides are today, where the old clans of MacNeills and Macdonalds are often divided through accidents of history into following the Presbyterian Kirk (mostly of the fundamentalist free variety) or the Roman Catholic. In the novel when the 'Sawbath' comes the protestants can only stand and watch their catholic cousins as they smuggle away the booty. 'But what happier day to liberate the whisky,' said the island priest to Danischewsky, 'than to spirit it away on the good Lord's day.'

A religious satire between staunch Free Presbyterians and devout Roman Catholics was too much for Balcon who considered religion an even more touchy subject than sex. The rivalry was written out of the film and the Catholic island of Barra became Presbyterian. In the film the Sunday congregation is seen leaving the Castlebay (Roman Catholic) church, its architectural high orders in heady conflict with the normally unadorned stark meeting places of Free Presbyterians. Mackenzie, a convert to Catholicism, island life and Gaelic must have smiled: he was born in West Hartlepool of English and American parents, who were accomplished actors.

The story as it was developed became anathema to Mackendrick. He had been brought up in the Presbyterian tradition which had imbued him with a code of morals, a work ethic and a sense of duty. To him the real Barra was not his Scotland at all. 'Really it is nearer, in many ways culturally, to Ireland than to Scotland.' Mackendrick argued against portraying the islanders as a bunch of

107

booze-obsessed Irishmen. The Russian-Jewish Danischewsky held the opposite view. He was beginning to see the ever partying locals in his film more romantically as a small isolated community at odds with foreign authority. Perhaps he saw the happy islanders as a traditional Russian-Jewish village or 'stetl': such as would later give the impetus to such musicals and films as *Fiddler on the Roof*. And it is interesting to note that the seemingly echt Scotch kitsch schlockbuster spectacular *Brigadoon* had its origins as a central European Yiddish tale set in just such a 'stetl'. In *Whisky Galore!* it was precisely such a bogus view of fatigued romanticism that Mackendrick was fighting against. After all there had not been a film made in Scotland up to that time without its heady draught of sickening schmaltz. Mackendrick always dreamed of correcting this, of making a historical picture that brought forward the dichotomies of life up on the edge of Europe. His long term plans to present the dilemmas of Mary Queen of Scots almost got made, itself axed when Universal Studios were bought out in 1969. Mackendrick has never made a film since. He has become the greatest film teacher in the English speaking world. But as Charles Crichton said recently, 'He is an even better filmmaker, head and shoulders over all of us at Ealing.'

Back on Barra the producer and director were beginning to drift further apart. Mackendrick now felt that the Englishman Captain Wagget was the only ethically true Scotsman on the island and proposed that he should be seen as a laird wearing the kilt (an instantly recognisable type even in the Highlands today). Creative tension was about to snap. For Danischewsky it was getting altogether far too confusing and he pulled rank. He maintained that only in Scotland would a tartan laird have any meaning. The whole world would be confused if Wagget wore anything other than trousers like any other tweedy Englishman.

Mackendrick would have to wait till *The Maggie* to have his revenge in the form of a kilted Scots laird speaking in the accent of the ascendency.

One of Danischewsky's first strokes of genius, which seems to have helped more than any other factor to shape the emerging 'Style Mackendrick', resulted from the chronic shortage of accommodation on the island. As Mackendrick tells:

> Danishewsky couldn't find a big enough house for us all. So he farmed out the experienced London actors into rooms and lodging houses with the islanders. This taught me something that I have used ever since, which is how to take professional actors, trained actors and put them up against the amateur. The result is that they feed off each other. The professional actor gives the scene the pace and the amateur keeps the professional actor honest.

To see this in action in *Whisky Galore!* look at the celebration ceilidh sequence that begins with the mouth music (port a beul) as it builds into

108

In this myth (and to a certain extent in reality too) much uisgebeatha disappeared into hiding places and down the islanders' throats. Here Wylie Watson hides the cratur while the expressions of Gordon Jackson, Joan Greenwood, Bruce Seton and Gabrielle Blunt let us see how serious a business it all is.

the reiteach dance and try and distinguish, from their performances, the actors from the locals, the professionals from the amateurs. The Barra extras felt at home in front of the camera because they were at home. Philip Kemp in his illuminating new Mackendrick book, *Lethal Innocence*, quotes Gordon Jackson as saying, 'We corrupted them all – they were high-powered actors and actresses by the time we left'. He remembered: 'The old post-mistress saying to Sandy at one point, "I don't think I'd be in this shot, Mr. Mackendrick. I wasn't in the other angle".' In the end integrity won out. *Whisky Galore!* escapes the condescension of the 'Kailyard' school from the tension between the actors and islanders. It was the one wonderful gain from the long protracted shooting schedule. Perhaps the only scene which fails this test comes when the islanders are forced to turn back from their whisky plundering mission because the Sabbath bell rings. In the book the two island communities look across their sectarian divides. But in the film it is the only time we are asked to laugh at, rather than with, the islanders.

Although Mackendrick's films are seldom overtly political, in *Whisky Galore!* the islanders are bent on upstaging their white settler laird. Highland crofting and fishing communities, with their inbuilt traditions of work sharing, land tenure and the open fishing rights on loch, river and sea – all find expression through the actions of the islanders within the film. When the climax is reached (that masterful low angle shot of peering faces into that golden hoard, underpinned with the music of *Scots wha Hae*) we hear, 'Let each man take what he needs'. Is this an old or a new way of thinking? In 1948 there would be an optimistic revolutionary ring to this; 'Praise Marx', perhaps, and 'pass the whisky!'.

Just as the film derived inspiration from the real islanders, something similar happened to the look of the film. The landscape and huddled houses of Barra suggested to Mackendrick how the action should develop. Since all the interiors had to be built and shot on the island (mostly in the Craigston village hall on the west of the island) even these had an unstudio authentic (islander inspected) feel. In lesser hands that would have been enough, but Mackendrick's master stroke in the finished film is to confront us from time to time with questions pivoting on cinematic style. He forces us to relook at that look; to question just what is cinematic reality. *Whisky Galore!* opens with mock solemnity, the narrator (the inexplicably uncredited Finlay Currie) rolling his declamatory pentameters over the seas of the Hebrides as each portentous statement is undercut by the images and actions on the screen.

As we hear of the plight of 'the islanders frugal living' we see them guddling lobsters out of the sea. The film gets its first laugh when over a panning shot of rolling seas the narrator continues, 'to the west there's nothing, except America.' An impromptu throw away at the recording as Charles Crichton recalls the session. It is as much a parody of a Grierson-produced documentary of the time as of most Scottish film-making for the next thirty years to come.

By the time the production was in full swing, the 'fillums' (as the islanders affectionately called the production team and actors) were part of the conspiracy of Compton Mackenzie's myth-making machinery. The story and film of *Whisky Galore!* was the culmination of a legend spun out of one single wreck among the thousands of ships that were sunk at the beginning of Hitler's war. The plight and plunder of the SS *Politician* (*Cabinet Minister* in the film) was fuel to fire-side story-telling (many of The Coddy's tales were woven into the book and the film). Mundane looters were transformed into mythic island heroes. Stories of their feats grew proportionately to the flow of the precious cargo as it was spirited across the islands and toasted around the peat fires.

Most of what we now know of the historic Hebrides has come down to us through the Celtic tradition of story-telling. Compared with Ireland and Wales, Scottish Gaelic, as a written language, was comparatively late. In the Hebrides history soon became enshrouded in myths. Heroic feats would soon overtake prosaic realities, as stories passed from hearth to hearth down through the generations as Celtic Whispers.

Story-telling is how Gaelic survived the many onslaughts on its existence from the homogenising imperatives of English. The *Whisky Galore!* saga was an insider story of a community against outside authority. Above all, here was a story that struck at the quick of the imagination; manna from heaven; the water of life restored to a war impoverished island; the Hebridean stuff of dreams. In the divided kingdom of the Scottish mind whisky can be the gift of Highland hospitality or the curse of the demon drink. Stevenson works out these polarities in *The Strange Case of Dr Jekyll and Mr Hyde*. For Compton Mackenzie whisky was exclusively a benign spirit; a catalyst of island hospitality.

Whisky was the civilising basis of life at the heart of 'Suidheachan', the huge gaunt bungalow Mackenzie had built for himself in 1935, named after the Gaelic for 'the sitting down place,' where a hunting MacNeill of Barra (island legend had it) used to take his rest above the cockle strand.

In *Whisky Galore!* whisky becomes the film's rationale, the mother liquor, the life-giving force that World War Two (reduced to a whisky drought) has denied the islanders. The wreck springs from divine intervention. It is the islanders' inalienable right to pick from the shores of providence.

In the bar scenes Mackendrick uses his island crofter extras to demonstrate that peculiar smile, half grin, half grimace, that says so much about the bitter-sweet world of the north. The hiding of the whisky is a wonderfully choreographed sequence, Mackendrick's answer to anyone who says that storyboards are redundant. The switches and movements within the frame are in perfect counterpoint to the cutting and music.

As the film pours on, whisky swirls like a hero through a near alchemical range of transformations. *Whisky Galore!* now becomes a series of themes and variations on the water of life. In the hands of the island doctor (played by James Robertson Justice – a launch pad

Joan Greenwood's poise and beauty (aided by the lighting) hold centre frame in the crowded ceilidh scene which was in a 'hall' constructed inside the real village hall in Craigston. Although trained as a dancer, apparently Joan Greenwood did not provide the twinkling feet for the close-ups.

for his later *Doctor* series) whisky is the restorer of life. An old 'bodach' is resurrected miraculously on his death-bed by his prescription of whisky, as the dismal expressionist shadows dissolve into bright rays of sunlight. Even the pedantic tone of the narrator is transformed (and in a masterful touch) the pentameters now lilt with a hint of a slur.

The dosage increases. 'Four whiskies and the man's a giant,' boys become men in preparation for their wedding night as the doctor becomes a clan medicine-man. 'One more dram to bring you into the ring in the pink of condition'; 'In one gulp or Catriona will be wearing the breeks'. Mrs Campbell's protected son is initiated into his nuptial rites, which will not end until she herself falls to temptation. Before the reiteach is done we see her down-turned lips slowly rise to a smile. What mythic powers the whisky has. Who could have forgotten her loathing of the demon drink as she roared earlier at her son, his eyes all ablaze with Scotch courage, 'Satan is in you, drunken debauched – bringing that wanton creature to my very door.' And then reaching for her final damnation, one that will forever deny him his island home, 'You can go up to Glasgow'. Surely this time she has gone too far. With whisky now chasing his Celtic blood through his throbbing arteries he skirls his pipes and drowns her hectoring out in front of a photograph of his piping father. Past and present, form and content, camera moves and sounds, all flow here to make the most telling scene in Scottish cinema. It is only when you see the production stills that you realise that for this shot alone a two storey interior/exterior set was built on a Barra headland.

Could it ever have been so graphic in colour? The black and white photography gives it that extra shift of the imagination, as true to the Highlands as the near monochrome washes of a Daniell print.

Whisky's qualities leap to the alchemical mythic when the islanders are on the verge of being snared by the excisemen; a bottle's worth in the petrol tank, then whoooomph! The lorry lurches into hyper space; over the hill in a frenzied flight. 'Freedom and whisky gang thegither', as that old exciseman Robert Burns once said, 'Tak aff yer dram'.

Then there is that superb performance of Wagget as played by Basil Radford whose nemesis has to be whisky: six bottles (which the authorities hold him responsible for) wrongly boxed in an ammunition case. Even his wife rocks in laughter as he falls off his high moral ground.

To ensure something of a flow of the Water of Life in his own life, Mackenzie augmented his writings by extolling Grant's Standfast in a memorable series of magazine ads. The war was an abominable interruption which denied him his sacred dram. The wretched Germans, he lamented, had even bombed distilleries and whisky bonds at Leith and Glasgow and exacerbated the drought of whisky as the nation's reserves were shipped to America for much-needed dollars. So when the SS *Politician* hit the rocks off Eriskay, it was clearly 'a gift from almighty God'. The question of looting just did not enter. Mackenzie in real life was unambiguous about the morality of plunder. 'What

Coals to Newcastle! Or, in this case, imported studio rocks to boulder-strewn Barra. An Ealing plasterer and painter lower an imitation stone over a real one. Most of the studio rocks only lasted until the first decent drop of rain.

112

comes from the sea should go to the people.'

In Mackendrick's film when we meet our first group of islanders (actors and locals) the central figure is the postmaster and great story-teller of Northbay, John MacPherson, of 'The Coddy' as he was known throughout Barra and the islands far beyond. 'It was not surprising to hear he had taken part in the film during the shooting of *Whisky Galore!* on the island of Barra,' wrote the Gaelic scholar John Lorne Campbell (and frequent guest of Mackenzie's) in his foreword to *Tales Told By The Coddy.* 'In fact, with such a personality he could have had Hollywood at his feet. Indeed it can be said that it is possible that the author would never have written the book if there had been no "Coddy".'

The Coddy played a pivotal role in and out of film. As postmaster he had numerous business interests (and monopolies) including selling fish, so Danischewsky hired him as his transportation captain (as they say on American movies). 'Unfortunately', Danischewsky remembers,

> He often arrived late, but The Coddy would brush aside my complaints with such philosophical observations as 'When God made time he made plenty of it,' and 'Time was here before you came and I dare say it will still be here after you have gone.

Soon there was little that could be organised on the film without the connivance of The Coddy. When an actor asked where he could find the film unit's WC; 'Man', he replied, 'the whole island's a WC'. He was not far from wrong for the summer of 1948 proved to be the worst for 80 years. The carefully constructed wreck which the crew had shipped up from the studios (and which Mackenzie had said in jest would not last a week) was carried away in a storm before a frame of film had turned on it. Artificial rocks were reduced to splinters. 'Surely you fillums were mad anyway, bringing rocks up here all the way from London', an islander accosted Danischewsky in the rain. As rain followed drizzle, and wind followed mist, the film schedule fell further and further behind. Weeks became months until 107 days had elapsed and the budget had more than doubled.

Reg Gibbons, camera department maintenance man, inspects a pre-shoot test using what looks like a sheep trough. Although the rushes were sent off each day for processing in London, tests were made using a few feet of film and processed in a temporary darkroom.

Ealing's first location film was itself edging towards the rocks. Whatever their differences at the beginning, both producer and director must have begun to share the view that their film might well be their last. When another Ealing director Charles Crichton happened to hear that the film was to be cut down as a second feature he offered his help. Balcon refused to have the rushes reprinted but offered Crichton time to reinstate what there was and then have a go at re-editing the film. Today all Crichton will admit to is restoring confidence in a film that had been scrambled through inexperienced editing. When he phoned Mackendrick to suggest a new way of cutting a sequence together, Mackendrick would reply that he had always planned it so. There was still some argument and some great scenes were dropped. Crichton remembers a sequence where the customs officer during his

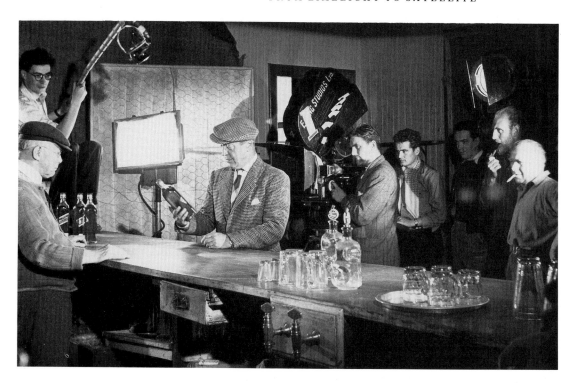

Basil Radford as the unfortunate Captain
Waggett, the Home Guard Commander of
Todday. The barman, played by James
Woodburn, insists 'there is no whisky!'
Herbie Smith (focus puller), Chick
Waterston (camera), Mackendrick, and
Gerry Gibbs (director of photography)
capture Waggett's quandary in the village
bar.

late night inspection wants to quench his thirst. As he reaches for the cold tap the audience would have known that a glass of *Highland Blend* was about to pour from the whisky-full cistern above. Mackendrick has acknowledged Crichton as the midwife of his film, a generous and creative act, for little money and no screen credit; very much in the spirit of Ealing.

Despite Balcon's first reaction the film soon became recognised as one of the great Ealing comedies. William Whitebait in the *New Statesman* gave it a resounding cheer: 'The makers of *Whisky Galore!* have planted themselves on the spot; and once there, they haven't succumbed to the holy awe of the unholy melodrama.' Foreign critics praised its play around the edges of reality; Mackendrick's directorial debut was compared favourably to the work of Rene Clair. As *Whisky a Gogo* it gave its name to pubs and discos all across France, boosting the sales of Scotch. As *Tight Little Island* it was the first Ealing film to make an impact in the States, where its theme echoed the deprivations of Prohibition, which had encouraged a nation of anarchist freebooting whisky concealers. The hated Volsted Act had only been repealed a few years before the onset of World War Two.

Scotch whisky sales benefitted from the great boost created by success of the film. But the parsimony of the trade hardly recognised what the film had done for their product. A night out at the Savoy and a bottle of Scotch were all the thanks given to Danischewsky and Mackendrick. Some Scotch myths you can never scotch.

114

Venus Peter: From Pictures to Pictures

Christopher Rush

In 1984 I wrote what I consciously intended to be my masterpiece: *A Twelvemonth and a Day*, rapturously received but variously categorised by critics, reviewers and booksellers as a novel, an autobiography, a social documentary, a prose poem; as fiction and as non-fiction. Partaking of all of these modes, it is a conscious evocation of the East Neuk of Fife of my childhood and of the slightly earlier Fife of the great herring fishing days, the days of the steam drifters. It is also an evocation of childhood through its largely autobiographical, part fictional, retelling of my own childhood.

This book follows the cycle of the seasons and the shore, charts the progress of the drifterman's year, and each chapter-month corresponds roughly to a year in the life of the narrator, my persona, taking him from age zero to twelve. The epilogue, the 'Day' of the title, records the end of childhood, the onset of adolescence, the break up of the family and the death of the community that nourished me, the disintegration of all the old fishing ways and characters and values under the influence of wider political forces, inevitable change, and human greed.

In the bitter spring of 1986 I received a phone call from a young man from London who introduced himself as Christopher Young.

This twenty-six year old stranger described himself as a film producer. The substance of his call was that he had just read *Twelvemonth* and wanted to make a film out of it. An all-important question was whether anyone had yet bought the film rights on the book. When I told him it was perfectly free there was an audible roar of relief. 'Stay right where you are', he said, 'and I'll be up on the next plane!'

When he arrived I was due for several shocks. One was that he was the son of Sir Roger Young, the Headmaster who had turned me down in 1979 for promotion. I had first set eyes on Chris Young, I recalled, when he was a ten year old standing in shorts at one of his father's 'At Homes' and politely offering me a cucumber sandwich. Not behind every innocuous plate of bread and cucumber does there lurk an embryonic film producer in school shorts.

Another shock was that this 'film producer' had never actually produced a film: the film based on my *Twelvemonth* was to be his first. From then on the shocks had less impact as I grew more used to the idea that the projected film was nothing more than the stuff pipedreams are made of and that my best course of action would be

The baptism, David Hayman is the Reverend Kinnear. 'At my baptism there was ice in the font . . . So the old beadle ran down the outer steps of the Kirk, to where a bursting sea was spraying the tomb-stones of my ancestors. He brought back a glimmer of cold brine in a brass collection plate. That was how it happened that the waters of the Firth, which had been wetting the bones of my forefathers for uncountable tides, were used that morning to baptise me . . .' (*A Twelvemonth and a Day* Christopher Rush p.2).

to proceed good humouredly with this penniless madman who seemed to have no firm notion of where the funding would come from. After all, like many well-intentioned zealots, he could be dangerous.

More surprises were to follow. I knew just enough about options on books to allow me to make the assumption that Chris Young would secure my agreement to some form of contract, get me to sign something, then go away and leave me in peace. Two hours later he was still seated in my study, sipping rum and telling me that the next stage was that I should write a 'treatment'. The word intrigued me but I had no idea what it meant. Carefully he explained. With equal emphasis I let it be known that I had last gone to the cinema about fifteen years before and that although I had watched the occasional film on television, I did not really belong to that world. In short, I was a book freak and probably the very last person whom he should involve in any way in the making of this film. Unperturbed, he assured me that I was the very man he wanted. Most people in the film world did not know how to write; that was why most films started off their lives with thin, glum little scripts which then had to be fattened and dressed in order to produce a decent movie. My alarm increased as I cottoned on to the correctly growing impression that he also wanted me to write the screenplay. There was vague mention of a possible director, though it seemed he had never actually directed a feature film. By this time I was convinced that Chris Young was mad, driven, or divinely inspired. I concluded that at the very least he was inspired and knew better than to try to escape from a man with a vision. I resigned myself to the idea of a very busy future.

From the time I was born my brain had begun snapping images with which it colourpostered the walls of my mind. This happens with everyone. The difference with me was that so many of the very early pictures had shown no tendency to fade. It is also true to say

116

that my mind works imagistically all the time and by instinct, but functions analytically only by deliberation and intent. Added to that, my imagination had been given much to feed upon in childhood, material that had scarcely been used up to the time I began writing at a fairly late stage in my life, and when I came to write *Twelvemonth*, my skull was a bulging portfolio. Hundreds of pictures came peeling away as I plied the pen, pictures heightened by authentic childhood experience and by years of suppression. In effect, a film had been winding itself up in the projection room of my brain for forty years, and in the process of literary composition that had produced *Twelvemonth* had unrolled itself dramatically during the nine months it took to write. So on reflection I was not too surprised that someone had seen a movie in the book.

But there was another sense in which I *was* taken aback by Chris Young's enthusiastic approach to me – and this was to present us with our first difficulty in writing the treatment. *A Twelvemonth's* structure of twelve chapters corresponding to the months of the year provides an eloquent symbol of the structural awkwardness faced by the film writer in trying to put across a story, a unified series of actual events.

The book has, in fact, no strong story line in terms of plot and must have seemed even to the most intrepid filmmaker to be little more than a series of disconnected impressions. To go for 'time' as the plot connector would be impracticable in terms of an eight week shooting programme and yet I could not envisage the story torn from its seasonal context. To show the boy narrator of the book ageing visibly in the course of the film would call for two young boy actors who would look reasonably alike – not an idea to be courted if it could be avoided, and yet the keystone of the project involved growing up and out of childhood. The closer the inspection the greater seemed the impracticability of making a film out of this book.

Gordon Strachan as Peter with the whale. Strachan was a Stromness Primary School pupil who was found under the producer's nose on the film's main location in Orkney. Not so the whale. The most expensive member of the cast, the sixty foot model of the sperm whale had to be brought on a lorry all the way from Bristol. Apparently it has been recycled by a local fun-fair operator as a kid's cinema showing cartoons!

117

Chris Young had quite clearly felt himself considerably moved by the vision behind the book and in the end he advised me simply to start writing – anywhere – and he was convinced that the vision would remain and work the trick, persuading the audience to accept the final results, whatever the penalties, whatever the flaws. In the final analysis the main character in the plot and the principal structural agent in the film would be the author's vision, the ultimate subjective reality that had begun the business and which we intended to objectify. Admiring Mr Young's idealism, I started to write.

Here it would be appropriate to present the introduction to the treatment which I had succeeded, with help from Chris Young, in producing by the Easter of 1986. This is what I wrote:

There are some people who spend their lives trying to resurrect the child within themselves – those first five years like the fingers on an artist's hand which sculpt our personalities forever. A few succeed in getting back to that unforgettable point in time (and beyond it) when the child first realised that childhood itself is not going to last, that the whole world is dying, and that time itself must have a stop. Out of that first moment of horrified recognition comes the story of our film – a man in search of his true self.

His search is triggered by a woman from his past, and takes him back to a childhood in the East Neuk of Fife between 1939 and 1950.

But what is important is not the time or the place, rather his memory of them. In this sense the film could equally be set among the olive groves of Calabria or the back streets of Marseilles. By the same token it is important that the memory is faithful to the hero's imagination and not necessarily to history – indeed this is the only level at which the accuracy of the characters and events of the story is of any significance. It is through the imagination and not the visible universe that the hero tries to reconcile himself to the real world.

Themes of life and death, hellfire and sexuality are reflected in the seasonal rhythm of fishing life, and played out by the vividly contrasting characters of the village, and more specifically the boy's imagination – seen clearly in his grandfather's tales – echo the boy's fascination with two women, parallel figures of fantasy, both of whom ultimately signal the loss of innocence but who lead the hero to a resolution of a kind – a painful but fuller understanding of himself.

The most obvious point which emerges out of this is that the concept of the film was, to begin with, rooted much more deeply in the structure and psychology of the actual book, that is to say the film was going to be a film a quest, an adult quest – an older man's search for the holy grail of his own identity. He finds that this sacred vessel is held by his childhood self and that the route to the Chapel Perilous is the path of the imagination. This was precisely that path that I myself trod in writing *A Twelvemonth and a Day* and rather understandably I began thinking about the film as a medium that would dramatise my own artist's journey, throwing in a little necessary fiction on the way.

Consequently the treatment opened with an older man's being glimpsed naked abed in a hotel bedroom – earlier versions ranged from Sydney to Venice – with an anonymous woman, her identity delicately blurred. A snippet of Italian opera acts as the trigger for his recollections and very swiftly the scene cuts to the man's five year old self pursuing his boyish antics in a fishing village setting. The entire film is conceived as a flashback.

As the film progresses, in this hypothetical treatment form, it becomes clear that the young boy is also engaged upon a quest. It is the forward-looking quest for understanding, which all human beings embark upon: understanding of self, other people, relationships, the world, the universe. His specific quest is given specific point and poignancy by the absence of his father, mysteriously away at sea, and whom the boy has never seen. Thus the backward looking quest of the grown man and the forward thrust of yearning young life are made to co-exist within the film as I first envisaged it. As the projected film reaches its end the two quests meet and merge with dramatic suddenness.

The point of mutual contact is a woman. In a word, what happens is that the unidentified woman who appeared with the man at the start of the film is now revealed as Miss Balsilbie, the young schoolteacher (not now so young) who has held him in thrall since more than twenty years ago when he was that little boy. The concluding narrative incidents that lead up to this sudden revelation are: the boy's realisation that his father (an imagined sailor) is in fact dead; and the actual death by drowning of his beloved fisherman grandfather who has acted throughout as a

Sinead Cusack as Miss Balsilbie. A member of a distinguished Irish acting family, Cusack had much theatre and television to her credit. Of the original, Chris Rush wrote, 'Miss Balsilbie's blouses were white roses that fluffed and fell as she breathed
. . . (she) reached out her white swansnecked, swansdowned arm, and her hand touched my exercise book . . . She squeezed herself into the desk beside me, tucking in her shimmering silk skirt. It rustled mysteriously like the quiet turn of the tide, fell over my knees in cool waves. It made me shiver' (*A Twelvemonth*, pp 80–81).

119

substitute father. At the end of an obviously failed love scene between
the grown man and a forty year old Miss Balsilbie – now shorn of the
stuff of childhood fantasies – the man looks out of the window of the
sea-girt hotel and howls in anguish. What he sees is his childhood
self running crying along the street. The two cries, man and boy's
become one as the grandfather's body is brought ashore. Death has
made its brutal intrusion into his world and the boy now comes face
to face with reality; he has left the Eden of the imagination. So has
the man: he cannot make love to this woman of flesh and blood. So
love and death change all things – the film is a duet of innocence and
experience.

Into the hamper of this treatment I packed away as many of
the *Twelvemonth* goodies as I naively imagined I could decently take
along to the film-goer's banquet. Quite apart from the scenes and
characters that do actually appear in the finished film, I squeezed in
the following: a great-grandfather; a sailmaking uncle; a much larger
clutch of eccentrics; a purely visionary Princess Paloma who remains
unseen (it is the HoneyBunch of the book who is actually washed naked
by the beadle) but who is filmed in the fantasy sequences inside the
boy's head; a leapfrog six years from a much younger to a twelve
year old boy. And there were in addition fishing scenes out at sea,
storytelling sequences, summer holidays and Christmas festivities, the
passage of the seasons, scenes in the woods and in the snow. The only
major omission from the book was the whale, which I never dreamed
a director would wish to tackle in a low budget film. The whole was
rounded off with the sudden realisation that Paloma is after all just
a fat sad old lady in tweeds; that the father is never coming back;
and that love as a dream and death as a reality are the firm truths
we must live with.

After much discussion the title of the film moved from 'The Birth of
Venus' to simply 'Venus'. At that point I suddenly recalled a local East
Fife fisherman nicknamed Venus Peter (in that inbred society, with
only a handful of surnames held in common, men were distinguished
from their namesakes by the names of their boats) and I said to Chris,
'What about calling it *Venus Peter*?' There was an eloquent bar of silence
followed by an audible sigh of satisfaction.

Meanwhile, following my treatment, I penned a synopsis of the
screenplay in the form of a list of actual scenes. The only new character
who appeared in this version was Captain Carnbie, my music teacher
of *Twelvemonth* who taught me the piano and played the organ in church.
He was brought in to be Miss Balsilbie's lover and so to act as the
betrayer of my youthful fancies about women and my idealisation of
adults. Apart from this the new version did not greatly differ from the
original treatment except for one seemingly small item: the introduction
of a telescope for Peter, as he was now called.

This came about as the result of a special screening of *The Tree of
Wooden Clogs* that Chris Young arranged for me. An Italian peasant
lops away part of one of the local landowner's trees in order to make

120

his son a pair of clogs so that the boy need not walk barefoot to school. The crime is discovered and the whole family is evicted from the Eden of their community.

I found that this film affected me profoundly. The rustic setting, the village characters, the work rhythms of a simple people, the exile from grace – all built up to an interesting parallel with *Twelvemonth*. Taking the device of the clogs, I decided to introduce the telescope as a symbol of emotional and aesthetic aspiration, of seeing further than you ordinarily see, and this was to give rise, in the screenplay, to the deliberately conflicting lines spoken by the Reverend Kinnear and Miss Balsilbie: the one saying that you must always see just what you see, the other insisting that you must see more. In the end, having escaped from his dreams, Peter sees more than he wanted to see, but in doing so he grows up, casts off his dying community along with his outdated childhood self, and prepares to enter the tougher adult world.

I wrote this version of the screenplay of *Venus Peter* (for a film of six or seven hours!) in exactly six weeks. Besides the problems of inclusiveness and scope, I now came to grips for the first time with the purely local problem of scripting and I found that this entailed something entirely new to me as a writer – writing something that was neither poetry nor poetic prose but bare unpoetic dialogue. In the first instance I had to make my characters speak like real people and not like literary archetypes: I did not wish to succeed in this *too* well. Secondly I had to resist my instinctive temptation to create atmosphere by surrounding the dialogue with my descriptions of what I envisaged would or should be happening on the set. This turned out to be impossible for me and I continued to do the work of the director and the camera with my verbal atmospherics and asides, all of which I knew would be pruned away from the final version of the screenplay. The trouble was that I had already seen so many of these pictures in autobiographical reality. I simply could not disentangle myself from the scenes when scripting *Venus Peter*.

Ironically I was unaware as yet that Chris Young's carefully chosen director was at that moment going through my literary works with an eagle eye. When we met for the first time it was evident to me that he had absorbed not only *Twelvemonth* but everything else that I had written, even my poems. He was busy building my vision into his own concept of the film so that he could recreate it faithfully. Nor did he even stop at my writings. We met several times and he questioned me closely about myself, my childhood, my literary philosophy, throwing up in the process images and information that had not made their way into print but were destined to make it onto the screen. Captain Marr's ship, for example, swinging above the pulpit in the kirk, came up in conversation and provided the film with its beginning and end and indeed one of its most potent images. Holding me in one eye and my gigantic screenplay in the other, Ian Sellar had ingeniously produced a new ninety-five minute screenplay which became the firm

Peter with the boat in the kirk. The original
was commissioned by an ancestor of
Rush's, a Captain Marr, and hangs in the
Kirk at St Monans, Fife.

foundation for the final film.

My first feelings about the new script were of impoverishment; so
much had gone. There was no framing adult quester, no structuring
of the story through the passage of nature. Indeed Nature was the
important single character who was dropped from my screenplay.

There were other characters who suffered. God and the Devil, though
not removed (they remain in Kinnear and Epp) were made to sit
much further back. The village evangelists were silenced. Even the
dead themselves appeared only fitfully, so it appeared to me, instead
of the longer sequences I had planned – and the human characters
were cut down like corn: great-grandfather, great-uncle, a younger
uncle, Captain Carnbie, a fistful of eccentrics, HoneyBunch (who
was compressed into Paloma) and an old schoolmaster for whom
I'd written a vivid and moving scene. In spite of the fact that I'd
been well warned about the inevitable narrowing of scope; in spite
of the fact that I could see intellectually that the losing of five hours
of screenplay made wholesale slaughter unavoidable, even so I was
rocked back on my heels by the blows when they fell.

What was it that made me keep standing?

Admiration, in a word. I was staggered by Ian Sellar's achievement
in managing to retain the essence of the vision while having to lose so
much of the actual writing. What Ian Sellar did was to dismantle the
whole thing and reassemble it using only a handful of pieces.

If there were losses there were also gains. Paloma – a mere product of
the boy's imaginings, to be seen against the real thing at the end of my
version, became instead, in Ian Sellar's screenplay, a real live princess,
weirdly, touchingly mad, an unspeaking Ophelia of the Scottish shores.
The boy's father was likewise dragged very much alive and kicking into
the arena of Peter's life. He could not have generated the emotion he
does by simply never appearing and being pronounced dead, no matter
how deeply that affected his fatherless son. The Reverend Kinnear had
already grown under my pen in the transition from novel to screenplay
and he had undergone further development.

Also impressive was the way the screenplay echoed the structure
of the book as a series of impressions, while retaining in its jigsaw
arrangement of images a tenuous but brightly insistent narrative thread.
On balance I concluded that I was looking at a potentially magical film.
On only one point did I lash out in furious disbelief, angrily defending
the corpse of my original creation against a violation that I believed
to be outrageously wrong: the ending. *A Twelvemonth and a Day* ends
with the death of my grandfather. It is a harsh ending, sudden and
cruel, but as such it reflects the way death often does intrude into
existence, the unwanted skeleton at the feast, freezing the dancers,
silencing the music of humanity, whether still or sad. The death of
the fine old fisherman symbolises the disintegration of the community
and its culture, of the old fishing and folk values. It also marks the
end of childhood, of imagination and dreams, and brings on the pale
glare of reality.

122

The screenplay now ended with Peter's father coming back, as it were, from the dead and grandfather's tragedy commuted from the ultimate death sentence to bankruptcy and the loss of his boat. I believed this to be too weak an ending.

In any case, so I argued, audiences want blood. Death, moreover, is the end of every story, I kept on arguing. All the great classical stories end in death and I wanted the film to adhere to the pattern of classical tragedy; I did not want my story to lose power in the end by being robbed of the stroke that everybody was waiting for. This potential loss of power I regretted so bitterly that I never gave in to the combined arguments of producer and director that they wanted a more positive ending that spoke of some kind of resolution, harmony and hope. In altering my conclusion I believed they were committing a major blunder and I staunchly opposed them all the way. It was only after I had seen the finished film that I was to change my mind.

Meanwhile the search began for a cast and a location. The latter at first presented us with something of a problem. It was natural enough that the first place to which I should take the filmmakers would be the East Neuk of Fife, the cradle of the whole experience. In particular I wanted them to see the Old Kirk at St. Monans. They were impressed by its setting and by the image of the ship over the pulpit which became an evitable part of the film. The trouble was that the surroundings no longer resembled the villagescape which I had described in *Twelvemonth*. The sea-battered, wind-torn and workaday houses of my childhood had lost their grittiness and now, courtesy of the National Trust, the seatown frontage resembled an Italian ice-cream parlour in its pretty colours and quaint postcard picturesqueness.

As an alternative I suggested the narrow, winding streets of old Cellardyke, a few miles further up the coast, but it was becoming increasingly clear than an even stronger atmosphere was wanted, one

Juliet Cadzow as the Princess Paloma, wild, silent and half-crazy. She was a composite of Paloma and HoneyBunch from the book. 'She smelled to high heaven. From six feet away you could have adored her; from three feet you could have died'. (*A Twelvemonth* pp 57.)

123

that would speak of a different world, autonomous, self-contained, microcosmic. A long search was instituted for this location, which took on, through the winter of 1986 and into 1987, the hypothetical aura of a lost world, a mythical place that now existed anywhere.

Until I remembered Orkney.

In some ways its treeless austerities, so different from wooded Fife, made it the very last place I might have suggested. And yet, with its port of Stromness so largely unspoiled, so like the working face of the St. Monans of forty years ago, and with its colossal skyscapes and seascapes expanding into infinity, it seemed the ideal spot in which to turn a camera around and never once run into contemporary Britain. I asked Chris if he had ever been to Orkney. No, but if I felt strongly about it, he would go. He did so, taking Ian Sellar with him. Quite simply they never looked back. The Orkney magic worked for them as it has worked for thousands. The question of the location was settled in a trice.

Having decided on a place, the next matter was how to people it with a fitting cast. Orkney was already peopled by a superb cast of potential extras and the presence of these highly individualistic islanders was another big plus towards the decision on location. As to the professional actors, there was no shortage of interest in the various parts but the vital question now needing to be settled was that of who was going to play the boy Peter.

The starting point was the hope that somewhere in the islands themselves there might just be a boy who would have the natural ability and who would be able to bring to the part something that a child actor conscripted from elsewhere would not have: a feeling of kinship with the sea-splashed environment that was to be the setting for the film. We found exactly what we were looking for in Gordon Strachan, who also provided us with something else: a strong sense of his own identity, perhaps in some degree caused by his never having known a father, the situation Peter finds himself in throughout most of the film. With his freedom from precociousness and self-consciousness, his ability to handle adults easily and not look as though he were acting, he was a triumphant find.

Not that finding him was easy. Every male child in Orkney of reasonable age was auditioned or assessed. And it was during this search for Peter that the typical Orcadian qualities of openness and hospitality were incidentally revealed. The search having proceeded quite far and no decision having been made, it was pointed out to Chris Young by a Stromness man that there was a crofter in one of the remoter islands who had two sons. Chris and Ian hired a boatman to take them to this island and the Stromnessian promised to telephone the crofter to forewarn him of the imminent arrival of a film producer and director to interview his offspring. The crofter was also to be told that on no account were his boys to be alerted to the fact that these two strangers were looking for actors. The idea was to keep things on a low profile and proceed as naturally as possible.

Dressed like a producer in his camel coat and accompanied by Ian Sellar – dressed like a director in his London designer's gear – Chris knocked on the door of the croft, his stomach trembling somewhat from a brisk passage over the waves. They were ushered in and greeted at once with whisky – no introduction seemed necessary beyond that provided by the communal bottle. Whisky stimulates the appetite and soon soup and scones and slabs of cheese appeared and were gratefully consumed. Then more whisky just to wash it all down. The drinking became serious.

After some time Chris asked the crofter if he could see his two sons. The boys were brought in from their playing, according to procedure, not wishing to make them self-conscious by telling them that they were really being auditioned for a film, Chris and Ian chatted to them awhile, got their measure, and allowed them to return to their ploys without anything's having been suspected. The convivial afternoon wore on in a deepening haze of whisky, after which the two movie men said goodbye and staggered to the waiting boat. It was just as the vessel was bobbing off on the swell that the crofter, clinging to the last minute to the ancient courtesy of spirit which had restrained him till now from asking the obvious question, but finally unable to govern any longer his islander's instinctive curiosity, now that the two men were decently off his island, shouted after them: 'Oh, by the way . . . why did you come?'

The promised telephone call had never been made.

And yet, in the true Orcadian spirit, the man had welcomed, fed and whiskeyed two perfect strangers according to the timeless laws of hospitality.

Orkney has always attracted a variety of accents and callers: Vikings, oilmen, Americans. A ninety-strong film crew had now been thrown at them and they had blotted them up quite happily. When I came off the St. Ola ferry the first thing I saw was a procession of people wearing fifties gear, dark suits and hats, snaking slowly southwards out of Stromness. Among them I saw my film mother, my father, my grandfather, aunts and uncles and a scattering of village crazies, clutched from the past. At the director's command they lapsed into a dramatic hush. It was a tense moment in the film: I felt as if I'd come to witness my own funeral.

That apart, what were my impressions?

Of the incredible slowness, for one thing, of making a film: a minute a day; a sentence a morning; an entire phrase turned round and round in the camera eye until it is perfected, like a pebble sculpted and polished by the sea. Of seeing my childhood images of life projected palpably on to miles upon miles of reels, hanging in black bunches of celluloid spaghetti, waiting to be edited; the ghosts of the past giving employment to the actors of today; Juliet Cadzow being washed down by Alex McEvoy in the cold Orkney October through sixteen takes and as many tequilas; and the warm, sturdy Ray McAnally playing my grandfather with a depth and a compassion that brought tears to

125

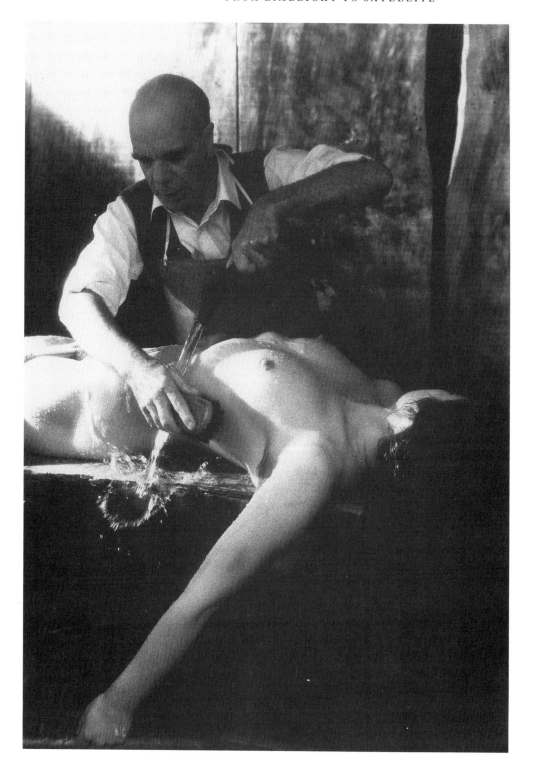

the eye. And of the colossal human jigsaw that goes into the making of a movie.

Everybody except financiers was in great humour: the Orcadians because the film had become in a sense 'theirs', complete with 200 extras, and because the town tills were tintinnabulating. And the actors too because they simply loved the script. The more I talked with them, Ray McAnally, David Hayman, Sinead Cusack, Emma Dingwall, the more I began to appreciate that a screenplay is not something over which an actor normally does much enthusing. A beautiful script nonetheless was how they saw it.

When script became film, I saw the folk of my past resurrected anew, safely distanced and apotheosised while again for other people they had taken on a larger-than-life quality. This was especially true of Sheila Keith's Epp, a miracle of metamorphosis. No other character in the film was so close to the reality of the original live being as she was.

As to the differences between book and film – how do they ultimately compare in affecting the imagination? – I worried about this at first. Someone once wrote that a picture is the literature of the illiterate. But in some ways you have to be even more 'literate' to understand a piece of visual artwork.

A great painting can stimulate you endlessly because of its very wordlessness, its ability to avoid verbalised statement and feeling, to take anyone anywhere in the world, whatever his language, and say, 'Look! This is what it was like for me . . .' And what is a film but thousands of pictures? And if it is true that a picture is worth a thousand words, then there are millions of words in the many frames of *Venus Peter*.

There is an old saying that the pen is mightier than the sword and a rather more recent assertion that the pen is mightier than the *word*. But is the image mightier than the pen? I do not believe that there need be a war between the two, as some people in our time have supposed. A great film may convert a war into a wedding, a marriage between pictures and words.

There is a human impulse to make pictures out of words, just as words, music on their own, lead some men to make more music, to fit the words. Jonathan Dove's strong score for *Venus Peter* combines with Gabriel Beristain's heightened photography and the screenplay by Ian Sellar and myself, to produce a warm fusion of the arts, a trinity in one.

Of course reading a book and seeing a film are two entirely different experiences and *Venus Peter* goes off on voyages of its own that do not concern the book. For one thing the book is highly inclusive: it simply contains everything that I could remember. The film is much more selective and in that sense more artistic than the book, since art is ultimately a selection from reality. Where *Venus Peter* perhaps succeeds more emphatically than *Twelvemonth* is in its presentation of two distinct levels of experience: the realistic and the poetic. I believe that *Twelvemonth* is wholly submerged in its own poetry. *Venus Peter*, on

OPPOSITE
Alex McAvoy as the Beadle and Juliet Cadzow as the filthy Princess Paloma. 'So Alex Fergusson, the old beadle who had baptised me with salt water, was the man who did out of pure Christian charity what not a single woman in the place would have dreamed of doing – he washed her. Took her through his burnside cottage, out to the back garden and into his wash-house, stripped her bare buff, laid her down like a sleepy queen on a big old-fashioned scrubbing board, and gave her a good soaping and rinsing before he let her go'. (*A Twelvemonth* p 57.)

127

Sheila Keith as Epp, the landlady who fed the boy poker-broken pan-drops. 'She stood as straight as the poker still gripped in her white hairless knuckle, and with which she looked as ready to crack my skull as please my palate.' (*A Twelvemonth* p 7.)

the other hand, shows a boy of heightened sensibilities experiencing poetic fantasies, while all around him is a world of hard economic fact, a world falling apart financially. It is plainly absurd to call *Venus Peter* a romantic film as some dimmer critics have ridiculously done. The film peels off romanticism frame by frame in its bitter recognition of economic reality, while at the same time exploring the richness of a poetic experience. There is the world of difference between poeticism and romanticism. It should also be understood that realism need not always mean the inevitable grittiness of urban deprivation, violence and the four-letter word. It is possible to be realistic and yet still see the beauty of living, of imagination. *Venus Peter* is in its own way a fiercely realistic film.

People have said to me, 'Oh, but the film is so different from the book!' They should bear in mind that *Venus Peter* was never intended to be merely the film of the book, even though at one point I did imagine it could be done. *A Twelvemonth and a Day* is the book that *inspired* the film *Venus Peter*.

They should also remember that literature is not an autonomous structure of verbal signs of any more than a stone is just an independent object lying on a beach. It is tied by various umbilical cords to its multi-maternal sources: history, politics, tradition, other literary works, the author, his biography, his socio-economic circumstances. And literature, alive and kicking, latches on to every reader that looks in its face and encounters it humanly, each with his own interpretation; latches on indeed to each new generation; each century.

In this way it becomes the property of the world, of Everyman. And if that man be a filmmaker he simply adds another layer of meaning, because writing a book is rather like throwing a stone into the vast sea. A series of concentric circles is set up and starts moving outwards, to disturb a very small area of that sea. The further the circles get from the centre of the original experience, the more blurred they become, the less they have to do with it; and yet they are wider than ever, taking the experience further. The filmmaker adds another circle, that is all. Or perhaps he too throws in a stone, into the centre of those brimming circles, overlaying the circles with rings of his own. The concentric circles wed one another and a new work of art is created.

In a way a filmmaker becomes a critic when he decides to make a film out of someone else's book, and the actors in the film also become critics when they interpret the characters they play. I was pleased to learn that many of the cast of *Venus Peter* had taken the trouble to read *a Twelvemonth* before filming began.

Now in *A Twelvemonth and a Day* I idealised my grandfather, turning him into the archetypal fisherman, the embodiment of the spirit of the sea and of all men who have gone down to the waters to do business in great ships. I surrounded him with all the poetry my imagination could muster; he strode through the book clothed with literary and biblical allusions, existing only in images, stories, poetic lines and a folk sensibility. In the screenplay he was simply given a few sentences to say and all that incidental verbal atmosphere was sucked up the lum. I knew that everything depended on an actor who would recapture that atmosphere and fill the film with it.

My first thought had been of Fulton Mackay, who had read the original treatment when he sat on the panel of the Scottish Film Production Fund and had voted us the money to start the project rolling. Fulton's death robbed *Venus Peter* of a potentially fine grandfather. I had also seen Cyril Cusack play an old fisherman in Bill Forsyth's television film of George Mackay Brown's *Andrina* and he ranked high with me – not that he was ever approached. In the end the part went to Ray McAnally who carried in his own aura of sturdiness and warmth, depth and understanding, to an extent I should have scarcely thought possible. He brought something else too – the stillness and self-possession of the realist who will not be untrue to himself no matter what the crumbling world around him dictates, because he knows that realism lies in being true to your own ideals: only the idealist is the true realist. In his humanity and integrity Ray McAnally crystallised and hardened the grandfather of the book out of the Celtic twilight of my imagery and thrust him solidly on to the screen, a tough old man at peace with himself and his world.

In the case of the Reverend Kinnear the process was reversed. A straightforwardly realised character in the book, a no-nonsense man of the cloth, with a huge fist and a tongue with a tang, he retreats in the film from easy categorisation, escapes caricature altogether and in David Hayman's brilliant portrayal takes on the curiosity of an enigma, a man playing his professional part on the world's stage, dropping the mask from time to time to reveal the layers of other selves hidden beneath, jostling perhaps in uneasy and maybe even tortured confusion. Kinnear indeed was one of the characters who took on a life of his own in the penning and yet refused to let even

Peter is rushed to safety in a pram after nearly drowning. Shot in The Street in Stromness, the Orkneys being chosen in preference to the book's Fife setting. The £1.2 million budget was scraped together by producer Chris Young. As well as money from the Scottish Film Production Fund, British Screen, Channel Four and the British Film Institute, Young persuaded the Orkney Islands Council to contribute £60,000. The Council felt the money was well spent. Local authorities throughout Scotland are looking more seriously at this kind of investment.

129

the author see just what it was that he wanted to be. I discovered during the shooting that David Hayman was well aware what had happened during the translation from book to screenplay and carried on the process in his acting.

Another miracle was Princess Paloma.

The real princess from Tahiti, married to a Fife sailor and brought back by him to live in the East Neuk, was dead before I was born. I was long fascinated by her gravestone however and found out about her what I could, which I fictionalised a good deal when writing *Twelvemonth*. Here she symbolises the wildest poetic fancies of my boyhood, never actually making an appearance as such until the very end of the story, when something completely different from the expected vision fleetingly emerges.

In the film she is made real – an object of awe but not of dreams. Perfectly tangible, she is in fact the result of a combination of two characters. Into her role she incorporates Paloma and HoneyBunch, one of that race of wandering female eccentrics that people village and shore. It was HoneyBunch who was washed down by the old sexton. It did become clear during the various versions of the screenplay, however, that we would have to cut down on the considerable collection of crazies from the book. One of the obvious dangers lay in running much too close to the winds of Scottish whimsy and in this case the two characters were simply packed up together in the one portmanteau.

The very palpable Paloma again represents a change from the misty sequences of verbal images that constitute the princess of the book. This very palpability of projection could be seen as one of the penalties of filming the story at all. On the other hand she is made to work on the screen on a dramatic level: in the pages of the book she lived a purely lyrical life.

Then there is the dreamship – another invasion from the poetic

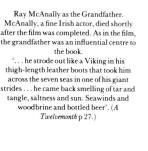

Ray McAnally as the Grandfather. McAnally, a fine Irish actor, died shortly after the film was completed. As in the film, the grandfather was an influential centre to the book.
'. . . he strode out like a Viking in his thigh-length leather boots that took him across the seven seas in one of his giant strides . . . he came back smelling of tar and tangle, saltness and sun. Seawinds and woodbrine and bottled beer'. (*A Twelvemonth* p 27.)

130

Peter Caffrey as the father. The boy's visions of his imagined father took some people by surprise. The expectation by some of the critics of the film was that it remain an untroubled and untroubling piece of fey 'realism'.

world on to the actualities of filming. Perhaps it is just too real as it sits in the grass like the set for a television advertisement. On the other hand it could be argued that Ian Sellar succeeded in bringing on to the screen the poetical dreams of one who never saw them as mere dreams at the time.

As I lived out my life in the St. Monans of the late forties and early fifties the visions I saw were as real to me as the fishbones and crabs' toes that littered the piers – at times even more real. So when Peter looks through his telescope he does not see a blurring of reality but a ship and a princess that are as concrete as the substantial Ray McAnally. Thus the film reflects the cruel dichotomy of experience: grandfather's boat, the *Venus*, was no more real in the end than the dreamship. It had no economic reality, was lifted out of the water like something that didn't belong on the sea, and was spirited away in the end into another element. In the Platonic sense it was the dreamship that actually possessed more reality than the *Venus*. Paloma too was wafted off to the social reality of an asylum, and looked no more appropriate in the big car than was the *Venus* on the loader, gliding incongruously along the street. Both Paloma and the *Venus* have become symbols of the disintegrating elements of the world they inhabit. Thus dreams and reality are alike seen as both real and unreal. Only one thing seems to remain – the eternal sea from which life emerged, the symbol of human destiny.

'The sea is everything.' The message is beautifully modulated by Ray McAnally in his closing soliloquy.

It is an ending which I immediately came to accept as the right one in spite of all my earlier bluster and concern for the classical tragic pattern. For one thing, hearing the words spoken in Ray's grandfather's storytelling voice, muted, secretive, intimate, and heard against the image of the glimmering sea, would have convinced me just in itself

131

that here was an experience with a stillness which tragedy could not touch.

But there was more to it than that.

Finally what happened was this. I came to see what Ian Sellar had seen from the beginning with the benefit of an objective outsider. *A Twelvemonth and a Day* ends, as I have already pointed out, with a brutal and laconic suddenness. Grandfather drowns, the family breaks up, the fishing declines, the community dies, and there is an end of it. With great deliberateness I switch from a lyrical to a curt prose style on the last page of the book, chronicling the death of the dream quite unsentimentally.

But Ian never looked at my story in that way. What he pointed out to me was that in fact I had *not* let it end like that. I had gone out, left my village behind, and grown up. But in addition to that I had done something positive with my experience. My world was not simply put up on a shelf and left behind me like a ship in a bottle. On the contrary I had kept it alive within my mind all these years. I had in fact written a book about it and had helped in the making of a film about it. There was something at the end of *A Twelvemonth And A Day* which deserved to be acknowledged. Ian called it 'the unwritten chapter': it is not actually *in* the book but it *is* the book. This view made a big impression on me.

After all, the book is largely a celebration. It ends with a lament, yes, but the conclusion of a work is not necessarily its ending, its last word, as it were. Ian was determined not to allow the elegiac ending to put its stamp on the film, to let that harsh conclusion take away from the celebratory impulse that largely created and informs the whole. For Ian Sellar the unwritten chapter of *Twelvemonth* had to show itself in the smile on Peter's face just as the film ends. Harmony, happiness, resolution, positiveness, the celebration of life itself, these are the keynotes of the story, in spite of greed, discord, hatred and grief. For it has to be said in conclusion that this is *my* story and that I was fortunate in finding a director who recognised its authenticity and set out to universalise it in a film which tells the *whole* story. It is a film which does leave me with a certain smile. For it is the film not of a book but of a life that continues.

Bill Douglas's *Trilogy*

Andrew Noble

To raise immediate passion to poetry in this way requires a vision of unconditional clearness, like that of a child.

Edwin Muir

My first viewing of *My Childhood* and *My Ain Folk* had an overwhelming impact which subsequent viewings have deepened rather than diminished. Undoubtedly part of its power came from its ability to resurrect my own early memories of wartime Scotland. It also opened a later seam of memory. As a Cambridge post-graduate student in the mid-sixties I had my first opportunity to view a stream of classic world cinema. I was both learning and hiding in Cambridge cinemas. They were places of escape from those anxieties that tend to accrue to the souls of Scottish aspirants at the centres of English cultural power. I felt neither I nor Scotland had much to offer; several English dons were not unwilling to corroborate this. Thus seeing the *Trilogy* provoked a double-edged shock of recognition. Here were Scottish films rightly belonging to the highest level of what I had seen in Cambridge. Furthermore, here were films which contradicted my personal, national Cambridge doubts because they overwhelmingly confirmed the authenticity and the creative possibilities of being Scottish.

I saw the complete *Trilogy* in Glasgow in the late-seventies. I took my friend, Jim Drury, with me, troublingly aware that Jim, an adopted child of the Lanarkshire coal-field, quite uncannily mirrored in his own life so much of what was being projected on the screen. Jim was and remains the most extraordinary man I have ever met. The higher business of the spirit was manifestly at work in him and but for his premature, cruel death would have emerged in creative writing. His life, tragically, was not allowed to imitate that of Douglas. Strongly influenced by the pain of my friend's Scottish childhood, I did not on that occasion do justice to the *Trilogy's* longest, third part. I thought Jamie's adolescence in *My Way Home* less well handled and Egypt a significantly lesser location than Scotland. Now I see these judgements as quite wrong and a significant part of what I want to say concerns the wholly organic nature of the three parts and the need to view the *Trilogy* whole.

The invitation to write on these films touched some deep personal places. It also evoked in me a profound sense of honour undercut by

133

My Way Home, Robert Blatchley, Stephen Archibald. Under the watchful gaze of Robert, Jamie begins to find his own way home to life.

an almost equal degree of anxiety. The *Trilogy* does induce in me both a shocked and awed silence. In a manner I associate with the greatest Russian fiction and film, it induces thoughts that lie too deep for tears. Dostoevsky postulated that the intelligibility and, hence, acceptability of the very universe was most acutely based on the problem of the suffering of children. After such aesthetic experience what mode of criticism is either desirable or acceptable?

Yet, if we carry the Dostoevsky analogy further, one is aware in reading him, or viewing Douglas, of an apparent paradox. Along with the savage, relentless emotional demands they make on themselves and communicate to us we are aware that we are being propelled into a heightened aesthetic, cognitive awareness of an intensity compatible with our overwrought emotions. As David Robinson has remarked of this creative ambivalence at the heart of Douglas's work: 'The effect is volcanic. You are always uneasily conscious of a seething eruptive emotion just below the cool surface.' What, then, the *Trilogy* demands of us is the head's subtle attention to an innovative use of image, narrative, language, natural sound, song and, not least, silence. This is because no conventional forms could possibly cope with the fraught heart's areas of feeling and being which are under exploration.

Of course, films such as Douglas's make stringent demands on an audience's feelings and hence intelligence. Many children respond instinctively to them. Retainers of childhood, that indispensable element of creativity, respond intuitively. Those adults enclosed in the sentimental prison houses of conventional cliche trained to demand

134

escapism, resist them. As a French critic remarked:

> The complaint of some of those who have seen the films is that
> they are depressing, an idea that I have never been able to come
> to terms with. What is truly depressing to me is the use of cinema
> to manipulate, to cheapen, to degrade, to falsify, and, of course, to
> bore. Supposedly 'happy', 'uplifting', and 'meaningfully optimis-
> tic' movies which attract huge audiences are very often depressing
> in exactly that way. Douglas's subject matter is, admittedly, hardly
> joyful or even very pleasant, but what he has done with it is an
> entirely different matter . . . This is not a cinema for the lazy,
> but anyone who has patience and is willing to work a bit will be
> richly rewarded.

Douglas himself perceives the film as a ridge in his complex conversation with the audience. 'One thing I do', he has written, 'is hold back
from spelling everything out in many films. The film is an archetypal
middleman in a two way process.' This is not an elitist but actually
a profoundly democratic principle. Douglas seems to share William
Blake's belief that the good society is based on the creative arousal in
the individual of sympathetic imagination. In a closely related way,
he approves of Orson Welles's remark that 'a film is never really good
unless the camera is an eye in the head of a poet', reciprocating Blake's
remark. For Douglas the magic of the cinema is that mystery where a
mechanism, the camera, becomes a medium for the sensations of the
spirit. As he has remarked:

> What interests me is reaching into the soul of person, other than
> the mask presented so often. There is so much to be read in a
> person's face. I use the camera to read that face and it will speak
> volumes if you will listen to it.

Douglas, however, sees a constant erosion of our capacity to be still,
watch and know. Drama which used to be sacred, annual ritual
now pours from our TV screens round the clock. The narratives
we constantly absorb are of a stupefying banality. Beyond this lurks
the breakdown of narrative coherence into discrete sensationalism.
The money men, with increasing academic collusion, are interested
not in imaginative arousal but commercial reflexivity. We are losing
the power, in Simone Weil's sense, to attend and are increasingly
distracted. 'Distraction,' as Saul Bellow has remarked, 'is the American
byproduct of Nihilism.' Douglas believes that the potential of the
cinema has been mightily abused:

> Surely it is imagery that is the language of cinema, a brand new
> language that almost a hundred years after its discovery is still to be
> properly learnt! The silent cinema started to learn it but, ironically
> in my view, the 'talkies' put back the process. And television isn't

helping today. Sometimes I fear it may be a lost language.

Paradoxically, I happen to believe that stillness and silence are potentially very strong elements in the film language – something perhaps only Beckett and Pinter have attempted on the stage – and all too easily overlooked in the hyper-manic format of today's movies.

There has been, of course, considerable critical comment on the relation of the *Trilogy* to the silent cinema. Indeed Philip French credited him with reinventing that medium for his own purposes: 'forcing us to open our eyes to an eloquent visual language we have forgotten or never learnt'. Derek Malcolm cogently remarked of *My Way Home* that it 'still owes its chief visual debt to the silent expressionist cinema and its chief aural one to natural sound rather than dialogue'. The melodramatic conventions of the American silent cinema, whereon even a genius of D W Griffith's stature teeters, would, of course, have been a disastrous influence. Douglas's influence has been not such restricting sentimentality but the 'hard', often elliptically imagist narrative forms of European cinema. The most specific debt, recorded in *My Way Home*, is to the great Russian master, Alexander Dovzhenko. With Dovzhenko's intensely edited power of narrative goes that pristine capacity to see the objects of the world as if for the first time. Dovzhenko and Douglas share what James Agee has defined as 'one of the richest promises that movies hold, as the perfect medium for realism raised to the level of high poetry.' The perfecting of this medium comes at the time of editing. Douglas believes that editing is akin to musical composition so that, paradoxically, objects of the eye become subject to the ear. Hence he approvingly quotes Welles's comment to Andre Bazin: 'I search for the precise rhythm between one shot and the next. It's a question of the ear; editing is the moment when the film involves a sense of hearing.' The timing and pitch of the *Trilogy* is nigh perfect, bearing witness to the intensity of Douglas and his editors for it is only when editing that, as Welles says, 'the director has the power of a true artist.'

As a literary critic, I am no specialist in film criticism. Indeed, I largely avoid, as with literary criticism, many of its contemporary modes. In preparing to write this piece I, however, returned to Agee, an abiding favourite. I was astonished to find the proximity with what he admired and desired of film and Douglas's own admirations and work. Agee was in a constant state of witty anguish over the commercial abuse (perhaps refracted in his own alcoholism) of cinema as the true medium for rendering our fullest humanity. Consider, for example, these 1947 comments on two films, *Open City* and *The Raider*, in their employment of amateur actors with regard to their prescience for Douglas's work nearly two decades later:

Since I think so highly of both films I should take special care to make clear that this is not *because* they use non-actors, or are semi-documentary, or are 'realistic'. It is, rather, they they show a livelier aesthetic and moral respect for reality – which 'realism' can as readily smother as liberate – than most fictional films, commercial investments in professional reliability, ever manage to. If they are helped to this – as they are – by their concern for actual people and places, that is more than can be said for most documentaries, which by average are as dismally hostile to reality as most fiction films. The films I most eagerly look forward to will not be documentaries but works of pure fiction, played against, and into, and in collaboration with unrehearsed and uninvented reality.

Collaboration with reality seems to me to be the essence of the *Trilogy*'s achievement. Such collaboration offends against the quisling collusion of most cinema with safe profit. Even worse, it breaks down the barriers of false craft which professionals tend to erect around themselves. More due to principle than fiscal constraint, the *Trilogy* opens itself to the landscape and people of the Lothians. However much he may impose his creative will at the moment of filming and editing, this is done on the vital basis of Douglas's prior ability to listen, look and appropriately respond. He deeply believes in cinema as a communal act where, if you seek, it will be given to you and often from the most unlooked for places. Nothing could be further than the image of the meglomaniac director; Douglas spontaneously makes himself in directing and teaching the locus where people can discover and deliver *their* talents.

The most singular aspect of this, of course, is the casting of the *Trilogy* and the consequent quality of acting from its mixed professional and amateur cast. Both groups emerged from a set of coincidences both funny and fated. With regard to the professionals Douglas, ignorant of that Scottish scene, was sitting having coffee in The Laigh in Edinburgh. Unknown to him, the owner, Moultrie Kelsall, while apparently clearing tables was listening intently to his discourse on the actors he needed. As he was about to leave, Kelsall called him aside and listed a series of names which, when checked, was found wholly right. Douglas, going to visit an Edinburgh school for possible candidates, was actually accosted by Stephen Archibald and Hugh Restorick, playing truant and cadging a smoke. He saw immediately who he was looking for. Archibald was to repay his faith by acting as if it was the only chance life was ever going to give him.

My Childhood

No critical account can possibly do justice to the compression and complexity of Douglas's storytelling. Several critics have noted that these short films (48, 55 and 78 minutes long respectively) appear to contain far more than their running time would normally allow. In terms of complexity we are in the grip of what might be described as Douglas's binary vision. We see Jamie both from without and within. At

137

My Childhood, Stephen Archibald.
Douglas's images of Newcraighall are
sparing and precise but create a vivid
picture of the village.

one level we are objectively aware of a small creature whose humanity is, for most of the course of the *Trilogy*, being remorselessly extinguished. At another level we are subjectively inside Jamie's consciousness trying to piece together the corruption, often sexual, around him. In such identification with the child we have, of course, the perfect practical example of Douglas's belief that cinema should be about the arousal of sympathetic intelligence.

Jamie is discovered living with his brother Tommy and his maternal grandmother. Both their domestic situation and the old lady's health are on the point of extinction. There is minimal food. They are, along with scavenged coal, burning the wallpaper and furniture to keep warm. For Jamie emotional warmth is in equally short supply. He is only spontaneous with his cat and Helmuth, a German prisoner of war. He, Granny and Tommy do form a triangular bond but Granny is visibly exhausted unto death. Further this triangle is disrupted by Granny's anguish over her two lost daughters; one, probably Tommy's mother, dead and the other, Jamie's mother, incarcerated in a mental hospital. This anguish is heightened into rage by the intrusion of the two men who she believes destroyed her daughters and certainly failed their illegitimate sons. In this film Jamie's father is transitory, oblique and thereby disturbing. Tommy's father appears with a caged canary birthday present. He is a cloth-capped creature of linguistic and moral impoverishment who Granny loathingly denounces. Tommy, however, such is the elemental need of a son for his father, clings to the gift and saves it from Granny's enraged assault. Jamie's cat is not, however, so forestalled. In revenge Tommy batters Jamie's cat to death. The infinitely resurrecting cartoon world of Sylvester and Tweetie Pie becomes horribly, morbidly real.

A child's experience of death and death's power to kill the spirit are at the centre of the film and Jamie's consciousness. Depressed, culturally deprived, these people are mainly beyond speech. Jamie, however, hearing Granny crying of her lost children in her sleep, enquires of Tommy about what death is. The events of his young life are a series of quite brutal answers to this central question. The cat, Granny, his mother are dead by the film's end. Helmuth, his substitute father, is, ironically, repatriated. Jamie attempts escape by jumping over a railway bridge onto a passing coal train. We do not know whether this is escape or failed suicide. What we do know is that, utterly terrifying for a child, people enter and leave his life without apparent reason or control. Truly, from he that hath not, even this is taken away.

The melodramatic potential for this is incalculable. Douglas himself is wholly conscious of the compression and hardness that was needed to avoid self-indulgence.

> It is a deliberate attempt to contract the length of the feature film as it is accepted in the commercial cinema. I have pared down to reach for the essentials. The autobiographical factor is the main component. The childhood of the title is literally my childhood and the incidents I recount are, with few variations, things that actually happened to me. This is not a dreamlike film composed of languid memories. It is a hard film made up of elementary contrasts: a few big events that have a great importance and the silence and the sounds that surround them.

Contrasts there most certainly are. Moments of quietude, Granny's face in close-up seated with her two grandsons temporarily tranquil round the fireside, alternate with horrendous outbursts of emotional and physical violence as people, beyond the end of their tether, erupt. There is too an almost musical contrapuntality in the development of parallel yet subtly contrasting themes. See, for example, how the sequence of the miner returning from their underground shift lifting their laughing children on their shoulders is followed by Helmuth's performance of the same rite for a solitary, solemn Jamie. If he is outsider of the group, solitary figures are also often contrasted against a bleak, incongruously angled Lothian landscape. Movement across these grim landscapes of loss, impeccably timed, is also of enormous importance. Trains, buses and vans carry people unbearably away. See the terrible moments as Helmuth, in the bus of the returning German prisoners, moves vertically out of picture while Jamie runs desperately in a horizontal line towards it with a speed which will never allow him to make contact. In other sequences Jamie's movement across the landscape and out of shot seems derived from a desperate, centrifugal energy unavailingly used to allow him to break free from the hellish confinement of the pit village.

If there are contrasts there is also the employment of what might

139

be termed the creative fusion of contraries. The film, an apparent contradiction, has the feel of documentary realism and yet every frame seems perfectly composed. A small but telling example of this is the sequence of the Germans working in foreign fields. A momentary shot of almost abstract perfection reveals them all head down in the turnip field. The next shot is of a man, as in a documentary instruction manual, cutting the roots from a turnip. Parallel to this is a combination of the 'thingness' of things with their symbolic import. There is a quite extraordinary specificity to things. Jamie, for example, pouring hot water into a cup, the water overflowing on the coarse grained table, before he thrusts it into his Granny's sleeping hands as warming consolation if not nourishment. Apples, too, are most distinctly apples as well as being our most perennial symbols of desire and knowledge. These are, in Saul Bellow's terms, 'substantial, not accidental' symbols.

The acting, too, seems to derive from some sort of inspired ambivalence. Douglas seems to be able to get people to do precisely what he wants yet part of what he wants is for them to imaginatively express themselves. He is an inspired viewer of still faces and he also has the most acute eye for the nuances of gesture and movement. See Eileen MacCallum's marvellous cameo as the psychiatric nurse, the simpering, brutally hard face and the use of her back and buttocks as she imposes order on the bed containing Jamie's catatonically inert mother. See the way Bernard McKenna compresses the whole squalor of his relationship to his son, Tommy, into the thrust of his unmanned legs propelling his bicycle as rapidly as possible from the scene of the crime.

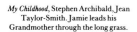

My Childhood, Stephen Archibald, Jean Taylor-Smith. Jamie leads his Grandmother through the long grass.

140

My Ain Folk, Jessie Combe, Helena Gloag.
The mutual loathing of Jamie's father's
wife and mother erupts between them.

My Ain Folk

A stunning sequence opens *My Ain Folk* when Tommy gets into the local cinema. For a moment the screen is flooded with a technicolour sequence from one of the *Lassie* films; that dog, so deeply embedded in the yearning consciousness of my childhood generation, who always made it home. This sequence gives way to the landscape seen as if framed through a proscenium arch. Suddenly the camera starts to sink and we realise, as blackness enfolds, it is viewing the world from a pit cage. We are, indeed, going underground and are about to enter the Freudian nightmare world of Jamie's paternal granny's Lowland home.

Jamie's father, due to Tommy spilling the beans, had existed troublingly at the periphery of Jamie's consciousness in *My Childhood*. In a sinister moment in that film he had slipped Jamie sixpence. What had initially seemed as a prelude to sexual abuse becomes, however, a single gesture which will be seen to sum up the whole of his guilt and inadequacy towards his son.

Bereft of Tommy, Jamie seeks refuge with his father's mother. It is just after VE Day. Sons are being welcomed back all over the land. Jamie enters, however, a hellish web of contorted sexuality, physical deprivation and emotional and physical violence. At the centre of this web is his Granny, like an inverted matriarch from O'Casey's Irish theatre. Jamie's father was a foundling. His adopted mother's insane love for him is ironically intensified by the fact that he is not a product of her loins. Her vain, crazed self-denial has, however, inevitably led to instinct being driven underground only to burst up in strange places and

141

My Ain Folk, Stephen Archibald. Jamie
buries his mother's pearls.

incestuous ways. The site where Eros most unhappily locates himself is
in the adjacent house where Jamie's father lives with his fancy woman
and another son. This woman also pleasured Granny's husband and, in
the course of the film, begins a frictive joyless affair with her other son
just returned, coarsened, from the war. All this, inevitably, explodes
in violent recrimination with the two women writhing on the ground
in the space between the houses.

Jamie lives his new life partly indoors. The verbal savagery of his
new Granny with her terrible oscillations between rage and infrequent
drunken sentimentality totally disorientates him. She is repeatedly shot
from slightly below with her arthritic back turned to the child so that
she bars him from the hearth's life-giving heat. Through the film he
is driven ever deeper into himself emotionally and, physically, into an
unsustaining outside world. Her insane, scouring respectability bars
the increasingly dirty child from the bathroom. His father washes him
in a cold burn but this physical intimacy only leads to a greater literal
and emotional space between them. Like a frightened animal (only
the whippet is welcome) he starts to wet himself in school, in the dog
basket, in the milk in order to disguise that he has been drinking it.
Not allowed to use the bleached lavatory, he excretes in the lane and
scratches like a dog to cover it.

Granny has it in her head that Jamie's mother had real pearls and
that Jamie knows where in his old home they are hidden. His response
to the crass wheedling is to rush to retrieve them and bury them. Her
response is to let loose her brave soldier son on him to beat the truth
out of him. In the film's horrendous sequence of violence we reach
a climax when Jamie's head hits the stove and he appears dead.

142

For Jamie the world war has been a mere prelude to the peacetime onslaught on himself.

Jamie's sole support in this is Grandfather. By a piece of schoolroom derived superstition he tries to invoke the death of his Granny. With dark visual wit, what we then see is an apparent stretchered corpse entering the house, as did dead miners, through the window. It is Grandpa being returned empty from the psychiatric hospital having been treated for acute depression. Partially restored, he and Jamie give each other some succour and collude against Granny. She is, as she always has been, far too strong for her husband. She sets mouse traps to prevent Jamie stealing apples for his Grandfather. As played by Helena Gloag, Granny is simultaneously terrifyingly, specifically realised and an awful demonic nursery tale archetype. Grandpa knows he is terminally ebbing and wants Jamie to institutionalize himself as he will soon be deprived of what little comfort and support he himself can give the child.

A flavour of the institution to come is given when Jamie accompanies Tommy's father to see Tommy. Cigarettes and banality are exchanged between father and son. Tommy is entering into the rituals of adolescence with the thieving skills of the institution. Left alone with Jamie, he inflates a contraceptive, which he has filched from the parental pocket. Jamie's appreciative laughter, the only time we

My Ain Folk, the influence of Dozhenko is revealed in Douglas's placing of single subjects which traverse the frame across stark landscapes and the vastness of the sky.

hear him laugh in the entire film, is still-born as the rubber bubble bursts and his face transforms itself into a look of stark recognition of his probably loveless, certainly accidental appearance on earth. When his father, taking most of his mother's furniture, drives off in his lorry into anticipated respectability with his mother's choice of a proper wife, Granny summons the authorities and Jamie follows Tommy into their van.

The film closes with a sequence which perfectly fuses Jamie's personal pain and public Scotland. We see the van crawling up the Mound in Edinburgh towards the home. As it leaves our field of vision a pipe-band swings into view. It first plays that Scottish song of lovingly remembered 'home and infancy', *The Rowan Tree*. This had already been sung by an old man to his displaced fellow villagers in an air-raid shelter in *My Childhood*. The band then breaks into that appalling Scottish ditty of good cheer and false promise, *Scotland the Brave*, as it descends from behind the castle to the other Edinburgh of Princes Street. Scotland's divided capital beckons.

My Way Home

My Ain Folk began in the cinema. *My Way Home* announces a subtle change of style and tone by pitching into the amateur theatricals of the home's nativity play. A nativity group composes itself on stage before the sleeping Provost. Jamie is discovered off-stage, kilted and bouquet-carrying. As he haltingly advances on the Provost, his wife and their tartan-sashed daughter, his trouser legs, slowly but remorselessly, roll down his legs. If he has escaped from a world of physical terror this incident brilliantly announces his entry to the world of adolescent uncertainty and embarrassment with absolutely minimal resources of prior affection.

The Head of the home, Mr Bridges, brilliantly played by Gerald James, is a genuinely kind man who perceives in Jamie latent talents and consequent self-destructive frustrations that mark him out. Inevitably, however, the home is a place of standardization. All the boys get mouth organs for Christmas. Jamie, never having had a present before, attempts individuality by painstakingly stamping out his name on it. For him, however, the mouth organs sound out a chorus of the damned. Music is not his creative talent; painting is, but he cannot express it. Frustration leads to his smashing rages or foetal shaped withdrawal to his dormitory bed. His mad mother's fate persistently beckons.

His father returns to take him 'home'. As indifferent as ever to his son's feelings, he brings with him the latest of his string of conquests. Jamie's sense of awakening sexuality is beautifully conveyed by the camera dwelling on the discrepancy between her splendid mini-skirted legs and her distressed, other woman's face as they journey homewards in the cab of his father's lorry. His father is back beside his mother with his first wife and son. Granny is now a ragged skeleton living next door in a state of dereliction. All the old hells and some new ones open up. Granny now wants to turn Jamie into the 'young prince' she so significantly failed to accomplish with her adopted son. His father, having got Jamie to dig up what are revealed as plastic pearls, wants to cut his losses by sending him down the pit. Jamie, to a chorus of jeers, stands in the living room, a coal-black wraith, announcing his intention to be an artist. 'If you were meant to be different,' he is told, 'you would have been born different.' Trapped, ruined people cannot bear exceptions to their rule.

He returns to the home which tries to find him appropriate employment as an errand boy at a gentleman's costumier's. Their attempt to dress him in oversized clothes as a 'gentleman' ends by his discarding them in a gentleman's public lavatory. Sent with a parcel to an Edinburgh public school he is mocked by a kilted boy for his inability to pronounce 'Gascoigne', the recipient's name. Trying to also find a home for himself he stays briefly with a woman of good Christian intent but a smile of unfocussed benevolence. Unlike Granny's, her hearth is open to him and an apple from her bowl for the taking. Jamie takes the lot and leaves like a thief in the night. The descending spiral continues to the down and out world of the Salvation Army Hostel, that sordid, bleary world of group eating and sleeping. The nadir is near as Jamie lies at night surrounded by the fallen muttering repeatedly 'I wanny die'. The last Edinburgh shot is of a blank railway-terminal indicator board revealing no destination. From his childhood trains have ambivalently suggested both a means of escape and of suicide. Wintry death has just been suggested by a shot of leafless orchard.

The next shot is of a new world. It is the desert seen from the back of a lorry as Jamie's Scottish voice in engaged in mutually near incomprehensible conversation with that of English, sophisticated, educated Robert. Even by his own extraordinary standards, the political and psychological compression Douglas achieves in this second half of a seventy-eight minute film is astonishing. In a few, partly comic vignettes such as rolling the sand flat or Jamie, the would-be artist, painting an infinite sequence of black and white bricks, the absurdity of the last phase of the British imperial enterprise is precisely caught. 'I served myself,' wrote Philip French, 'in the Canal Zone at that very time and am left speechless with admiration at the economy with which Douglas handles his material, the way in which a line of painted bricks in the sand, for example, becomes an image for the whole military life.'

The infrequency and often sheer wit of these allusive but so piercing historical insights which feature in *My Way Home* are present, if less wittily, throughout the *Trilogy*. For example, a whole world is conjured up in the first frames of *My Childhood* when the British soldier, his rifle abandoned among the prisoners and his back to them as he noisily urinates, turns and puts his hand to his lips to whistle the tractor homeward. *My Way Home* was released at the same time as *Yanks*, a heavily financed attempt to recreate the impact of Americans in Second World War Britain. Comparing these two films of the war

145

years, Derek Malcolm wrote in *The Guardian*:

> Schlesinger's film, not far short in length of Douglas's *Trilogy* and inevitably made, since it is clearly intended to take its place among the year's memorable commercial movies, with far more money, is also based on personal experience. Colin Welland, who wrote the original story and the screen-play with Walter Bernstein, did not do it merely as an exercise. Nor obviously, did Schlesinger. Yet I am bound to say that the Douglas *Trilogy* summons up more for me in any ten minute stretch the whole of *Yanks* put together.
>
> *Yanks* seems to me exactly what the Douglas *Trilogy* is not, and that is wasteful of its sometimes stunning effects. It refuses to do what Douglas does in every frame. It almost never commits itself. It is so carefully understated that, in the end, you wonder what exactly it is all about.
>
> Thus the well-recreated Lancashire town in which it is set remains stubbornly a place of fiction. Whereas the small mining village in which the *Trilogy* begins appears totally devastatingly real with half as much detail.

At a technical level one could make a case for Douglas's minimal economic resources dictating the inspired economy of his aesthetic. It seems to me, however, that great artists, in whatever medium, are spiritually attuned to the history of their times. Genius in the novel and film does perceive covert connections between private and public experience which is our life in history. There is, of course, that profound irony in the *Trilogy* that this unarguable sense of the forties and early fifties comes by way of our concentration on a nearly inarticulate child who is driven ever more in upon himself and whose soul is, in Simone Weil's phrase, 'monotonously, incessantly, and inextricably, steeped in pain'. Simone Weil also believed, however, that for the true artist there was a unique opportunity to perform his redemptive role if his personal pain was truly part of the historical pain of the times. Her words seem to me to go the heart of Douglas's matter:

> fortunate are those in whom the affliction which enters the flesh is the same one that affects the world in their time. They have the opportunity and the function of knowing the truth of the world's affliction and contemplating its reality. And that is the redemptive function itself.

The growing, redemptive relationship between Jamie and Robert is treated with brilliantly specific personal detail. In both Douglas's craft and moral vision William Blake's dictum that the good is done in 'minute particulars' completely holds sway. Hence Robert boning a kipper for Jamie provides an exact metaphor for a crucial, caring stage in their relationship. Discreet, unforced but substantial, symbols also exist. Insects, like Lazarus, emerge from the sand; Jamie's body

146

My Way Home, Stephen Archibald. Jamie's locker pin-ups of Marilyn Monroe are contrasted with Robert's portraits of 20th Century intellectuals, amongst whom can be seen Dovzhenko.

and mind also start to respond to sunlight. In a ring with others, unlike his childhood, who surround a scorpion which they intend to circle with fire, Jamie breaks the circle and goes to join Robert in his world of books and culture. His covert suicidal impulses are at last abandoned. Jamie also eventually leaves his Hollywood pin-up locker for the photographs, one of Dovzhenko, which decorate his new friend's wall.

This is carried forward by the inspired playing of the amateur Stephen Archibald and the professional Joseph Blatchley. A wholly fortunate last minute substitute, Blatchley gave what John Coleman described as 'an unselfish appearance of miraculous candour and simplicity'. The two of them are incongrous and wholly right together. Douglas also has a genius whereby his physical placing of characters is always so psychologically resonant. At one level Robert is Helmuth's replacement. Both Jamie's substitute fathers are non-Scottish speakers. With Robert comes an emotional warmth and physical contact missed since the German's departure. With Robert, too, comes a new homo-erotic depth. Jamie learns to say thanks, to smile, to see an arab child as even more deprived than himself. The world of books and pictures opens to him. He learns to take the lead. He now leads the pair of them to a mosque, where abruptly the camera pulls back, revealing them as a composed, diminutive pair in the middle of the abstractly patterned courtyard flagstones.

As they are about to be demobbed Robert gives Jamie instruction on how to get to his English home. The film then ends in, for the first time, a stunning sequence of non-realistic shots. To aeroplane noise accompaniment, the camera flows through the transformed,

147

translucently white painted rooms of his maternal granny's house. The artist can safely repossess his pain. Then there is a last shot of an English orchard in full bloom. It is the same orchard that had presented its dead winter aspect at the end of the Edinburgh sequence.

Some Scottish Conclusions

Comparing *My Way Home* to *Yanks*, Philip French remarked that such comparison 'defines the difference between real art and kitsch'. Since Scotland, the land that gave kitsch a bad name, has been a major fabricator of that eagerly sought commodity on the world market, it is wholly predictable that it would not prove a fruitful soil for a cinema of artistic truth. Indeed, such contemporary Scottish film criticism as exists seems preoccupied with diagnosing such Scottish cinema as exists as an exclusive by-product of the nation's, often tartan inspired, delusions. Weirdly, little attention has been paid to the fact that not the least of the *Trilogy*'s virtues is its cryptic but profound awareness of the politically exploitative presence of kitsch in Scottish life. A notable exception to this is James Campbell, writing thus of the *Trilogy* in 1979:

> Douglas was rejected out of hand by the Scottish Film Foundation (sic) in his attempt to gain backing for his project. 'Not a penny', he was told, the reason given being that the films would not present a sufficiently 'progressive' image of Scotland.
>
> It is impossible not to smile ruefully at the irony of this position, for the dominant theme of all Scottish art since the time of Burns has been the past: more specifically, one's personal past, or childhood; 'the need to discover a Scottish identity,' as it is often formulated. This admirable quest has been romanticised into weepy nostalgia, part of the pretence at a national identity which the Scots have been keeping up since 1707 . . . Barrie fertilized this lie, and to this day Scottish art remains steeped in nostalgia for pre-pubescent innocence. Since the cultural bourgeoisie of the country is besotted by this ideal . . . it is difficult for the artist who refuses to celebrate it to exist in Scotland: the lie cannot bear the exposure of art. It is precisely this innocence which Bill Douglas had to keep out of his film. Jamie, who never had a childhood, is the exact opposite of Peter Pan.
>
> In rejecting such infantile conceptions of his destiny, Jamie has replaced them with a true one, which cannot be restricted in place, but is nevertheless rooted in his Scottishness.

Though it is the single most significant item, this bourgeois inspired illusion of childhood paradise never quite lost is, by no means, the only Scottish fantasy to be exposed in the *Trilogy*. The Kailyard small town, pastoral and ahistorical, gives way to a pit village whose

148

people's lives have been blighted, maimed and distorted by modern history's savage industrial and military force. The pathos of this is quite brilliantly caught in the bonfire sequence which celebrates VE Day. The victorious villagers singing *Tipperary*, that song which masks the terrible pain of the earlier world war, with a St Andrew's Cross just perceptible in the night sky giving way to next morning's cold ashes. Another major staple item of Scottish kitsch, the cosy cottage, becomes a place of nightmare where feminine warmth and affection has given way to Granny's madly infected, definably Scottish will.

It is tartanry, the kilt and cult of 'Balmorality' which is, however, the most persistent element of Scottish fantasy. By 1800 aristocratic and bourgeois Scotland passionately desired to deck itself in the borrowed plumage of its highly liberal interpretation of the costume of its recently conquered Highland foes. This schism between Highlanders and their Lowland adaptors subsequently metamorphosed into a class division within Scotland as a whole. Douglas brilliantly catches this in two short, balanced sequences in *My Way Home* which painfully illustrate Jamie's inability, in action or language, to cross this Scottish social barrier. These are the sequences, already referred to, where he, in a kilt, is to hand over a bouquet to the provost's tartan-sashed daughter; soon followed by his confrontation with the kilted Edinburgh public schoolboy. The quintessence of this tartan derived, class-divided Scotland is most brilliantly encapsulated in the long held last shot in *My Ain Folk* featuring the institutional van and the pipeband.

Douglas, as an artist, knows intuitively what political commentators of the left, most incisively Antonio Gramsci, have analysed as the connection between bourgeois cultural display and performance and the use of these elements for political control and manipulation. One would, therefore, assume him to be the creative hero of radical critics of the Scottish media. To date this, absurdly, is not the case. In his *Scotch Reels*, Colin McArthur and his fellow contributors seem to have airbrushed the frames of the *Trilogy* from their memories. For example, Jim Hickey notes that the Scottish film event of 1972, the year of the release of *My Childhood*, was a Douglas Sirk retrospective at the Film Festival in Edinburgh! Following on a more than competent analysis of the origins and malign consequences of 'tartanry', Colin McArthur berates Scottish film culture for not keeping its 'historic appointment with the discourses of marxism and modernism'. He does, however, discover traces of what he desires in Murray Grigor's travelogue, *Clydescope*, in which Billy Connolly appears and perhaps James Joyce's influence is to be discerned. Behind this pretentious, dismal comedy of what passes for much of Scottish intellectual life lurk deeply unpleasant things. What such critics desire, one feels, are not works of imaginative truth but things to feed their arrested-adolescent, ideological self-righteousness. Indeed, they are half in love with what they rail against because they seek, like all ideologues, not so much art's true imaginative antidote to corrupt consciousness as possession of the enemy's institutional power. There are increasingly disturbing

My Way Home, Joseph Blatchley, Stephen
Archibald. The problem of boning a kipper
becomes a metaphor for the development of
the friendship between Robert and Jamie.

symptoms in contemporary Scotland of a left wing mythology as
dangerously delusion-filled as the bourgeois one it seeks to replace.

It is Gramsci, that sickly, inspired diagnostician of infected cultures,
who best defines for me this Scottish malaise:

> Certain countries are especially 'hypocritical'; that is, in certain
> countries that what one sees and what one does not see (because
> one does not want to see, or because whenever one does see it, it
> seems an exception or 'picturesque') are particularly contrasting.
> And it is precisely in these countries that memoir writers are few
> in number or autobiographies are 'stylized', strictly personal and
> individual.

The triumph of the *Trilogy* is that Douglas quite transcends the restrictions Gramsci describes though a decadent culture imposes on any artist
who seeks to represent both in his life and that of this creations the true
historical strains and sins of that culture. Part of ongoing Scottish bad
faith is that we are not generally aware of the cinematic gift that has
been made to us.

150

Bill Forsyth: The Imperfect Anarchist

Alan Hunter

The young Bill Forsyth did not burn with an all-consuming desire to leave his celluloid mark as the next Truffaut or Godard. In fact, he was not even seduced by the average cinemagoer's taste for escapism or an adolescent's idle worshipping of screen gods or goddesses.

The artist in him was nurtured and shaped by poetry, novels and his own vivid imagination. He envisaged himself as a pilot, a ship's captain or even a writer, but never as a filmmaker.

'I've probably stolen more inspiration from novels than from films,' he readily admits. 'Novels are much more efficient at creating an imaginary world. Movies are so limited by their own language and by the conventions that grew up so quickly. What I find distressing about movies, more than anything else, are the restrictions involved – that *theatrical* cinema has become *the* convention on the audience's part as much as on the industry's. Any slight wandering from that conventional shape is doomed; marginalised as art cinema or obscure or uncommercial or whatever. That's what's most distressing of all – to find out that the audience and the industry aren't interested in cinema. They are not interested in films. They are interested purely in the entertainment aspect of cinema.'

Forsyth perceives himself primarily as an artist, not an entertainer. His relationship with film is not as a story-teller, polemicist or propagandist but as an individual exploring a means of expression to which he has grown passionately devoted. His healthy disinterest in the mythology of the film industry, his disdain for the increasingly prevalent creation-by-committee process and refusal to pander to anyone's sensibilities save his own, place him in the modest ranks of filmmaking mavericks who dream in celluloid.

His popular reputation is not that of a rebel or subversive, but of a charming, couthy purveyor of pawky wit and incisive observation. However, as is so often the case, the stereotype conceals a much more complex figure of a writer-director who has never seen his work in terms of a career or an audience but only from the perspective of addressing himself to the potential of pure filmmaking.

Bill Forsyth was born in Whiteinch, Glasgow in 1946, the son of a

Production still from the making of *Local Hero:* Burt Lancaster, Bill Forsyth and Fulton Mackay. Forsyth – 'When it came to casting we had to fight a bit for the idea of Lancaster. It was suggested he would unbalance the film. But . . . he was the actor I had in mind for Happer from the beginning of the script.' (*Sight and Sound*, Summer 1983.)

plumber. He entered the film industry purely on a whim by answering an advert in the *Evening Citizen*. Stanley Russell of Thames and Clyde Film was looking for a young lad to join his small production company. Attracted by the exotic fantasy possibilities of the job and convinced that there had to be money in the film business, the impressionable schoolboy applied for the position and was as surprised as anyone when he was informed that it was his.

Chance and happenstance were therefore the strongest influences on Forsyth's embryonic career. However, within a short time, he became hooked on the medium itself.

'I think the exposure to moviegoing in a serious way and the Cosmo cinema were the biggest factors,' he recalls. 'First of all, I thought – wouldn't it be nice to be a filmmaker and, to do that, you have to watch films and find out what they're about. When I started to do that I found a kind of attachment to the European cinema that was around at the time. There was something exciting at the Cosmo every three days and I admired the work of Louis Malle and Jean-Luc Godard. You would go around in a leather jacket, smoking Gaulloise and trying to pretend you were French. I suppose it was a revelation really to find out that movies could be different to the run of the mill thing that would turn up at the Odeon, Anniesland.'

Work at Thames and Clyde could entail just about anything, from making the tea to editing, focus-puller to lighting. It provided Forsyth with a thorough grounding in the technicalities of placing image on celluloid and gave him the best education a future filmmaker could want.

'I was there about a month and Stanley asked me to write a script. I left school in February and in April he asked me to write this script for the Bank of Scotland. It was called *Order to Pay* and it was about cheque accounts. They were trying to encourage people to open cheque accounts in 1964 so it was quite pioneering, I suppose. He had one of these kind of left to right things with images and commentary and I think it was what the bank had produced. He asked me to expand it into a script, with no tuition or anything. I just had to take it away and do it. That was fun.'

Whether learning his craft on documentaries and sponsored films or working at the BBC (on *Z Cars* among others) or later, as a first year only student at the National Film and Television School, Forsyth was carefully fathoming his relationship to film and the potential that mainstream filmmakers seemed to largely ignore.

'The whole business of conceptualising cinema was there, was natural to me from the word go. It didn't develop into an interest in genre or anything else, it was absolutely pure film that I fell in love with; the stuff itself and the sheer business of being in a darkened room and have something engage your mind through your eyeballs. All that visceral stuff fascinated me with all the passion of a twenty year old – all the madness and devotion you can have. That's what I was like with film and condemned absolutely everything that was happening round me in cinema. I've probably retreated a bit from that stance now, and have certainly become a very conventional filmmaker in the way that I use film but inside me I think there still beats the heart of the anarchist.'

The iconoclast was very much to the fore when Forsyth began to make his own films. There now seems to be an element of confusion over which title was the first to bear the words 'directed by Bill Forsyth'. Further elucidation is not assisted by the fact that some of the early work he produced in the late 1960s did not indulge in anything as conventional as credits and titles informing one of authorial responsibility.

'*Language* was the first one followed by *Waterloo* but the first one that said "Bill Forsyth" was *Still Life With Honesty* which was a little film commissioned by the Arts Council about the painter Willie Gillies for his retrospective in 1969. I think I shared a directing credit with Martin Singleton because we were a two-man team at the time; he had a camera.'

Language and *Waterloo* appear to have been much more typical of Forsyth's aspirations at the time with the latter film taking a vigorously anti-narrative approach to its subject and utilising two ten-minute shots within its forty-five minute running time.

'My mind was heavily engrossed in this idea of what cinema could be; if it could only be torn away from this narrative human-drama bondage that had kind of captured it very early on. *Waterloo* was a human story that wasn't told in dramatic narrative but in a psychological monologue. There was lots of talking in it, incident, bits of poetry, information and what you were supposed to get from it was a sense of human loss and distance; emotional, physical and temporal distance. Some of the monologue came from a science-fiction film about someone who had just woken up in a space ship from a state of suspended animation. He and the crew had been asleep for sixty years so, when he woke up, he had the opportunity to reflect on the fact that everyone he knew on earth was dead. That was a jumping-off point to use other images and pieces of monologue to discuss that kind of distancing and loneliness.'

Waterloo begins in Forsyth's mother's home with his grandfather reading from a book, *The Marines Were Here*, and ends in a Glasgow bowling green following a human chain of events as the game unfolds. The intention was to create something hypnotic and poetic. When it was screened at the Edinburgh Film Festival, it cleared the George Square Theatre almost as quickly as a fire alarm. The film exists today in pieces, gathering dust under Forsyth's bed. He concedes that it is probably dreadful but derived a strange satisfaction from the public reaction twenty years ago.

'It was a Sunday afternoon in Edinburgh and there was a Tam O'Shanter cartoon on before and someone else had made a film about St Kilda bird life. It was actually more thrilling than disappointing or painful to have that kind of effect on an audience than to have them

153

That Sinking Feeling, the darker side of Forsyth's comedy: Alan Love, William Greenless and Douglas Sannachin discuss the pros and cons of suicide. Forsyth – 'The scene where the three boys talk about suicide has a couple of jokes, but the actual situation behind all the fun is that when we were making the film there was a case of two guys killing themselves, and there's been another case of that more recently.' (*Sight and Sound,* Summer 1983.)

sit there and not know what they were feeling. I think most of them just left because it was boring. I suppose that was the first moment I felt like a filmmaker because I had actually moved an audience. If not emotionally or anything else I had actually moved them out of their seats.'

Although Forsyth's experimental efforts may have gone unappreciated by the good folk of Edinburgh, he did receive an offer to screen *Language* at the Museum of Modern Art in New York. Seen as a soulmate to American underground filmmakers of the period by a visitor to the Festival, Forsyth was unable to follow up the offer. *Language* had been made 'after hours' at the BBC where he worked on a freelance contract and the film from the camera had been the print; there was no means to copy it.

Apparently unperturbed by a lost opportunity to gain recognition as a Scottish Warhol, Forsyth has nevertheless attempted to retain vestiges of his distaste for conventional narrative.

'I think film is very accessible and, in terms of what it demands that the audience brings to it, it has a very low threshold. An appreciation of painting is helped if you have read some books or seen a lot of paintings whereas anyone should be able to go in and see a film and it should get to them totally. Maybe I've just made a wrong interpretation and film is more complex, but, to me, if anything moves me in a film it is something really simple, dreadfully simple – it's never complex. It's either just an association of two ideas or a human situation or a movement from a character. I suppose I expect everyone to be capable of that and I try to do it sometimes in my own films. I think my anarchism now is at a kind of silly level. In the last film or two what I've been doing is taking on basic, mainstream narrative subjects and trying to subvert them in odd ways which is healthy but it's not a productive exercise.'

In the 1970s, Forsyth pursued a 'hand-to-mouth' existence as a partner in a production company that made three to four sponsored or documentary films every year. In retrospect, it seems folly that he and his colleagues should have believed that feature films could be regularly made in Scotland given the lack of a feature film tradition here, not to mention the theoretically insurmountable question of attracting finance.

'Within a year of entering the industry I was desperately committed to filmmaking – there was no other form of expression I could envisage. I don't have any skill as a painter and I was too lazy to seriously contemplate a life as a writer; film was my natural, instinctive medium. I wasn't alone, I was with other people who wanted to do the same thing so we sustained each other's dreams and talked about the feature film at the end of the rainbow. It slowly got to the stage where we'd talked about it so much and dreamed about it so much, that there was no point in not doing it. We were just ready.'

Modesty and brevity on Forsyth's part conceal some of the other factors that lead to his 1979 feature film debut as the writer-director of *That Sinking Feeling*, 'a fairytale for the workless'. By the 1970s, many of Forsyth's generation had served their apprenticeships and moved on to the development of their own production companies. The Scottish film community expanded and fortunately the amount of available work grew proportionately as sponsors like the Highland Board commissioned more projects and people were successful in attracting new sources of sponsorship.

Discovering that it was possible to make a reasonable, albeit precarious, living at that level of the industry, Forsyth's generation individually and collectively were then free to address themselves to the question of how they might set about fulfilling grander cinematic ambitions. In a simplistic sense the notion of a Scottish feature film was an idea whose set time had arrived.

'People did things in different ways. We really admired someone like Mike Alexander, for instance, who pursued a very steady course. He made narrative films with his own resources – first a ten minute one, a twenty minute one, a half-hour one and then a Children's Film Foundation sixty minute feature with a story and a script. You could see him steadily moving in one direction. At the start everyone had these huge ambitions and then gradually you could see – he's quite happy at the BBC, he's a good documentary guy. People like Charlie Gormley and I just kind of lived it in our heads. It wasn't a matter of moving towards something, it was simply that, in our minds, we were already there, however fanciful a notion that might have seemed to others. "Being a filmmaker" was where my head was – and that's a very seventies expression.'

At the time, the Saltire was clearly in the ascendant. Scottish nationalism was to reach the peak of its political potency in terms of popular votes and seats in the Westminster Parliament whilst the demand for some form of self-determination was widespread enough to force a referendum on the issue, however biased in its constitution. It is therefore possible to view the Bill Douglas trilogy, *Long Shot* and ultimately *That Sinking Feeling* as products of that era and also cultural reflections of political ferment.

That Sinking Feeling – comic acceptance of poverty: Robert Buchanan – cornflakes can function either as a staple diet, or, elsewhere in the film, as the readiest substance on which to overdose in a suicide attempt.

'I'm not so much convinced it was Scottish Nationalism,' Forsyth reflects. 'But, maybe it was. Maybe that resurgence in Nationalism meant that we were forced to look at ourselves as a nation because we had this event in 1977 called *Cinema in a Small Country*. My contribution was to think up the title. We were isolated; even joining the trade union then gave you a sense of having arrived. At the Edinburgh Festival in these days we'd be in the same room and whisper "don't look now there's Jeremy Isaacs". There was no connection. It's bad enough rubbernecking it at Cannes but in Edinburgh it was pathetic.'

Forsyth believes it was the formation of the Association of Independent Producers that provided Scottish filmmakers with an entry into the wider world of British movie making.

'Before BAFTA *Scotland*, BAFTA used to have a recruitment drive up here. We'd all join, they'd say "Thanks a lot" and then twice a year when you were in London you could go there for a drink. When

Comfort and Joy, Bill Paterson. 'The ship in the background is the Waverley, the only paddle-steamer left on the River Clyde, and an echo of a bygone age when the river was 'a high road to the ends of the earth', as the script said. I realise the enormous risk that I am running by including such a romantic representation of Scotland in the film. Already I can hear my accusers declaring that I have fallen once more into the gaping trap that awaits ever Scottish film-maker, the dreaded Tartanry and Kailyard. Or maybe I have strayed into a new and more terrible area of sin called 'Dockyard'. I await my sentence. The truth is that the Waverley was tied up for the winter and we couldn't move it, honest. The metal bollard was extremely cold for Bill Paterson to sit on. It would be impossible to make films in Scotland without thermal underwear.' (Bill Forsyth, *Sight and Sound,* Spring 1984.)

the AIP started, in order to strengthen their position, one of the first things they did was to send someone up here to organise. He came up basically to take our money, go back to London and forget all about us. We all gathered one weekend and suggested that they start an AIP Scotland and that's what happened. With that connection people were suddenly up and down to London and you were meeting people from the BFI instead of waving at them from a distance. What AIP did for London independents it did for us two-fold because it gave us an identity and a straight route into London. That all happened around 1977-79. So, it was simpler for me a year or so later to capitalise on that communal feeling of something having to happen, to stand up and say "I'm going to make this film, who wants to help me?" Everyone, in the spirit of the times said "I'll give you a camera" or "I'll give you three weeks of my time" and we went out and did it.'

That Sinking Feeling very directly stems from Forsyth's involvement with the Scottish Youth Theatre whose members he envisaged as perfectly fitting the bill to populate the cast of his script *Gregory's Girl*, a tale of schoolboy infatuation, football, romantic longing and unexpected resolution. Initial attempts to secure funding for that particular enterprise met a stonewall of rejection and indifference. As a reaction of this soul-destroying process and also as payment for the debt of gratitude he owed to the Scottish Youth Theatre members, he wrote *That Sinking Feeling*, the story of a gang who raid a factory full of stainless steel sinks.

Made on the kind of budget that makes a shoestring seem lavish, *That Sinking Feeling* received a triumphant reception at the 1979 Edinburgh Film Festival. Amidst a further round of surprising rejections, money was finally forthcoming for *Gregory's Girl*. Forsyth was becoming a familiar talent; attracting critical kudos, awards, media flattery and genuine interest from within the film community at home and abroad. David Puttnam, one of the many who had turned down the opportunity to produce *Gregory's Girl*, wooed Forsyth with a notion that became *Local Hero* and *Singles*, a 1974 script, finally emerged a decade later as *Comfort and Joy.*

One small indication of Forsyth's swift rise was his changing status at the Edinburgh Film Festival. In 1979, the low-budget, 16 mm *That Sinking Feeling* was a 'discovery' energetically promoted by a cast and crew pasting the city with posters twenty-four hours before its premier. In 1984, *Comfort and Joy* occupied the coveted opening night slot to a sell-out three thousand audience at the city's Playhouse Theatre.

Four feature films in five years is quite prolific for a contemporary director and allows the careful viewer to build a fair picture of the universe that Forsyth inhabits; his interests, concerns, style and content. Forsyth believes that his films are universally misinterpreted and misunderstood; viewers latch on to certain obvious elements and assume that they have unlocked the door to his entire psyche never looking beyond the qualities of charm and humour to examine the recurring themes of loss, loneliness and isolation.

156

Gregory's Girl, the certainties of choux pastry are weighed up against the fickleness of girls: Clare Grogan, John Gordon-Sinclair, William Greenlees.

Comfort and Joy, for instance, tells of a radio disc-jockey who reaches a crisis in his life when his girlfriend deserts him at Christmas and he is left with only the banality of his work and the distress of the happy families that surround him in his personal world. Drifting along in search of enlightenment, he becomes embroiled in an on-going ice-cream war between rival branches of the Scotia Nostra.

In Forsyth's eyes, the film was an anti-war story that was partly inspired by the *Private Investigations* track on the Dire Straits album *Love Over Gold* in which 'a solitary person was trying to solve a kind of enigma that he'd maybe created for himself.'

Immediately before the release of *Comfort and Joy*, one recalls Forsyth's genuine amazement at just how funny the audience and the critics seem to find his scripts. 'I was convinced that the film wasn't funny all the way through when we were shooting it. I thought it was a really serious film and I was quite happy about that. It was only when we showed it to twenty or thirty people who hadn't read the script that I was very surprised to find out people were actually laughing at it. I was genuinely surprised, I didn't expect a humorous response at all.'

The serious facets of *Local Hero* were also less obvious to many viewers. Ostensibly about a small Scottish community cannily exploiting the rapacious greed of a large American oil company, its surface storyline is the packaging that conceals an engagement with familiar Forsyth terrain of loneliness, isolation and a search for identity. The character of whizzkid American businessman Mac (Peter Riegert) is a man who doubts the validity of his own apparently bleak lifestyle when confronted with the camaraderie, companionship and community spirit of the Highlands, however avaraciously it manifests itself.

Like Dickie Bird (Bill Paterson) in *Comfort and Joy*, he is on a journey of self-discovery in a world that is portrayed with all its faults and foibles intact. There are no purely good or purely evil characters

157

Local Hero, Peter Riegert (left) and the
telephone box. From the movie's
beginning, the character of MacIntyre is
defined as a telephone man, and during his
stay in the village the callbox represents a
precarious link to the outside world of big
business. By the movie's end the tone has
changed from satire to pathos as the phone
box, MacIntyre's last remaining link to the
village, rings out unanswered.

in Forsyth's universe, merely fallible, well-rounded human beings composed of virtues and vices, compassion and callousness. Mac may be seduced by the beauty of the Highland way but the villagers are not paragons of virtue; they will contemplate dispatching wise old Ben (Fulton Mackay) when he stands in the way of their collective gain.

The fact that viewers and critics will latch on to his most evident qualities of humour and quirky observation before addressing themselves to the melancholy or cruelty in his work has constantly bemused Forsyth although it would never cause him to question what he genuinely wants to say or the most efficacious means of expressing certain sentiments.

He once said, 'There's always something you want to say. I would not want to make a film that didn't say anything. I'm not interested in getting into something that's just a piece of entertainment, a James Bond or an adventure film.' More recently, he explained that with *Comfort and Joy* the frustration was 'because people found it slightly amusing it wasn't amusing enough because it kind of tickled them and, in their estimation, didn't follow through because it didn't seem to want to tickle them all the time. I admit that I'm probably more to blame than anyone because the audience is there and they have their expectations in movies and it's difficult for the individual filmmaker to turn things around. The thing is you get categorised so quickly. It's easier for Wim Wenders to present a film to an audience and have them respond in the way he wants because he hasn't been categorised in the way I have but if you make one or two films and they're kind of labelled as lighthearted and charming and beguiling and Celtic twilight, then you are in deep trouble. If you put yourself as being challenging from the word go, then the audience is perhaps more alert and probably smaller as well.'

In *Housekeeping*, which Forsyth adapted from Marilynne Robinson's novel, he found material that was 'more like the kind of films I wanted to make than my films were'. Set in smalltown Canada in the 1950s, it recounts the story of two orphaned girls and their complicated relationships with a succession of older relatives and their eccentric aunt Sylvie (Christine Lahti).

Forsyth was attracted to the story because of its underlying sadness and air of melancholy that is redolent of *Local Hero*. To many commentators, Sylvie appeared an attractive free-spirit whose unwilling inheritance of the girls liberate them from a repressive life and set them on the road to some glorious adventures. Forsyth, however, saw a cruel irony in the whole situation.

'To my mind the entertainment was in the idea of these two girls, in a situation where they had no choice, latching on to whatever was given to them and all that was given to them was this completely inadequate loon. Like these ducks when they come out of the egg – the first thing that they see, they love it and follow it about. The fun in the situation for me was in standing back from it and seeing these completely inadequate people forced upon each other. She turns up for a long weekend, the old aunts leg it out the door and Sylvie's left with the kids. All these things strike me as being funny. I think that's humour and I suppose I'm in serious trouble if nobody else thinks that.'

There are few things as subjective as humour; one audience's joke is another's evidence of mental instability. Forsyth is charged with being charming and he may well be guilty. During the making of *Local Hero*, David Puttnam observed; 'I think his particular strength is as a communicator. I think he's got a very, very wonderful vision of people. Not so much life as people. Bill has a unique ability to feel out the best in people and he has an innate belief in the best of people. He's a remarkably uncorrupted and unsoured man.' Forsyth himself would probably argue that he takes delight in moments of perversity and that behind all laughter there is an essential cruelty or hurt, hence the similarities he has acknowledged between Glasgwegian and New York humour.

'It is the humour of despair, the humour of the gallows. The humour of awful circumstances or predicaments. I think that is where humour comes from. From situations where the only way out is to laugh, for survival's sake. At the bottom of every joke is a piece of despair, you can't produce a laugh without it. If someone falls on a banana skin you get a laugh but someone gets hurt.'

The major characters in Forsyth's films are often at conflict with themselves or their surroundings and his fine observations of these tensions have caused quirky and offbeat to be added to the list of Forsythian adjectives. However, rather than being a filmmaker who

Comfort and Joy, hard hearts and cornets: Bill Paterson, Iain McColl. Forsyth's stated desire 'not to sidestep the business of violence in big cities' led to the notion of an ice cream war which parodied the rival mobs of the Hollywood gangster movie. The real and murderous ice cream war which occurred in Glasgow just prior to the film's release suggested that Forsyth's (well-intentioned) balancing-act of violence and irony was an inappropriate method of coming to terms with the situation.

159

Housekeeping, a world of women: Andrea Burchill, Christine Lahti, Sara Walker. 'I suppose there are any number of ways you can approach a novel in terms of adapting it but I simply wanted to make a promotional movie for the book so I was quite wilfully slavish to the book. I didn't want to even have an attitude to the book or use it as raw material.' (Bill Forsyth, *The List*, December 1987.)

chooses to explore the odd and unusual, whether it's an ice cream war or a female soccer star outshining her besotted male rivals, Forsyth makes the distinction that he is someone who always finds eccentricity however apparently routine or mundane the setting.

'I think we're basically all odd. I think we all have a tension between what we think we are and what other people think we are. Everyone is like that and I just tend to highlight it. I think I could make a detective story, or something conventional like that, and end up having odd characters in it too. Strangeness is in everyone, it's just a matter of whether you choose to reveal it or not.'

In 1988, Forsyth was in Portland, Oregon filming a John Sayles script entitled *Breaking In*. Burt Reynolds played ageing safecracker, Ernie, an unambitious professional burglar who has carefully calculated the acceptable percentage risk in both his working environment and the way he relates to the world.

Mike (Casey Siemaszko) is a lonely, gauche youngster who has turned to crime more as a playful pastime than as a larcenous compulsion. The two men brush up against each other, like ships that pass in the night, in a compromised, low-key piece that the Goldwyn Studios saw as a buddy yarn and Forsyth viewed more in terms of fatalistic, pre-war Jean Gabin.

The experience convinced him not to work from someone else's script in the future.

'It's not very satisfying and also you're playing into the hands of the industry as well because at the end of the day, if it's your material you can say 'No, I didn't mean it that way'. If there is another voice there already the presumption is that anyone's interpretation is as valid as yours. Also, it's a matter of pride. Having got away with writing scripts and directing them there's not quite the same thrill in working from someone else's material. You feel that you're not inhabiting the full

160

space that you could or should. Writing is the most important part
of it because that's where the ambitions are running at full tilt.'

Comfort and Joy completed principal photography in Glasgow shortly
before Christmas of 1983. To date, Forsyth has not made another film
in Scotland. He appears to have developed an ambivalent attitude
towards his native land and any sense of responsibility that someone
of his stature might be expected to feel towards the attainment of a
flourishing indigenous industry. In 1982 he said; 'I am very fond of
my country. I've become more so recently the more I've become aware
of it. It's a delight to be able to present it to people on film – well this
is us, or that's what I think we are.' In 1990, he believes; 'We're not
Scottish, we're northern European and highly industrialised, developed
westerners. Whatever is uniquely Scottish about us would be so difficult
to put across in such a crass medium as film that it's not worth the
attempt. I don't think there is a need for a Scottish film industry
per se and I don't know what that really means – fifteen guys like
me, five Scottish films a year? It's quite a brutal stance to take. I
would maybe feel differently if I was a Senegalese filmmaker but I'm
Scottish at this point in the twentieth century. Maybe if I thought
movies were important then I would think it was more essential that
Scotland had them all to itself but because of the low opinion I have
of movies anyway that I don't. I think there are many more things
that we lack before that.'

As in virtually all instances Forsyth's only sense of responsibility is
to himself and his relationship with film, not to a career, an audience,
an industry or a country.

He is currently in Scotland writing a script with the working title of
Being Human. It will take place in a variety of locales during different
historical periods. He describes it tantalisingly as his *Last Emperor* and
it is the first pure Forsyth original since *Comfort and Joy* was realised.
In those seven years, he has matured as an artist and changed as a

Production shot from *Breaking In*: Casey
Siemaszko, Burt Reynolds, Bill Forsyth.
'The thing is, the producers wanted to
make a buddy movie about the way
odd-balls relate to each other, and I was
trying to make a film about how people *don't*
relate, how they can exist and work
together, but absolutely *not* communicate
whatsoever. Consequently, they
endeavoured throughout to lighten the tone
of the film, so despite my loyalty to it, I just
don't feel that my ambitions were realised.'
(Bill Forsyth, *Time Out*, Sept 1990.)

161

man; now a fortysomething father of two with a developing interest in the pastime of fishing, twenty-five years of experience in the film business and enough self-confidence to allow himself upwards of a year to research and write the new script.

By the time of *Comfort and Joy* he had mined many autobiographical feelings and observations and it was time to move on. *Being Human* may well reflect the interim lessons and his reflections on how best the anarchist in him can use the medium of film.

'I've always been more interested in the relationship of me and film rather than me and the subject matter of whatever interpretation was going on. There isn't any kind of progressive thing but in a straightforward sense I had actually run out of source material. I had taken this character, whoever he was – whether he was me or a version of me – from the age of sixteen to around thirty-five or so. The thing was totally mined and in a linear sense I had caught up with myself so that made the idea of going back into the material was uninteresting for me. One move was *Housekeeping* where I feel in love with the book so much that I wanted to possess it. It was an act of larceny. There are extraneous things as well; you think, well, now I'm in this kind of position I might like to go to the States for a year and you end up making a film like *Breaking In* just to experience something different, not for the joy of it or any ultimate filmic statement. That's when you become corrupt in the scientific sense of the word, imperfect or used, but that's what a career is.'

Bill Forsyth, the imperfect anarchist, is now at the stage of filmmaking he likes best; the conceuptualisation when you 'can't dream high enough or large enough'.

In the words of David Puttnam, he remains 'unsoured' and takes a positively juvenile delight in announcing; 'I've been walking up and down for the last three months stroking the typewriter saying "One day, one day you and me have got a date".'

Despite the twenty-five years of adventures in the screen trade, Forsyth is still possessed of a celluloid dreamer's hopes of what cinema could be and time, frustration or misinterpretation have not diminished his love of film or his pleasure in testing its capabilities.

'When I was nineteen I had hopes that, certainly by the time I had matured to the stage I'm at now, cinema would mean something different. It would be like those science-fiction things where you get wired up and have dreams and could choose to be a pirate or a cowboy and away you'd go for a couple of hours. That's what cinema meant to me and that's where I thought it would go; there would be a direct engagement between the filmmaker's mind and the audience's mind. That would dispense with the idea of having to appeal to another human being through a narrative. You can do that in a comic if you want to, it's nothing peculiar to film so it seemed to me to be a misuse of it. To be able to establish this direct link with the audience and their sensibilities was much more exciting. Working in film now is a continual tension but, in a sense, that's what makes it interesting.'

Sean Connery

John Millar

Sean Connery is Scotland's only movie superstar. Put as bluntly as that, it sounds like yet another of those fawning Hollywood-style accolades which are tossed about like so much confetti. But just think about that opening statement for a moment. It isn't at all extravagant. The more you analyse it, the more appropriate it becomes. For no other Scot in the cinema has had the international impact, acclaim, success or staying power of this son of Edinburgh.

At the time of the release of the box-office smash, *The Hunt For Red October*, he was described as one of the most bankable actors in the movie-making business. Again that was not an idle boast. Connery, who has gone from beef-cake (he won a bronze medal in the Mr Universe event before becoming an actor) to Bond and on to Oscar triumph, has had his share of film flops. But as he entered his sixties, Sean Connery enjoyed a golden streak of cinema glory.

The British Academy of Film and Television Arts (BAFTA) presented him with the Best Actor award for his convincing portrayal of the medieval monk detective, William of Baskerville in that atmospheric and intelligent whodunit? *The Name of the Rose*. There were no prizes, but much acclaim – again entirely deserved – for his portrayal of Harrison Ford's father in *Indiana Jones and the Last Crusade*.

The most satisfying moment, however, was surely in the spring of 1988 when he broke his Oscar duck by winning the Academy Award for Best Supporting Actor – deserved reward for his gripping role in *The Untouchables* as the veteran cop Malone, who teaches Kevin Costner's Elliot Ness the way to take on Robert De Niro's mobster boss Al Capone. Long after viewing Brian De Palma's excellent cops and gangsters movie, it's Connery's scene-stealing performance, from the first night-time meeting with Costner on a bridge, to his character's bloody death, which remains in your mind. A favourite moment is when Connery's Malone spells it out to Elliot Ness that in the war against Capone there aren't any rules. 'If he brings a knife, you bring a gun. If he sends one of yours to hospital, you send one of his to the morgue.'

And even when recent movies, such as *The Presidio* and *Family Business*, were not all that they might have been, Connery's presence remained considerable. A highlight in the patchy thriller, *The Presidio* sees Connery's provost marshal give a bar-room brute a real hiding, just by beating him with his thumb! In the hands of many other actors that scene would be laughable, but when it's the six foot three-inch frame of Connery delivering the attack you are convinced.

The Name of the Rose perhaps Connery's greatest acting challenge and one he rose to admirably – he played a virgin.

163

Indiana Jones and the Last Crusade back in bondage?: Harrison Ford, Connery. Steven Spielberg 'George (Lucas) wasn't thinking in terms of such a powerful presence for Indy's father. His idea was for a doting, scholarly person, an older British character actor. But I had always seen Sean Connery. Without a strong, illuminating presence, I was afraid that Harrison Ford would eradicate the father from the movie. I wanted to challenge him. And who could be the equal of Indiana Jones but James Bond? . . . There are only seven genuine movie stars in the world today and Sean is one of them.'

It's been reported that Connery's fee for *Highlander II* - the sequel to the time-tripping adventure fantasy in which he acted Christopher Lambert and all-comers off the screen – is £2 million for a fortnight's work. And there was said to be more big money – $5 million this time – for his starring role in John Le Carre's *The Russia House*. Not bad going for the lad, born into a tenement home in Edinburgh's Fountainbridge, who once earned thirty-three and a half pence an hour for modelling in a G-string for students at the Edinburgh College of Art.

Thomas Connery became one of the most famous deliveries at Edinburgh's Royal Maternity Hospital on 25 August 1930 and the environment into which he was born didn't suggest that an international movie career was beckoning. The family was typical Scots working class. His father was a lorry driver and young Connery left school at 13, without any examination certificates. (That lack of academic qualification was remedied back in 1981 when Heriot-Watt University conferred the honour of Doctor of Letters upon a highly flattered Connery.)

Like most kids of that period, Connery was introduced, while he was still a schoolboy, to the notion of having to work for financial reward. So, before and after class, he had part-time jobs as a milkboy and butcher-boy. After leaving school he had several jobs, which included a stint as an undertaker's assistant when one of his duties was to polish coffins. But all these different types of employment were simply preparing him for the role in life to which he was really to take a shine.

The route towards international film success started the way these things are supposed to . . . at the bottom. He got his first taste of the greasepaint in 1951 when the athletically built young Scot won a place in the chorus of *South Pacific*. But it was the role that an already established actor did not play which really pushed Sean Connery into the limelight. Jack Palance had portrayed the burned-out boxer Mountain McLintock in an American TV production of *Requiem for a Heavyweight* and in 1957 the BBC wanted him for their version of the drama. The chisel-featured Palance was unable to oblige and eventually Connery was chosen for the role. And, as David Shipman says in volume two of his book *The Great Film Stars*, the result was 'a remarkable performance'. Sean Connery was off and running, though some less than memorable movies, such as *Darby O'Gill and the Little People*, *On the Fiddle* (which in the USA had the baffling title *Operation Snafu*) and *Tarzan's Greatest Adventure*, were to come and go before he hit paydirt.

Producers Harry Saltzman and Cubby Broccoli were looking for the actor who would be James Bond in their production of Ian Fleming's *Doctor No* and Connery was one of many actors considered. Despite the fact that in 1962 he could scarcely be described as a household name at that stage of his career, Connery was not slow in coming forward during his meeting with Saltzman and Broccoli. He had a tendency to punch the table to hammer home his point. What finally convinced the producers that they had found 007 was Connery's confident swagger as he walked across the street. From that moment, the boy from the tenements of Edinburgh had walked into the chapters of film history.

With seven Bond adventures – including his comeback *Never Say Never Again* - Connery established himself as a box office sensation. Ironically, it's said that Roger Moore – who stepped into 007's shoes after Connery – had been the original choice to play Bond. But, as far as most film-goers are concerned, the publicity people got it right

Production still of *From Russia with Love:* Connery, Daniela Bianchi. With Bond in untypically vulnerable repose and 'the girl' in untypical possession of the gun (not to mention directly confronting the viewers gaze) this shot almost seems to subvert the traditional Bond ethos. Presumably, however, the message is intended to be – she may be a Soviet spy but having sampled the Bond libido she's more likely to protect than to attack 007.

Never Say Never Again, last tango: Kim Basinger, Connery. 'Good to see you again, Mr Bond. Let's go back to the gratuitous sex and violence, I say,' says Q.

when they decided upon the slogan Sean Connery *is* James Bond.

No one sipped a vodka martini, embraced the heroine or blasted the villains better than Connery. He was also in a class of his own when it came to delivering those famous one-line quips, which added a dash of humour to his Bond outings. My favourite Connery Bond movie, *From Russia With Love*, contains two perfect examples.

Scene one is the shooting by Kerim Bey (Pedro Armendariz) of a Spectre baddie who is trying to escape by a trap door which opens in the mouth of a picture of Anita Ekberg on a movie billposter promoting the comedy, *Call Me Bwana*. After the dead villain topples to the ground, Connery says . . . 'She should have kept her mouth shut'. Scene two comes at the end of the movie when Rosa Klebb (Lotte Lenya) who has a poisoned spike in the toe of her shoe has tried to kill 007. Titania (Daniella Bianchi) comes to Bond's rescue and shoots Klebb, Connery looks down at the body and quips . . . 'She's had her kicks'.

During the height of their success, films like *From Russia With Love* were banned in the Soviet Union. No doubt that memory brought a smile to Connery's face when he was cast as the Lithuanian submarine commander in *The Hunt For Red October* or when he was on location in Moscow, cast as a womanising, boozing publisher in *The Russia House*.

Throughout the Bond excursions, and for several other movies, Connery wore a hair-piece. But, unlike some who need, indeed seem to rely upon, these make-up aids to preserve their screen image, it hasn't mattered to the Scot's fans whether or not he wore a wig. In fact some women have said that Connery looks sexier in the roles where he hasn't bothered with a hair-piece.

166

He has also refused to let his natural soft Scots burr become a hang-up. When you cast Sean Connery in a movie that's exactly what you get. So we've seen him, Scots accent and all, as an Arab sheikh in *The Wind and the Lion*, a Spaniard in *Highlander*, an old Irish/American cop in *The Untouchables*, a high-powered Norwegian cop in *Ransom*, a Saudi diplomat in *The Next Man* and the Lithuanian hero of *The Hunt For Red October*. With some actors it might matter, or even irritate, that the accent always remains the same. With Connery it is of no consequence. What does matter is his undoubted towering screen presence.

Since 1974, Sean Connery has been one of our tax exiles. Much of his time is spent with his second wife, Micheline at their home on Spain's Costa Del Sol. 'I didn't take a long time mulling it over,' he said of his decision to live outside Britain. 'It was really a series of events – the 98 per cent taxes I was paying and the possibility of making three films outside the UK, which meant I was not going to be here for 36 weeks of the year.'

Despite his exile, Connery's Scottishness has never been disputed. The actor who has 'Scotland Forever' tattooed on his arm – a legacy from his spell in the Navy – has remained true to his roots. It's because of his Scottishness that he made the Clydesider documentary, *The Bowler and the Bunnet* and he only starred in the 1971 Bond, *Diamonds Are Forever*, because it meant that The Scottish International Education Trust, a charity he set up, would benefit by $1 million.

During his Bond age, Connery set about proving that he didn't have to be packing a Walther PPK to make his mark on the movie screen. In the late 1960s he was seen in a wide variety of films, from *The Hill*, a harsh drama set in a North African prison during World War Two, and *Shalako*, in which he was cast as a western guide in charge of a group of European aristocrats on safari in 1880s New Mexico, to *The Molly Maguires*, set in an 1870s Pennsylvanian mining community, and *The Red Tent*, where he played the polar explorer Roald Amundsen.

That variety shouldn't have come as a surprise. Even in the early stages of his career, Connery was all for tackling roles as diverse as Vronsky in *Anna Karenina* to the punch-drunk boxer in *Requiem for a Heavyweight*. And Connery has continued to ring the changes in his selecting of movie roles. He was the leader of a gang planning a robbery in Sidney Lumet's inventive thriller, *The Anderson Tapes*; the police inspector at breaking point as he interrogated a suspected child abuser in *The Offence*; a space-age version of Gary Cooper's *High Noon* hero in *Outland* and an old-in-the-tooth Robin Hood in the under-rated *Robin And Marian*.

Stories of his strong-willed attitude to his profession have passed into legend. It's said, for instance, that he refused to sign on for Alfred Hitchcock's *Marnie* until he had read the script.

Not all of his choices have proved wise, but then, the film you sign up for doesn't always turn out to be the movie that's screened in the cinema. Films in the 'those he'd probably prefer to forget' category,

Never Say Never Again. Connery's last fling as Bond and his most tongue-in-cheek performance as the revived icon of the 60s. In his mature years as an actor, Connery is receiving the recognition which eluded him in his Bond years. In 1990, BAFTA gave him the Tribute Award in recognition of his 'outstanding contribution to world cinema'.

Production shot from *The Man Who Would Be King* with Connery and Michael Caine. 'As long as actors are going into politics, I wish, for Christ's sake, that Sean Connery would become king of Scotland' – John Huston.

most likely would include: *Meteor*, that disaster of a disaster movie about a hugh chunk of rock hurtling towards Earth; *Cuba*, the fairly mediocre drama set during the beginnings of Castro's revolution; *Sword of the Valiant*, a version of the saga *Gawain and the Green Knight*, in which he played the latter role; and that tedious futuristic fantasy, *Zardoz*.

Connery has said that he is drawn to film scripts which he finds interesting and stimulating. But there is sometimes another reason why he'll take on a role. An example is Terry Gilliam's *Time Bandits*, in which Connery had a cameo appearance as the Greek King Agamemnon. After the inevitable round of golf at Gleneagles, Connery explained why he had accepted that offer. 'The problem was that they couldn't get the film off the ground. So if I did Agamemnon, then they could get the other actors.'

With such a high-profile, whether he wants it or not, whatever Connery does is news. So when he withdrew from the filming of *Rosencrantz and Guildenstern Are Dead*, rumours began to circulate that he had throat cancer. The truth, thankfully, was less dramatic. The growths on Connery's vocal chords were not malignant, but he now has regular check-ups to ensure that his throat reminds in good order. During the time of this throat ailment, Connery chose not to talk at all for a month, to see if this rest would help. Apparently he opted for that period of silence because the actor who starred as the cinema's best-known secret agent has a fear of hospitals.

He certainly doesn't fear confrontation, particularly when he feels that he has been wronged. And if that wrong affects the Connery bank balance then you can be assured that he will go all-out to remedy the situation. That has been the Connery way all along.

When he felt that he was not receiving just reward for his part in the success of the Bond movies, he dug his heels in until a better arrangement was struck regarding his fee for the 007 adventures. After the success of his partnership with Michael Caine as two soldiers of fortune in John Huston's memorable version of the Rudyard Kipling story, *The Man Who Would Be King*, he sued the film company for cash – a figure said to be £109,146 – claimed to be owing.

'I've never cheated or stolen from anyone in my life,' said the straight-talking Scot. 'And I would be quite happy to stick anyone who steals from me in jail.'

His most famous excursion into the courts was when Connery was awarded £2.8 million damages against a former financial adviser. Then there was the lighter-side of the legally aware Connery when a French newspaper suggested that he wasn't slim or sexy enough to continue being Bond. Connery, who was able to prove that his waist-line was still within an inch of what his measurements were at the time of the *Doctor No* outing, sued and won.

Connery also likes to be a winner out on the golf course – whether he's sinking putts at Las Brisas, Marbella or at any of the British courses which welcome the 12-handicap actor. Even when he's taking part in a pro-celebrity match, Connery's interest is in being triumphant. He was once a good enough footballer to have been able to play at the sport's professional level. Interest in that game remains and he was seen among the crowd supporting Scotland when the 1982 World Cup finals were held in Spain. But it is golf about which he is passionate. His wife Micheline has confirmed this in Kenneth Passigham's biography of Connery when she's quoted as saying . . . 'Sean's a terrible loser, but you know what they say. Show me a good loser and I'll show you a loser.'

Predictably, because of the canny Scot reputation, Connery chooses to carry his own clubs round the golf course. An appearance, witnessed by a colleague, at the Royal and Ancient Club at St Andrew's also suggests he remains a down to earth bloke. He drove to the course in a very ordinary family saloon and his low-key appearance surprised other visitors. Three blue-rinsed American matrons were goggle-eyed and reacted with a 'Is that who we think it is?' when they spotted Connery on the first tee. My colleague recalls that Connery sent his first drive out of bounds, but doesn't say whether it was the presence of the gobsmacked fans who made him miscue the shot.

Those golfing ladies are not alone in being over-awed merely by being in the presence of Sean Connery. Hardened newspaper hacks have the same sort of experience.

Another colleague turned gooey-eyed when he recounted having his lunch-time pint interrupted when he spotted Connery – or 'Big Tam' as he's still known to Edinburgh folk – walking past a boozer in the capital. The drink was put down on the bar while the veteran journalist hastened to the doorway to confirm that it was indeed Connery, jacket

Highlander high camp: Connery, Christopher Lambert. *Highlander* was an important film in Connery's 1980's ascent to super-stardom, allowing him an opportunity to utilise Bond-style traits such as authority and irony while sending up the larger-than-life persona. In a film where a Frenchman was playing the eponymous Scotsman, enrolling the assistance of (arguably) the world's best-known Scotsman to play a Spaniard was the necessary tip-off to enjoying the film's self-consciously flamboyant humour.

169

Production still from *The Hunt for Red October*. A new wig, a new nationality (Lithuania), same old accent. Connery is such a big star that scripts are woven round his Scottish accent (*Family Business*) or it is just accepted by producers and audiences.

slung carelessly over his shoulder, sauntering down Edinburgh's busy Rose Street.

A fascinating quote, from a man who appears to be very careful about every word he speaks, illustrated much of the Connery philosophy. In a profile in the *Observer* newspaper, he was quoted as saying . . . 'I suppose more than anything else I'd like to be an old man with a good face, like Hitchcock or Picasso. They know life is not a popularity contest.'

Movie-makers have recognised that Connery does indeed have a good face. It's a face brimming over with character, charisma, experience and strength. Those famous features were used to great effect in the opening shot of *The Hunt For Red October*. The screen is filled with Connery's eyes, then the camera gradually pulls back until the audience is held by Connery's face – complete with steel-grey beard and wig – in all its grizzled glory.

Though he had forty-four films under his belt before finally winning an Academy Award nomination for *The Untouchables*, Sean Connery can look back on his cinema career with pride. Not only has he reached the stage where he can be referred to – like Brando, Cagney, Gale, or Steiger – by his second name alone, he has also had far more pluses than minuses in an industry where, as far as box office results are concerned, every new movie can be a venture into the unknown.

What's more, I am inclined to the view that we have yet to see the very best of Sean Connery. In his sixties it could well be that this very excellent Scottish actor will have more opportunities to hold aloft glittering movie prizes in the same proud manner in which he clenched the Oscar in a victory salute back in 1988.

The Hill. Connery's struggle to establish a career outwith the 007 movies saw him appear in a number of challenging and unusual films but in the public eye he remained Bond. 'The problem with interviews of this sort is to get across the fact, without breaking your arse, that one is not Bond, that one was functioning reasonably well before Bond, and that one is going to function reasonably well after Bond.' (*Playboy*, November 1965.)

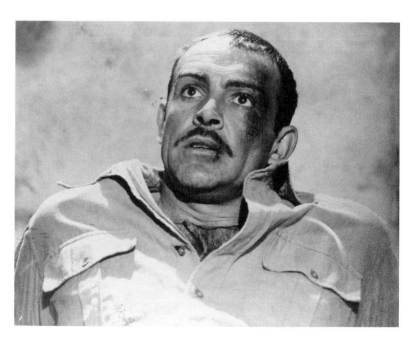

170

Pictures in a Small Country: The Scottish Film Production Fund

Ian Lockerbie

Not everybody noticed at the time, but March 1982 was an historic moment in Scottish film culture: public funds were at last allocated for the Scottish Film Production Fund, officially charged with promoting film production in Scotland.

There had already been a lengthy history of film production in Scotland. By the early 1980s there was also an enterprising new wave of Scottish film makers who were getting films made against the odds, without having waited for the Fund to come along. Murray Grigor, Charles Gormley, Mike Alexander, Douglas Eadie and, of course, Bill Forsyth are merely the best known of this new breed of directors.

Nevertheless, while the Production Fund is only one part of the filmmaking scene in Scotland, it is a particularly important and central part. Its establishment put film as a creative art on the same footing as those other arts that have for long enjoyed public funding through the Scottish Arts Council. No less than literature, music, painting and drama, film can now claim to have a publicly recognised role to play in creating a distinctive Scottish cultural identity.

The importance of film culture in a broader sense had already been recognised, of course, in the establishment of the Scottish Film Council, as early as 1934. The paradox was that the government grant to SFC had never included any element for film production. While funding for the other arts was totally devolved to Scotland, Scottish filmmakers were still, at the beginning of the 1980's, expected to apply to the one source of public funds for production in the UK, the BFI Production Board in London.

Some colourful tales have been told about the selective blindness of the BFI Board, at that time, to Scottish submissions. To be fair, it must be recorded that more recently the BFI's support for Scottish film, both in partnership with the Fund and independently, has been extremely positive. But equally, it has to be said that the special needs of Scotland cannot realistically be expected to be a major concern of a body located in London. However confidently one can now look to the BFI to play a willing role in Scotland, it is self-evident that there are cultural priorities and objectives that can only be properly appreciated from a base within the country.

SFC proclaimed this repeatedly at the end of the 1970s and the beginning of the 1980s. Encouragingly, it had an enlightened ally in the Scottish Arts Council. SAC saw the need for a Scottish cinema with the same clarity as SFC, but, having a much larger budget at its disposal, it was in the fortunate position of being able to do something about it. In 1980 it established its own Film Committee under the chairmanship of Rod Graham, with a remit to embrace film for its own sake as well as pursuing the more traditional 'art film' concept. Within a short space of time that committee had helped to fund films like Mike Radford's *Another Time, Another Place* and set many interesting projects in motion.

When SFC's arguments finally bore fruit in March 1982 with the allocation to it by the Scottish Education Department of an ear-marked fund, SAC was far sighted enough to join forces with SFC by combining the resources that each now had for production. By June 1982 both Councils had formally agreed to establish the Scottish Film Production Fund as an independent body with a budget of £80,000 to disburse in its first year.

This brief history makes it clear that the Fund's remit is a cultural one. While it has never been insensitive to the requirements of the industry and the market place – on the contrary, as we shall see – its priorities are distinct from those of industry-led initiatives. Its essential objective is to take a leading (not exclusive) role in building up a Scottish cinema. It exists because, while visual literacy demands an acquaintance with cinema from all over the world (and the work of SFC admirably allows this to happen), a self-respecting national culture cannot simply consume the images of others. It needs to produce its own images of itself and reflect its own sensibility in what is the major art form of the twentieth century.

It is far too early for any thorough going-assessment of the Fund's progress, but there is already enough of a track record to take stock of what has been accomplished, to look at problems it has faced, to ask whether its objectives and mode of operation are right for the job and to consider its policy options for the future.

I was the Fund's first Chairman; since 1989 Sir Denis Forman has been Chairman and Penny Thomson became the first full-time Director. What follows is a purely personal account of the Fund's early performance.

Going About It

The Fund Committee worked out its own detailed policy. Our remit was this:

to foster and promote film and video production as a central element in the development of Scottish culture, by the provision of financial assistance to such individuals, production companies, production groups or cultural bodies as are deemed appropriate.

We could have chosen to concentrate on certain areas of filmmaking rather than others, and on certain stages of the production process. Broadly speaking the development of a national cinema was interpreted to mean the support of works that fell within the mainstream of contemporary film and television. This allowed for a range of different kinds of film not excluding the odd avant-garde or experimental work, and occasionally, an amateur or community production. But the preference was clearly for professional work, capable of appealing to substantial audiences. There was thus a predictable match between policy and membership of the Committee, with its high proportion of distinguished practitioners. Similarly, the relationships that have developed between the Fund and applicants, notably as far as financial arrangements are concerned, have increasingly resembled those obtaining in normal commercial practice. While outright grants are often made, the Fund has also sought to make investments in the productions it supports, by recovering a percentage share in the profits or achieving some other form of financial return.

Colin McArthur, then of the British Film Institute, published a typically challenging article in the *Glasgow Herald* about the Fund's establishment in which he expressed the fear that it would be set up without a properly wide-ranging debate on what it should be doing.

> SFC/SAC will not publicly raise the question of what kind of cinema does Scotland need, will instead convoke a group of individuals connected with film and television to advise on the spending of the fund and – to the extent that they publicly address issues of policy at all – will talk about responding to individual projects of merit and encouraging individual talent.

Against such a pragmatic approach, situated within current professional practice, he argued for a radically different way of spending the available money which would locate the work of production in much broader social communities:

> Instead of the fostering of individual talent, it [his model] proposed the formation of groups round specific locations. Instead of a series of disparate one-off projects with no particular audiences in mind, it proposed an ongoing address to specific identifiable audiences; and instead of seeking subject matter in the imagination of particular film artists it proposed a subject matter which is socially agreed to be important.

The critique of mainstream cinema that McArthur implies is one worthy of respect. Many would agree that, in a fully-fledged film

173

After the Rains. A Winton Hill Animation
film produced with the financial assistance
of the Scottish Film Production Fund.
Animated and directed by Jessica Langford
with the production facilities of the
Edinburgh Film Workshop Trust, *After the
Rains* deals with environmental issues using
archetypal images which recur in cultures
and cosmologies throughout the world.

culture, there is a need for alternative concepts and practices of filmmaking. But that is not the situation in Scotland. It can be argued that, in the specific circumstances that we actually faced, the pragmatic mode of operation adopted by the fund was not only defensible but preferable. What Scotland needed most urgently – and still needs – is a body of films substantial enough in volume and range to satisfy the tastes and interests of a diversity of audiences. It is by no means certain that, by promoting widely disseminated work at the grassroots, we would have achieved anything other than the continued absence of Scottish images from our screens and the continued frustration of a fair number of Scottish filmmakers.

The approach that we adopted was not, in any case, innocent of debate and self-interrogation. Our choice of projects was not a series of arbitrary one-off responses to proposals of merit, but fitted into a policy framework with clear objectives. If commercial appeal was frequently (but not invariably) one of our main criteria, it was always subservient to cultural relevance and artistic worth, and it was there because cultural relevance that cannot reach audiences is, for practical purposes, a contradiction in terms. What the Fund has done, in effect, is to furnish the material on which the debate that McArthur calls for can take place. If the films we have supported are not the kind of cinema that Scotland needs there is ample evidence now on which to rehearse the case and influence future Fund policy.

Penury

Knowing where we were going was never a problem for the Fund, but the serious lack of the wherewithall to do it certainly was. Our original £80,000 of public money grew to over £100,000 by 1988. In the meantime, we had persuaded Channel Four to be a sponsor, contributing £35,000 per annum. In 1989 Channel Four generously increased its annual contribution to £50,000 (inflation-proofed) and BBC Scotland joined it as a backer to the tune of £64,000 per year for three years, against a commitment to provide a one hour film for broadcast on BBC Scotland each year.

While the near tripling of funds over seven years seems a healthy growth, the total amount available even now is puny when set against the actual costs of film production. Fortunately, lead times in the development of projects are long, so that a large allocation of money to any one film is almost always spread out over more than one financial year. This, together with the fact that other projects do not always develop as expected, produces a fairly flexible cash flow and allows the Fund to 'stretch' its money over many more projects than its total resources would seem to an outsider to justify.

The progress of *Venus Peter* is a good example of the flexible management of resources that has been practised with many other projects as well. It was the Fund which put up the original development money for the film. This enabled the production team to develop a screenplay from Rush's original book. Such was our faith in the project that we then committed £70,000 in advance to the film before any other investments were in place, and subsequently put in another £25,000 to complete the budget package.

Thus, by phasing its contribution, the Fund was not only able to contribute over £100,000 to *Venus Peter* out of annual budgets that were each barely more than that figure, but, more importantly, it was able to play an instrumental role in attracting the rest of the £1.3 million necessary for the making of the film. The real credit for the production rests with producer Chris Young and his associates, and it is more than possible, given his determination and skill, that he could have persuaded the other backers (BFI Production Fund, British Screen Finance, Gavin Films and Orkney Island Council) to make up the Fund's contribution, had we not agreed to participate. But one can equally suggest that the Fund's faith in the project, and its willingness to go into its financial limit in support of the film, considerably eased its progress and might even have been crucial.

There is a limit, however, to what can be done with financial juggling. It is only a marginal alleviation to a state of penury. The level of funding has always meant that only a small proportion of those who apply can expect support. Worse, it has meant that the Fund could never be more than a minor partner in projects that it decided to back. Virtually every award that has been made has been conditional on the applicants raising at least fifty per cent, (usually more) elsewhere. In the case of a major undertaking, such as a full length feature or a documentary in more than one part the Fund's stake must inevitably be extremely small.

Penury also makes it difficult to play a pro-active rather than a reactive role in commissioning work. From the start, the Fund was anxious not simply to wait for applications to come in, but to initiate its own projects and choose its own partners to carry them out. With the experience and understanding of needs that have now been accumulated, that desire must be felt even more keenly today. But with available funds so heavily oversubscribed, such an initiative would have meant turning away even more applicants, so the ambition, at least until 1989, had to be put into cold storage.

Leaving aside the frustration that all this entails for the Fund – keenly felt when the credits go up on the screen – the consequence is that Scottish filmmakers are still condemned to take the plane to London before they can dream of making a film. It is a truism to say that British cinema generally has been heavily dependent on Channel Four, but nowhere is that more the case than in Scotland. Even if it is argued that, with such an expensive art form as film, funding for large projects should rightly be sought outside as well as inside Scotland, it remains true that, in absolute terms, support for Scottish film still lags well behind that for the other arts. On the most modest calculation of adequacy, it should be possible for small and middle scale productions to be financed wholly within Scotland, but that is still a distant goal.

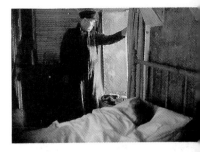

Ray McAnally and Gordon Strachan as the Grandfather and the Boy in *Venus Peter*.

175

Getting On With It

Development, especially script development, is a very necessary area of activity, and the one where money goes furthest, since applications are for relatively modest sums, in film terms. In the Scottish situation where opportunities have been so few, there are inevitably plenty of aspirants with ideas they want to promote. Add to the fact that the Committee has always been keen to give a chance to new talent, and one can see why it would have been easy to over-invest in development activities.

That would have been a mistake. It is a sad fact that even when major writers are involved, far less untried ones, there is a high mortality rate in speculative script development. Looking back over those that the Fund has commissioned, and which have not yet gone further, is a sobering experience. It is true that, lead times being long, it is always possible for a dormant project suddenly to come to life and move into production. While it is heartening when this happens, the facts of life counsel caution in this area. Without by any means disengaging from development activity, the Fund quickly concluded that it was even more important to follow through on initiatives, by concentrating on those with a realistic chance of success, and by working as near as possible to the point of production.

What filmmaking means to the general public, of course, is the production of high profile feature films. The acid test that the man in the street will surely apply to the Fund's efforts is whether he has seen one of our films on the box, or at the local cinema.

By that test, our rating will not be very high, but it will not be particularly low either. The limiting factor has not mainly been penury – there are ways of coping with that as we've seen – but the general dearth of major feature projects in Scotland. The Fund has been involved in a very reasonable proportion of all Scottish features since 1982. Occasionally, its role has been very modest, as in the case of Cary Parker's *The Girl In The Picture*, where we simply supplied funding for a pilot shoot that enabled the producers (Paddy Higson's Antonine Films) to secure the full budget elsewhere. But in other cases, whether it be *Every Picture Tells A Story, Living Apart Together, Venus Peter* or *Play Me Something*, our participation was a genuine element in the budget, within the limits already described.

Some puritanical observers would not agree, arguing that the Fund's overall share in a feature budget is so small that it can never be more than 'top up' money. Rather than a real partner in the project, they would see the Fund as being merely in the industry's eyes a convenient piggy-bank to be plundered for the final slice of funding. This was a criticism levelled in relation to the first feature we supported, Charles Gormley's *Living Apart Together*, where it was alleged that our contribution of £25,000 was a waste of money because such a small sum could easily have been found elsewhere by the main backers.

That argument overlooks the considerable merits of *Living Apart*

Tin Fish, Jon Morrison, Craig MacDonald. A National Film and Television School film produced in association with the Scottish Film Production Fund. Written and directed by Paul Murton, *Tin Fish* deals with the effects on the inhabitants of a Clyde Coast village of the presence of a US nuclear submarine base.

Together, which had the qualities of accessibility and stylishness that the Fund wanted to promote. Since we would certainly have supported it more substantially, had we been able to do so, it would not have been logical to hold back on the grounds that we could only play a minor part. Even more important is the general issue of the Fund's relationship with our leading filmmakers. It would be absurd and tragically self-defeating to take the view that, as soon as a Scottish filmmaker achieves prominence and moves into the big budget league, he or she can no longer look to the Fund for support. On the contrary, it is vital, and in everybody's interests, to keep faith with our most successful talent, and to work together with a sense of mutual advantage on even the biggest projects.

However, a film culture is not built with features alone. It needs a diversity of genres exploiting the many different possibilities of the medium and appealing to different interests.

Perhaps the encouragement that the Fund has given to animation will turn out, in the long run, to be just as important as its contribution to features. Despite the fact that Norman McLaren, one of the world's great animators, was a Scot and partly learned his craft at Glasgow School of Art, animation, with a few notable exceptions, has been largely absent from the scene in Scotland. Now with the elegant work of Lesley Keen, Donald Holwill and Jessica Langford being supported by the Fund (and by others) there is a spreading interest in this most fertile of cinematic arts, and the chance of a strong Scottish school of animation establishing itself.

RA: The Path of the Sun God. A Persistent Vision Animation Production for Channel Four Television in association with the Scottish Film production Fund. Written, animated and directed by Lesley Keen, *RA* is a three part animated feature on themes from Egyptian art and mythology.

Other new seams of activity have been opened up, sometimes without the need for massive resources. A good example is the relationship that was built up with Scottish students completing their training at the National Film and Television School at Beaconsfield, and at one or two other institutions. Provided that certain criteria were met, the Fund at an early stage agreed to supplement the institution's own budget for final graduation films to enable the students to make the film in Scotland and on a slightly more ambitious scale than might otherwise have been the case. The aim was to allow young professionals to enhance their first opportunity to make a film for the general public.

This policy was an unqualified success. At modest cost, it produced a set of films that were simultaneously showpieces for their makers and their institutions, and satisfying works for the public. To have made *The Riveter* with our help may have played a part in Michael Caton-Jones's rapid progress to become director of *Brond* and then of the widely acclaimed *Scandal*, and has certainly resulted in a short film that is authentically part of Scottish cinema.

The same is true of other NFTS productions that were supported, notably Ian Wyse's *Fall From Grace*, Gillies Mackinnon's *Passing Glory* and Douglas Mackinnon's *Ashes*. In all these instances, the skills being supported were those of the director, but the Fund is no less interested in giving opportunities to students in other professional grades, not least that of producer. The ideal is to build up a base of professional expertise

177

that serves the wider film environment while also adding regularly to the body of films available. There is no doubt that the continuation of this rewarding formula will be among the Fund's priorities for the future.

A Missing Link

The graduation pieces draw attention, however, to a curious missing link in the chain of production: that of the short fiction film. All the films in this category have been fiction shorts which have considerable advantages as a training ground for first-time directors (as well as for more experienced filmmakers). By definition, it is relatively cheap and allows limited money to help more people. Unlike more specialised genres, it gives exposure to many aspects of the craft, including direction of actors. Like the short story, it is a form that can be a complete aesthetic experience because of, and not despite, its brevity.

In a well-ordered universe, therefore, one would expect a body in the Fund's situation to be very active in the field of the short film. Unfortunately the reverse is true. Apart from the graduation pieces, there have been few good proposals and, with one or two exceptions, few projects supported.

The explanation for this strange state of affairs is to be found in the shrinking number of outlets for the short film. In commercial cinemas it has virtually disappeared, being considered a disproportionately expensive form of programming. Even in publicly supported cinemas its position has been severely eroded by the financial pressure that they, too, are under. Both British Screen and the BFI Production Board have fought a rearguard to defend the genre, but their efforts have not been matched by policy initiatives at the level of exhibition. Until this happens, the short film, despite its obvious merits and its distinguished place in film history, will be a threatened species in the cinema.

In action at the Mousa Broch in the Shetlands. Penny Thomson produced and Rosie Gibson directed *The Work They Say Is Mine*, an examination of the role of women in Shetland life.

That need not be true as far as television is concerned. Bearing in mind that the half-hour slot is a favourite programming unit in television and considering the average costs that obtain in that sector, it remains a mystery why channels are not interested in promoting good short films in their schedules as a strand that would compare well in cost with other quality programmes. A fairly modest investment annually by the main Scottish channels, supported if necessary by the Fund, would make a dramatic difference to the opportunities open to Scottish filmmakers.

As it happens the Fund's most notable venture in the short film, Jim Gillespie's *Happy the Man* took the form of a three way collaboration with producer Paddy Higson, (once again!) and Scottish Television as co-investor and exhibitor. Although the film is an intriguing, imaginative piece that works well at both a popular and a symbolic level, and has deservedly received serious critical attention, it is no secret that it did not please the decision makers at STV. Nevertheless, it is a safe bet that it will live on and be shown to audiences long after the innumerable, nondescript half-hours that fill the schedules week in, week out have been forgotten. The Fund should be unrepentant about having backed it and should press television companies to undertake more ventures of this kind. Everybody would gain, Scottish cinema not least, from a re-forging of the missing link.

Documentary

Until enterprising action does something to rescue the short film, the main area for regular production investment by the Fund is likely to remain what it has always been: the documentary.

There are excellent documentary film makers in Scotland and the Fund is fortunate to have worked closely with many of them. One of our earliest projects, Rosie Gibson's *The Work They Say is Mine* on Shetland women (produced by Penny Thomson, now Director of the Fund) may have been matched in quality by subsequent productions but it has never been surpassed. The two series by Brian Crumlish and Christeen Winford *Roots of Homelessness* and *Into Nicaragua* are major documentaries that can stand up in any company, as can Diane Tamme's *Innocent as Hell*. It is particularly satisfying to have worked in a sustained way with Timothy Neat through *Hallaig, Tree of Liberty* and *Time is a Country*, right up to a fine culmination in *Play Me Something*. All these and others (Ken McGill's *Mud and Guts*, Sarah Noble and Paul Murton's *Site One*, David Rea's *Dancing to My Shadow*) make a distinguished record of production of which the Fund can be proud.

Being involved with documentaries immediately raises for the Fund the whole question of its relationship with television. Some aspects of that relationship are applicable to all kinds of production, while others are specific to documentary. As far as general involvement is concerned, the Fund has always accepted that it could not operate realistically without a close association with television, especially Channel Four. It did not see that situation as problematic, and has always placed production for television high on its agenda of activities.

What it has been anxious to ensure, however, is that it should not become an all-purpose adjunct to television, from which support is routinely sought. Quite regularly in the early years applications were received for projects which, while worthy in their way, did not obviously require funding from a source outside television itself. What the Fund looked for was projects that not only had cultural relevance and artistic merit, but also stood out from normal television programming and justified an intervention on the grounds of their unusual nature. In practice there was never much difficulty in applying such a judgement and thus achieving complete freedom of action in our choice of projects.

As far as the specific case of documentaries is concerned, the relationship with television has been wholly positive in that it has given the

The Easterhouse band *Scheme* rocking the *Glasgow Pavilion* in Diane Tamme's *Innocent as Hell*. The film provided core material for the Scottish Film Council's media education pack on rock music, *Local Heroes*.

films access to audiences that are very much greater than documentary has enjoyed in the past. Globally, despite competition from other types of programme, documentary is making as powerful an impact on audiences and as a great a contribution to the social and cultural life of the country as ever it did. The substantial investment that Channel Four and all the other broadcasting companies make in the genre is one of the most admirable features of current media practice and the Fund has been right to devote a large slice of its resources to it as well.

One problem, however, if one looks at the situation in the light of the Fund's broader objectives, is that in television documentaries tend to be ephemeral experiences and lose their identity by being immersed in the relentless 'flow' of television. On the whole such films do not fall into the privileged category of programmes that are regularly repeated. Viewers may thus remember the message delivered by specific films and have their understanding of the subject increased. But they have little chance of getting to know the films as individual entities or taking their interest in any one film further. Some films may acquire an alternative life on community and other specialised circuits, but in the main, after their one showing they are lost to the general public.

In cinema films remain accessible and can take on an extended and ever-changing life by being seen again at different times and in different contexts. The main solution to the problem of the ephemerality of documentaries in present practice is thus to restore the films to the domain of cinema, in the same way that many feature films now enjoy a double life by moving between the two media. At the simplest level, this means providing exhibition prints so that films can be seen on cinema circuits. The Fund has already responded to this need without restricting itself to films initially supported by itself. Two films which seemed to us worth promoting in this way, although we were not otherwise involved with them were David Halliday's *Northern Front* and *Gramsci*, a fine fiction-documentary by Mike Alexander and Douglas Eadie.

At a more sophisticated level, what is needed is a properly conceived exhibition policy, in which the Fund would ideally join forces with other agencies, notably the Scottish Film Council. Here the problem has not yet been fully addressed, but there is little doubt that an energetic attack on the issue would bring dividends.

It has to be recognised, of course, that even when restored to public attention, documentary as a genre is not the greatest of crowd-pullers. By the same token a body which gives significant support to documentaries earns less public kudos than if it were concerned solely with more instantly appealing products. But that has not deterred the Fund in the past and should not deter it in the future. Even when resources increase, it should not be tempted to follow the crowd into undue concentration on glamorous fiction at the expense of documentary. There are still innumerable subjects in Scottish life and society that need to be placed before a discerning public with the particular impact that documentary can give. John Grierson's conviction that the 'creative treatment of actuality' is a genuine and vital form of cinema has been amply proved over the years, and the Fund has done well to demonstrate its faith in that belief.

The Future

The public profile and active role of the Fund was improved by the decision in 1989 to appoint Penny Thomson as full-time Director, whose first (successfully completed) task was to secure extra money to pay for her post.

The Director has been active, for example, in pursuing connections with various European projects that potentially Scotland can tap into, including the MEDIA 92 Programme, Babel for minority languages, EFDO for subsidising the distribution of low budget European films, the European Script Development Fund with its headquarters in London, and EAVE for encouraging young film entrepreneurs, in which Penny Thomson participated as an official observer. Like many things European, these projects will no doubt prove to be hedged round with daunting procedures and difficulties of access, but it is heartening that the Fund has been quick off the mark to tackle them, and one can be sure that the claims of Scottish filmmakers will be energetically represented.

The natural line of progression for the Fund is for it to take the pro-active coordinating role in film production in Scotland. Implicit in this role is networking with all other film agencies to ensure financial and institutional support so that Scottish films are properly publicised, filmmakers are trained and films are produced in this country. The very active IFPA, and other associations within the industry itself, including BAFTA Scotland, are powerful initiators themselves, and there is no reason why there should not be a happy and active collaboration between all the parties involved. But with the authority of public body status and funding behind it, and a growing record of enterprise, the Fund has now reached a position where it will be the prime mover on the scene.

The imminent inauguration of a professional training course in Scotland will predictably bring a new constituency of clients to the Fund's door. Another development area will be that of production in Gaelic.

One of the biggest tasks for the future, to be embarked on as soon as possible, is the promotion and marketing of Scottish cinema. It is not sufficient simply to produce good Scottish films and wait for them to be widely appreciated. That there is a latent interest in Scottish cinema is obvious from the enthusiastic response to the films of Bill Forsyth and a few others. But that interest has to struggle against a process of cultural conditioning which promotes only certain brands of cinema and marginalises those that do not conform to the preferred model. We thus live in a cultural environment in which Scottish films

181

Production still from *Silent Scream* featuring Iain Glen, whose performance as convicted murderer Larry Winters won him the 1990 Berlin Film Festival Best Actor award, the Silver Bear. The film also won the Michael Powell Award for The Outstanding British Film of the Year at the 1990 Edinburgh International Film Festival.

can appear on Channel Four without a word of comment or analysis appearing in the Scottish press or the arts programmes of Scottish television channels. A Scottish filmmaker, Murray Grigor, can receive the well deserved Reith Award 1990 for a distinguished body of work and even the quality Scottish press accords the event a desultory line or two at most.

The film agencies need to ensure that there are many more opportunities of seeing what is now the considerable output of films of different kinds and to give audiences the chance of meeting Scottish filmmakers and taking an intelligent interest in their work. In the first instance this kind of effort would form part of the well conceived exhibition policy that has already been referred to. The responsible body in such matters is the Scottish Film Council which has the capacity to foster systematic programming in regional film theatres and organise special events of various kinds, and has done so already on many occasions. However, the Fund's close relationship with the industry and connections with filmmakers could be a valuable support to SFC and provide, through a combined approach, a higher profile and impact.

An alliance between the two bodies would certainly be required for what would be the most challenging venture of all – the mounting of an annual Scottish Film Festival. Contrary to popular assumptions there would be easily enough material for such an event, if each year's output were suitably mixed with retrospectives, exhibitions, master classes, debates and discussions. The backlog of ignorance about the history of Scottish cinema is such that it would take several years of retrospectives simply to bring the public up to date. Meanwhile new works, from graduation pieces to feature films, will be steadily increasing and assuming a greater proportion of each year's festival. If the first event were to be a five or six day programme confined to the evenings, this would already be a mammoth step forward compared to the exposure that Scottish cinema currently receives. And it can be confidently predicted that it would be only a year or two before the scale would escalate to include daytime programming as well.

There is, of course, a precedent for such an initiative in the annual Celtic Film Festival which has been running for several years, with good Scottish participation. However, without questioning the excellence of this event, it clearly does not meet the needs that now exist. Leaving aside the fact that it is held in Scotland only every four or five years, it has always been more of a festival for professionals than for the public. In this respect, it need not be threatened by a new festival with wider cultural objectives and a more concentrated focus on the general public. Indeed, there is much that a new initiative could learn from the Celtic Festival, not least in the substantial part that television material plays in its programming. A Scottish Film Festival would, indeed, like the Fund itself have to embrace television and cinema in its remit, and take the inventive use of the moving image in all its forms as its central criterion of selection.

For anybody who has seen such an event being established and thriving in other small countries, there is no doubt about the enormous stimulus it gives not only to public interest and national pride, but also to actual filmmaking activity. A national culture develops by speaking to itself in a variety of ways, including celebration of its achievements. When we remember with what timidity Glasgow Mayfest emerged on the scene only a few years ago and compare it with what it is today, we can see the self-generating power and spin-off effects of such ventures. There is no reason why a Scottish Film Festival should not follow a similar trajectory. The sooner we launch one the better.

Conclusion

When the Film Production Fund was first mooted and then set up, nobody was in any doubt about the uphill task it faced. For obvious financial and commercial reasons filmmaking does not easily thrive in small countries. Yet it has by now been demonstrated that in Scotland there is the invention, the talent and the technical skills to make films that express a distinctive sensibililty and outlook on the world. All that is needed are agencies and mechanisms to allow those qualities to thrive.

Production still from *Silent Scream* featuring Iain Glen and (right) David Hayman. *Silent Scream*, an Antonine Production funded by the British Film Institute and Film Four International in association with the Scottish Film Production Fund, deals with the final hours of Larry Winters, an inmate of the Barlinnie Special Unit.

The Fund is an important agency which has already achieved a great deal on the slenderest of resources. What it and the film community now deserve is a recognition by its government sponsors that the case for a substantial increase in funding has now been fully proven. With a doubling, or even a tripling, of its public money the Fund would still be no better resourced than a medium sized theatre, and it would certainly do as much for the common good, with the extra funds, as any theatre or arts centre. John Grierson, who got most things right, used to say that a serious remit called for a proper remittance. Let us hope that the Scottish Office will take heed of the old master's message.

There are many other issues concerning the Fund that merit discussion but cannot be broached in a short chapter. The question of its relationship to the two founding bodies, SAC and SFC, and where exactly it has its constitutional being, is one that will have eventually to be addressed. The balance of its committee between London-based and Scottish-based members might seem a simple, practical matter, but it is one that could have certain implications if the balance tipped the wrong way.

Many other policy and constitutional questions will come sharply into focus if the prospect of a Scottish Assembly were to become a reality. Of all the arts bodies, the Fund is arguably the one with most to gain from proper arrangements for determination in Scotland. It is hard to believe that legislators, with an understanding of the importance of the arts as an expression of national identity, will not see the case for a greater role for cinema. Those who care about film and Scottish culture would do well to start thinking now about that eventuality.

List of films and video productions supported by SFPF, 1982–1990

Abbreviations – *FF* feature film, *D* documentary, *A* animation, *FS* fiction short, *CS* comedy sketches

1983
LIVING APART TOGETHER, director Charles Gormley, Film on Four, Channel Four, *FF*
GREAT EXPECTATIONS, director Sitar Rose, non-broadcast project, *D*
LOCH NESS MONSTER MOVIE, director Ian Rintoul, non-professional project, *A*

1984
EVERY PICTURE TELLS A STORY, director James Scott, Channel Four, *FF*
FALL FROM GRACE, director Ian Wyse, NFTS graduation film, *FS*
HALLAIG, director Timothy Neat, Channel Four, BBC Scotland, *D*

1985
ORPHEUS AND EURYDICE, director Lesley Keen, Channel Four, *D*
TWO-REELERS, director Tom McGrath, non-broadcast project, *CS*
FOLLOW THE FLOW, director Mary Walters, non-broadcast project, *D*
SITE ONE, directors Sarah Noble and, Paul Murton, workshop production, *D*
THE CLYDE FILM, director Ken Currie, non-broadcast project, *D*
ABSOLUTE, director Ken McGill, *FS*

1986
THE WORK THEY SAY IS MINE, director Rosie Gibson, Channel Four, *D*
INNOCENT AS HELL, director Diane Tammes, Channel Four, *D*
PASSING GLORY, director Gillies MacKinnin, NFTS graduation film, *FS*
THE RIVETER, director Michael Caton-Jones, NFTS graduation film, *FS*
HAPPY THE MAN, director Jim Gillespie, Scottish Television, *FS*
MUD AND GUTS, director Ken McGill, Channel Four, *D*

1987
ROOTS OF HOMELESSNESS, director Brian Crumlish, Channel Four, *D*
THE JOURNEY, director Peter Watkins, *D*
COMPELLANCE, director Bob Last, BFI, *FS*
TREE OF LIBERTY, director Timothy Neat, Scottish Television/Channel Four, *D*
TIME IS A COUNTRY, director Timothy Neat, Channel Four, *D*
GRAMSCI, director Mike Alexander, Channel Four, *D*
1686, director Neil Mackintosh, RCA graduation film, *FS*

1988
EVERY WOMAN'S FEAR, Glasgow Film and Video Workshop, non-broadcast project, *D*
SMALL CHANGE, director Sonya McAngus, non-broadcast project, *D*
INTO NICARAGUA, director Brian Crumlish, Channel Four, *D*
FACTS OF LIFE, director Laura Sims, NFTS graduation film, *FS*
HILL STREET, director James Mavor, non-broadcast project, *D*

1989
DANCING TO MY SHADOW, director David Rea, BBC Scotland, *D*
WALKING ON ICE, director Bill Kirkwood, non-broadcast project, *D*
VENUS PETER, director Ian Sellar, BFI/British Screen/Channel Four, *FF*
PLAY ME SOMETHING, director Timothy Neat, BFI/Grampian TV, *FF*

1990
RA: THE PATH OF THE SUN GOD, director Lesley Keen, Channel Four, *A*
AFTER THE RAINS, director Jessica Langford, *A*
ASHES, director Douglas Mackinnon, NFTS graduation film, *FS*
TIN FISH, director Paul Murton, NFTS graduation film, *FS*
ALABAMA, director Jim Shields, NFTS graduation film, *FS*
THE WHY?S MAN, director Murray Grigor, Channel Four, *D*
SILENT SCREAM, director David Hayman, BFI/Channel Four, *FF*
THE WALL WALLAH, director Graham Maughan, *D*
CITIZENS THEATRE GLASGOW, director Diane Tammes, Channel Four, *D*
PRAGUE, director/writer Ian Sellar, *FF*

The Impact of Channel Four

Charlie Gormley

The impact of Channel Four? On the Scottish film community? From a Scottish viewpoint it's not the impact that's important, the real question is: did we get a result? So I questioned David Scott at Channel Four and listened to Gus Macdonald at Scottish. They have all the figures relating to audience shares and percentages of budget collated and set out in graphs. But somehow the figures don't help, short of turning you into a Scot Nat. It's like reading a report on a football match that lists the corners and free kicks and leaves you to guess the result.

One definite result is the impact on the speech patterns of most of us who get involved. What do the numbers look like, we ask. Do the numbers stand up? That's budget speak. And we learn to discuss money obliquely and in sections. We talk about the downside and front end. I remember the writer Willie McIlvanney getting quite cross with me because I insisted on talking *movie money* and he wanted to talk *film* and *quality*. Your argument's safe from distortion here Willie, for I intend the supreme cop-out – this is a personal view.

The first time I met Jeremy Isaacs he was the Programme Controller at Thames Television and I was a little drunk from hanging round a sponsored reception at BAFTA in London. The occasion was the launch by Penguin Books of the paperback of Gordon Williams's *Hazell* stories that Thames had made into a series. And I was there because I knew the Paisley-born author. I had never met a man as pro-Scottish as Isaacs, not even in London. So we talked a little about film and he said what wonderful filmmakers we had up in Scotland and I explained that I intended making a film about three Scottish media writers and that Melvyn Bragg was interested. Isaacs nodded and said that if Melvyn dropped out I could tell David Johnston at STV that he was happy to talk network if David was interested. What with the not so dry white wine swishing about on top of what had been downed before, I wasn't quite sure of what I had heard. It was simply a shock to speak to a serious television person and have him field the pitch on the spot. Anyway Jeremy asked me how David was and, flushed with first names, I said he was running around with a fist full of fivers trying to buy back the franchise. The sober Isaacs asked me to repeat what I had said and I did. And thought no more about it except to wince privately at the memory. Within a year Jeremy was in Glasgow with a Peter MacDougall script of the *Sense of Freedom* story and a contract from STV to make it. But even before he signed the deal my sometime partner Bill Forsyth and I heard that Jeremy had also helped encourage STV to put up half the £200,000 budget for *Gregory's Girl*. We figured he was mildly embarrassed that the BFI had turned us down flat with the story a couple of years before when Jeremy was still its Chairman. So if Jeremy Isaacs was Channel Four, and he was, then we got an early hint of what was in store. Cameraman Mick Coulter told me of the stunned silence that greeted the opening of the camera truck on *Gregory's Girl*, when he and Bill got their first sight of the mountains of 35 mm gear that went with real picture making. After an artificially extended film childhood, it was sweet relief to be asked to play with the grown-ups.

But first the 'Back Story'. It was John Grierson, he of the trenchant phrase, who insisted that Films of Scotland had a remit but no remittance. And it was the main source of film finance in Scotland before the Highland Board weighed in with extra help. It was then virtually impossible to make and sell films for the local TV stations, largely because the film and television union, the ACTT, was in reality two unions – one for people inside the TV stations and the other to cover the fast-diminishing movie studio personnel and the rumps of freelancers. The mistrust was almost total. Even when a filmmaker sold a film to local television, as did Mike Alexander, it was likely to be blacked before it was screened, on the basis that the TV section of the union had no way of monitoring the production and ensuring that the rule book had been adhered to in all its fine print. Much easier to pull the plug on it and give tacit support to the official union line that freelancers were not free at all but casualised labour. The real movies that got made like Bill Douglas's *Trilogy* and Bill Forsyth's *That Sinking Feeling* and *Gregory's Girl*, either got some modest funding as 'art' movies or were made for next to nothing on the goodwill of the technicians.

Only the Children's Film Foundation offered a crack at a minutely budgeted 35 mm 'theatrical' production. The kind they showed at the Saturday morning matinees. But before you got near those ABC Minors and the Rank equivalent, you had to undertake a post-graduate course in the Henry Geddes school of filmmaking which ignored how visually sophisticated the young audience had become, and insisted you opened every sequence with a wide shot so the kids would know for sure where they were. But it was 'pictures' and we littered the Scottish landscape with young Londoners holidaying with uncles and aunts in the Highlands, learning to guddle salmon and befriend sheep dogs before the coastguard and the police and the fire brigade rushed in for the grand slam ending. Of all the cliffs in all the world, why did he have to fall off mine?

I'm sure it's the same the unsubsidised world over. Still long before JOBFIT and its clones, the Scottish film community had devised ways to run a year-long training scheme for an annual intake of new film assistants; had stitched together a modest Film Production

Fund and put our union house in order sufficiently well to find broad approval with the TV boys. We were even sufficiently devious to wrap ourselves in the Scottish flag, the national comfort blanket, and threaten politicians with an old fashioned Scottish Office notion called the Goshen Quotient – the idea of a civil servant who worked out that Scotland was due or deserved something like 11.1% of the national cake. We never got halfway close to Goshen so we weren't impressed by the envious remarks on Scottish film success by Welsh filmmakers at an early Celtic Film Festival and we were right not to be. Within a decade we watched as employment in the Welsh TV and film industry climbed to twice the numbers Scotland had. Thanks largely to the Government sponsored Welsh language channel. Still, we had access to Channel Four. And it was a network channel. It had a Scotsman at the helm and a sprinkling of Scottish commissioning editors. Surely there had to be a way in.

B A Robertson and Jimmy Logan in *Living Apart Together*. Logan has acted in films since *Floodtide*. He is described as being a 'real pro'; his 'method' is to jump into the part on the word 'action!'.

In the first years Channel Four was designed and built for the independents. A publishing house with no studios to fill and no tradition of how and where to spend its money. The Scottish independents were ready and waiting. Unfortunately we had no TV skills. We could make documentaries or we could try for the Film Four slot. Talk shows and light entertainment and current affairs were outside our experience and our interest. I can only think of one producer who behaved like a true TV man. Steve Clark-Hall took off for the south with an idea for a long running series for older viewers. And he got it.

The magic wand that Channel Four waved was not Jeremy's gutsy drive and David Rose's nous. It was new money to back realistic budgets. A good production manager with a pocket full of tenners can get you out of more problems than even your script can get you into. Cash. The magic ingredient. The true and tested route to film success. For success in the movies is to get a film to make. What happens later when the critics have their way with you or the public stays away in droves, is something else. Still, win or lose, it was heady stuff for a cottage industry weaned on a diet of industrial documentaries and new town films.

Living Apart Together was my first 'theatrical' film backed by Channel Four at a budget of £350,000. There is nothing wrong with low budget productions. It suits the national temperament and mirrors the newspapers' liking for 'heroic' local filmmaking. I often think that a small part of the *Gregory's Girl* success was that it came out just as Lew Grade's big budget *Raise the Titanic* was sinking ignominiously. In underfunded pictures the required level of chance taking and pure luck, even if you grant the necessary talent, is enormous. You can't afford to re-shoot and fill the obvious gaps – you have to buy what you got on the day and make the best of it in the cutting-room. As a general rule it is best suited to the non-Hollywood, open-ended, enigmatic 'art house' type of film. So with unerring ease I embarked on what the Americans would call a 'backyard musical'.

Alan Sharp once told me that in this business if you start out

187

unwitting you pretty soon get witting. That's what I imagine happened to me on *Living Apart*. The problem is that the long climb up the learning curve reaches its peak of knowledge and understanding after the picture is shot and cut and scored. You are now in good shape to make a film but the only calling card you have is the film you just struggled through and learned from. Your head might now be filled with smart picture making insights and commonsense solutions, but the only evidence is to the contrary and it is up there on the screen for all to see.

Of course some people were already nosing the way ahead. Iain Smith had moved south to work for Puttnam and hated our back home methods of filmmaking. He was persuaded by Puttnam's views on the 'compartmentalisation of talent' which sounded to me like producer talk for 'divide and rule'. If you keep the writer and the director apart you have fertile ground for the kind of creative tension that only a producer can solve. At home Paddy Higson had climbed up through the production manager and line producer roles to get within sight of producing. And only producing. The rest of us, Smithy insisted, were making no serious attempt to enter the real film world. Expecting to go on writing and directing or producing and photographing when we could barely compete in one department. Puttnam was then in the ascendant and by his rules Smithy figured maybe only two or three home based Scots could cut it in the big London playground. And only if they specialised and worked hard. It seemed profitless to ask if you were one of the magical two or three.

Barbara Kellermann and B A Robertson in *Living Apart Together*. Kellermann was the only established movie actor in the group. To get her, producer Gavrik Losey pressurised agent Dennis Sellinger for a decision hard against the Yom Kippur festival.

188

Tom Conti, Helen Mirren in *Heavenly Pursuits*. It is unusual for 'name stars' to work in low-budget Scottish movies. Conti came into the picture because he was impressed by the screenplay.

Mercifully for us Channel Four was different, both from our experience and the rules of the 'business'. It was full of hunch players. So, rough and ready as we were, we got to make the classy documentaries and the mini series and the pictures for Film Four. I remember being called upstairs after a screening of my first effort and being asked, in all seriousness by David Rose, if my producers were treating me all right. What a studio to work for!

It may have occurred to the more than cursory reader that I have not said a word about Scottish culture or a separate Scottish identity. I haven't even said 'Scottish Film'. It is not a thoughtless omission. I have always viewed filmmaking as intrinsically international. The ordinary cinemagoer isn't familiar with French cinema or Swedish cinema because of Truffaut or Bergman but because Truffaut and Bergman made international films. I went to see a Fellini picture not an Italian picture. And while film can give a wonderful sense of place, a sub-text of heightened reality, there are so many things that film can't do or doesn't do well. It is a poor medium for pamphleteering. It's just too oblique for the heavy 'punch line' addicts. The twists and turns of the traditional screenplay tend to subvert any polemical drive and undermine an attempt at reasoned argument. As anyone who ever wrote a 'movie' will tell you, the trick is to catch your ideas and wrap them up in digestible emotions. The logic for what you are saying comes last. And you work backwards through your drafted screenplay so that the means can justify the end.

189

Helen Mirren, Brian Pettifer in *Heavenly Pursuits*. After *Pursuits*, Mirren was accused by a TV company of being 'too difficult to work with'. She sued the accusers and accepted an out of court settlement which vindicated her behaviour. Gormley had attested that she had successfully contributed to a low-budget movie which had demanded plenty of action and some stunts. *Pursuits* came in on time, under budget. Hiding out of focus is Brian Pettifer, an unlikely priest, wearing a Glasgow Rangers t-shirt under his cassock.

A million frames ago Mark Littlewood photographed a young couple necking in the Princes Street Gardens. At a Films of Scotland meeting the puritanical streak in John Grierson demanded the scene be cut. That was not the Scotland he wanted to project. So what would pass muster as a 'Scottish Film'? Would you go for the stinging realism and sharp wit of Peter MacDougall's Greenock films or veer towards Murray Grigor's explorations of cultural imperialism in *Scotch Myths*? How about John McGrath and the network televising of his mammoth promenade theatrical pieces? Sure as hell, if the local critical backbiting is to be believed, it wouldn't be Bill Forsyth's films. Bill, it seems, has gone from winning the game for Scotland to vaguely letting the side down. Of course this is just academic chit chat and maybe I read it wrongly but to my mind it underlines a problem the academics have and rarely talk about. There are simply too few 'Scottish films' for a true pattern to emerge. And those that do exist are too much talked about.

Graham Greene once said that the average bright sixth-former could drive a bus through the attitudes and ideas in which his beliefs were rooted. I'm on his side when it comes to reflecting on this wee nation. And yet to hear Nigel Tranter talk about a man who lost his memory, and draw the comparison with a nation that forgot its stories and its heroes, compels attention. But then why should a Scotsman be surprised by the Jekyll and Hyde in his nature? It was in a note prefacing *Sunset Song* that Lewis Grassic Gibbons suggested that if the great Dutch language should disappear and a Dutchman wrote in German, he might be forgiven for importing into German certain Dutch words that had no true German equivalent, and with them the rhythms and cadences of his native tongue. What Gibbons wanted was the same forbearance for his writing in English. It seemed a fair plea when I first read it and it still does. But a film script unlike a book, is only a staging post, a blueprint for a form to get it up on the screen where it belongs, it needs funding. Just like moon rockets. When Godard opened *Tout Va Bein* with an almost endless sequence of cheque signing to prove how films got made, we nodded sagely. But it did not need anyone out of France to tell us that. Any film with any 'theatrical' pretensions going to cost two million dollars minimum. Which is a powerful amount of money to raise before you can get to your work. And very very little of it can be raised in Scotland. You get out the begging bowl and you get on a plane.

By the time I had made *Heavenly Pursuits* a 'Scottish Film' had become, in the minds of some critics, a definable entity. Its comedy moments would be 'light' when they were not 'whimsical'. A 'slight' piece relieved by 'deft' touches. Which was not how I viewed a film about life and death and people by underprivileged kids with learning difficulties. But as Margaret Thatcher never tires of saying, 'you can't buck the market place'. *Pursuits* proved to me that – outside of maverick, one-off 'hit' movies – it is possible in Scotland to make films with sufficient production values and star power to compete in

190

the States with American films that cost from five to ten times more. Of course you better have a good story and fight for good players in all departments and a star name or two and throw in the 'bits of business' and stunts that give a film a movie look. At least that's what I figured I'd learned on *Living Apart* and tried to apply in *Pursuits*. Which is not to say there are no moments when I want to hide behind the couch when it turns up on late night television. After all who is better placed to know the difference between how things are on the screen and how they might have been.

In a recent John Logie Baird lecture Scottish Television's Gus Macdonald read out the figures that proved that outside the most modestly conceived efforts, the Scottish nation could not financially support a film made exclusively for Scottish consumption. The TV boys have their own Goshen Quotient that dictates that if an episode of *LA Law* costs fifty thousand dollars for a UK screening, the Scottish pay around four thousand dollars for the privilege of showing it. And the Yanks accuse the Japs of dumping. He advised aspiring producers to go for the larger British market with programmes they were prepared to pay to show. Of course it was only an argument set out to prove the game plan Scottish are presently running with. But the numbers, as we say, are inescapable. Channel Four provides a hedge against the relentless pressure of the numbers. And as a network station with a sense of duty and obligation, it can and does stand the numbers on their head. In the last three years their budget spent in Scotland has jumped from £2 million to £4.5 million and last year to £6.3 million and local independents cornered the major share of the total. At last Scottish producers were learning to make 'television' and not rely on the occasional biggish spend on drama and film. Surprisingly most of us would chart that improvement from a most unlikely happening, one of the annual visits by the Channel Four brass to talk to Scottish IPPA – visits that are normally conducted in an atmosphere of friendly acrimony. There are even tales of bread rolls hurled at unsympathetic Londoners. Three years ago the weapon that won the day for Scotland was silence. Jeremy Isaacs knows his stuff well enough to sometimes be tempted to speak on his feet. He was half way into a lecture on what a fair shot Channel Four gave Scottish producers, and by way of illustration started to calculate how well we did in terms of our numbers and our audience share. Up till then we had been screaming about the metropolitan preferences of the commissioning editors. So Jeremy did the head calculation and we all held our breath for once. The figures were so bad that, still on his feet, he initiated a Scottish slush fund to seed programme ideas. As they used to say, give a man money, watch him act funny.

By the time I floated the idea for the yet-to-be-made *Van Diemen's Men* or – *Tender Hearted Men* if you prefer a selling title – the basic costs of my films had gone from £250,000 to almost £1.2m to £2.7m at the last count. And there is more than inflation involved, or even an inflated view of their worth. For my money *Tender Hearted Men* is a modern story that just happens to be set in the Australian past. And that's a problem. When I wrote it nobody told me Aussies were sick of 'costume drama'. I can argue all night but it is a limiting factor when I need to raise Australian money. So there I am with a script a lot of people like with around a million earmarked in the UK and a war on my hands long before a camera even turns. Of course if I can interest a couple of heavy duty stars I can probably diffuse the prejudice. And say I do? I am right back where I was with *Pursuits*. With a film I like but one that needs to get super lucky. And why? Because I am only talking production budget. The last time anyone talked to me seriously about successfully launching a film on the American market, they were projecting a spend, on advertising and prints, of three million dollars. That's a lot more than *Pursuits* cost to make. And it's a lot more dull as a topic of conversation than the zinger in the second act climax or the spare elegance of the dialogue or the neat way you've handled the actors. It is also a very far road from Scotland and the native obsessions. And even back home the film world is not standing still but in constant flux.

So three cheers for us even if we still fall far short of Mr Goshen and his minimum quotient. And Film Four International? I'm told that it can take up to a year for an unknown to get a script rejected. At one point the department was receiving around four hundred scripts a week. It seems to me that the British Establishment has managed its classic absorption technique. One day Film Four is those daft wee films on the Channel nobody watches and the next is the saviour of the British Film Industry. We must be the only industry on earth that manufactures more saviours than films. But don't take my word for it, ask about. Or better still watch the opening credits on any British Film of late and you will see that the backers tend to outnumber the stars. A Palace film in association with Film Four International and British Screen and British Satellite Broadcasting of a You Know Who film. The new money that was is now old money and there is just not enough of it. Roll on Film Five.

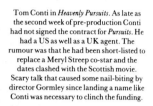

Tom Conti in *Heavenly Pursuits*. As late as the second week of pre-production Conti had not signed the contract for *Pursuits*. He had a US as well as a UK agent. The rumour was that he had been short-listed to replace a Meryl Streep co-star and the dates clashed with the Scottish movie. Scary talk that caused some nail-biting by director Gormley since landing a name like Conti was necessary to clinch the funding.

Fiction Friction

Gus Macdonald

The increase in production of television drama is one of Scotland's export success stories of the past decade. This is an important advance since fiction on tape and film is the dominant commodity in an international entertainment industry that is globalising at a rapid rate. Deregulation will open up opportunities denied to producers in Scotland by public service structures, over the past thirty years. However to move forward in the more competitive nineties Scottish producers must now develop products that more consumers want to watch. It is particularly important that fiction films spearhead the drive to increase our market share of television production.

(Apologies for the business jargon: it is a reaction to subjective twitterings about television which disguise the truth that in a high tech, labour intensive, public service industry of some cultural importance, Scotland has allowed itself to be marginalised without much protest.)

Three examples underline the consequences of decades of systematic stunting:

> Wales today with *half* the population of Scotland has *twice* as many people working in television and related activities – almost 5,000 to our 2,500.
>
> Yorkshire Television in Leeds makes more network productions for ITV alone than all the producers in Scotland – Scottish TV, Grampian TV, BBC Scotland and sixty independent production companies – make for all four UK network channels.
>
> In 1990 ITV network commissions worth £60 million will be made by British independent production companies. None of those companies will be Scottish.

The most likely way our undernourished industry can strengthen its economic base in increasingly competitive times is through our ability to sell stories. While encouraging a talent for telling stories with universal appeal, it is vital that we also create our own space on Scottish screens for stories only Scots might feel for or even understand.

Scottish viewers provide five million reasons for thinking small, for finding ways of making watchable drama which is affordable when the average production cost of network drama is £400,000 an hour in the UK. American television drama costs twice as much. Budgets this big mean that at present every Scottish-made story on television has to be submitted first to the UK networks in London to be approved and paid for. The ability to broadcast Scottish stories internally for

A Sense of Freedom directed by John Mackenzie and starring David Hayman as Jimmy Boyle. The film shows hardman Boyle's small-time gangster life in Glasgow and follows him into the degradation of Scottish prison life, stopping at the moment of his transfer to the experimental Special Unit in Barlinnie Prison, Glasgow. Mackenzie also directed *The Cheviot, the Stag and the Black, Black Oil* and *Long Good Friday*, television and films which showed tremendous promise which has not been fulfilled. Hayman, seen in 'dirty protest' in the still, continued his involvement with the Special Unit in *Silent Scream* based on the life of inmate Larry Winters.

193

The Campbells stars Malcolm Stoddard as Dr Jones Campbell. Scottish Television's attempt at an historical soap which fits into North American as well as Scottish markets.

Scottish screens will become more probable if external success allows us to expand the domestic production base. But breaking into the fiercely competitive international sales market from the small underfunded base that exists in Scotland today will not be easy.

For producers looking west from the UK, one great problem is that viewers in the biggest television market in the world, the United States, are profoundly insular. Foreign programmes are rarely seen on the American networks – PBS accounts for most of the present two percent non-US share. Looking east, some markets like Germany, Italy and France are large. But European broadcasting is wracked by deregulation and language is still a huge barrier. What chance then for a small country like Scotland with meagre finance, a thin spread of talent, and a stunted production base? The international examples set by the Danes, Irish, Norwegians, Belgians, Dutch or Finns are not encouraging.

Scottish Television has played a major part in encouraging feature films and TV movies in Scotland with this backing for the following stated:

Sense of Freedom, by John McKenzie and Jeremy Isaacs
Gregory's Girl, directed by Bill Forsyth
Ill Fares the Land, directed by Bill Bryden
Comfort and Joy, directed by Bill Forsyth
Double Jeopardy, directed by Jim McCann, *Taggart* 90 TV movie
Killing Dad, produced by Iain Smith with Palace Pictures and British Screen
Love Knot, another *Taggart* TV movie, directed by Peter Barber-Fleming
The Big Man, directed by David Leland from the William McIlvanney novel
Taggart, Movie III, directed by Alan Macmillan

Nine films made by Scots over the past decade. Television through Channel Four has also played a role in most of the other films made in Scotland. Let us therefore look more closely at the economics of buying and selling fiction. As an ITV Network Controller I am a member of the Film Purchase Group which each year views and buys about $60 million of films and series mainly from America for ITV and Channel Four.

The international trade in television drama and movies can be alarming, particularly to producers. But the good news for the broadcasters is that to buy American half-hour comedy in 1990 costs: *Roseanne* and *Cosby*, on Channel Four, $16,000 (about £10,000); *Wonder Years* and *Golden Girls*: $15,000 per episode; *Cheers*, $13,000, for a network screening plus perhaps a repeat run or two. ITV buys jointly with Channel Four who take those comedies that don't rate highly enough for a mass audience channel like ITV. One hour rates are, for example, *Thirtysomething*, Channel Four, $25,000; *L A Law*, ITV,

$22,500; *Baywatch* – a big hit, Californian hunks in trunks, minimal wardrobe costs – maybe $50,000 an episode.

Scottish Television's size, based on advertising revenue, is about 5.5 per cent of the ITV network so that is our share of network costs. So divide by twenty to see how much it costs to fill a half-hour in central Scotland and attract quite a large audience with bought-in, foreign programmes. Those popular sitcoms from the US cost only £500 for a half hour. For quality drama like *LA Law*, £750 an hour.

ITV, like BBC, has a self-denying ordinance that limits foreign programme imports to 16 per cent of transmissions. The new EC suggestion is a 50 per cent maximum so if our UK trade barrier collapses due to deregulation, domestic TV drama production in the UK will become small and even more competitive.

The larger warning is clear. Independent producers sometimes protest when offered the going rate for regional production on TV and BBC which is about £30,000 an hour. That's what we average on in-house production. If this seems low for a market of five million Scottish viewers, protesters should remember those import prices for popular American programmes. A big movie, if it costs ITV $2 million, still only costs us £30,000 an hour in Scotland.

There is more bad news for producers with visions of fortunes to be made in foreign sales – two receipts for overseas sales of *The Campbells*, a 100-episode series which Scottish Television co-produced in Canada. Big sale to Malta: price per episode thirty pounds. The other sale was to Zimbabwe: price per episode – thirty-five pounds.

In this increasingly hostile free-for-all, Scottish producers have one great advantage – England. While English producers – to expand – must fight their way into those tough foreign markets, east and west, Scots producers have, just over the border, an audience ten times larger than their own. The new Broadcasting Act promises 'free and fair' access to the networks which serve the fifty-five million British viewers. And since Scottish producers at present take a very small UK market share, successful expansion into England could double or treble the production of network programming in Scotland if we ever approached parity.

My rough estimates of the present position is as follows:

Total ITV Network Production in 1990   £360m

Scottish Television's Sales	£13.6m
Grampian Television's Sales	£0.4m
Scottish Independents' Sales	Nil
Total for Scotland – 4 per cent -	*£14m*

Total Channel Four Network Commissions for 88/89   £140m

Scottish Television	£1.3m

Mark McManus as Det Chief Inspector Jim Taggart in the *Taggart* TV movie *Double Jeopardy*. The series is a major network success for Scottish Television. As John Caughie said in an earlier article, 'he may be a stereotype, but he's our stereotype'.

Grampian Television	£0.4m
Scottish Independents	£2.8m
Total For Scotland – 3 per cent -	*£4.5m*

Total BBC Network Production £500m

BBC Scotland, Total – 3 per cent	£15m
UK Network	£1,000m
Scottish Network Production	£33.5m
Scotland's Market Share	*3.3%*

Bookie starring Maurice Roeves. A Scottish pilot series which, although it gained over eight million viewers, was not sufficiently popular to make it in network terms.

In the UK context £33 million, three per cent, is not a lot, but ten years earlier network sales were insignificant. In future what might Scotland's proper proportion of UK production in return for providing 10 per cent of UK network viewers? Double the present output and the creation of perhaps a thousand new jobs? If you think ambitions of this scale are inflated, ethnic haverings, compare them with the annual output of English regional companies for the independent networks.

Granada TV	in Manchester	£50m
Yorkshire TV	in Leeds	£45.5m
Central TV	in Birmingham	£62.9m

However, any hope of expansion in Scotland on a significant scale requires a hard-eyed look at the present performance of networked drama. My analysis suggests that we should start by making our fiction programmes more appealing to British audiences. Just three years ago, thirty years late, under IBA pressure, the ITV system began to open up and regions like Scottish were at last allowed to compete albeit on a limited scale, for network access. We made good use of our opportunities.

Leslie Grantham as boxing promoter Eddie Burt in Scottish Television's *Winners and Losers*. Grantham's ex-star status in BBC's *EastEnders* did not carry over to this pilot series. In spite of an audience of 8 million, it was not felt to be the right kind of audience and it was dropped by the network.

In those three years, Scottish Television's network sales have gone from £3 million to £13 million and the great majority of sales are in fiction. You can see that we have outperformed comparable 'regional' ITV companies down south, who had also been shut out of the UK production market.

Scottish	5.5%	13.6m
Anglia	6.6%	7.7m
HTV	6.3%	7.2m
Tyne Tees	3.6%	5.7m

Scottish independent producers have special problems. The £2.8 million in commission from Channel Four in 1988/89 is not impressive spread across some sixty indie companies, almost a tenth of the total sector in Britain. The total commission figure jumped to around £6.3 million in 1990, stimulated by Glasgow's City of Culture year. Let's hope that can be a springboard towards a target of ten per cent of Channel Four's commissions.

The most worrying area for the Scottish independents, and for all of us in the industry in Scotland, is their current failure to break in to ITV while English independent companies in 1990 will get £60 million of commission from ITV. ITV, like most consumer markets, has its distortions, its special niches, and its own currency of 'Audience Research'.

One hundred million pounds of ITV productions will be made by indies in two years time. It will help all of us if Scots indies get a decent share. Scottish Television would like to hear from them as often as we hear from English independents with projects looking for help to penetrate the ITV market.

Soon Scottish independents will also have the chance to compete for twenty five per cent of the BBC's huge two channel output, less populist than ITV but for that reason likely to encourage even more intensive competition from independents south of the border. But throughout the world, the most watched, most traded forms are fictional: movies for TV, occasional single plays, film series, soap serials and sitcoms.

BBC Scotland's current drama output is distinguished but there is still not enough of it on the network, about the same as in 1980. However its creative range is wider than that of Scottish Television because the BBC networks still schedule single plays. The absence of commercial pressure also allows them the freedom to make excellent, expensive series like *Tutti Frutti* which, to our surprise up here, did not attract large audiences down south.

Expansion from Scotland on a significant scale requires that we take a hard look at the present performance of Scottish-made networked drama. We must make our fiction programmes more popular with British audiences.

Take ITV drama first. ITV's experience is that *Inspector Morse, The Bill, Poirot, Coronation Street* or *Taggart* in peak time will beat American movies on BBC or American comedy on Channel Four. ITV policy is therefore to invest at £400,000 an hour to fund popular, quality drama. To be judged a success on ITV at peak time series should get over nine million viewers. Between nine and seven, survival is uncertain. Under seven million in peak and drama series are unlikely to be recommissioned on ITV. By this criteria of popular appeal, Scotland has produced only one big hit over the past ten years, *Taggart*. Now in its seventh year *Taggart* has had a run of thirty-nine one hour episodes and three ninety minute movies for TV. Finding such a winning format in UK network drama is difficult event for big players. Consider the competitors on ITV in recent months and the series cancelled.

Saracen Thirteen one hours from Central TV SAS style derring-do. Averaged seven million – not recommissioned.

TECX Detective series set in Belgium. Thirteen one hours from Central TV, started at seven million and was pulled off halfway through the run when it was at 4 million and still sinking.

Harvey Keitel as US serviceman Carl in BBC's *Down Where The Buffalo Go*. Produced by Andy Park (*Tutti Frutti*) and scripted by Peter McDougall (*Just a Boy's Game, A Sense of Freedom*), *Buffalo* gave full opportunity for one of Keitel's powerful, mannered and troubled performances.

197

Dunroamin Rising with Russell Hunter. Hunter has been a stalwart of Scottish theatre, television and film for decades. His screen career spans from *The Gorbals Story* to such contemporary TV drama as *The Justice Game*.

Yellowthread Street Designer Hong Kong cops, from Yorkshire TV, 8.7 million, respectable but dipping. Not recommissioned.

Capital City Thirteen hours from Thames TV about a bunch of merchant bankers. 7.4 million. Got recommissioned for another run on the basis of its 'good demographics'.

Scottish Television launched two new pilot series in the last two years hoping they might run parallel to *Taggart* on the network.

Bookie 8.4 million. Not quite good enough in this race.

Winners and Losers Again set in Glasgow, 8.0 million. Pretty good but not recommissioned. A rival company's research department said, its demographics showed it had a 'lager lout' audience: young, male, working class!

Other lethally low ratings of ITV series recently all under 7 million.

The Free Frenchman Central TV: expensive period. 6.7 million.

Game Set and Match Granada TV: complex, international locations and Ian Holm as Le Carré's spy. 5.1 million.

Small World Granada TV: witty, intellectual, academic. 4.8 million.

The One Game Central: A mystery thriller written by a Scot, John Brown. 4.7 million.

After The War Granada: Frederick Raphael's biopic about literate intellectuals. 4.3 million.

On ITV, therefore, one Scottish hit and two Scottish misses and a lot of aborted development. Switching to the BBC networks – a selection of their recent popular dramas in 1989 and 1990.

Bergerac	12.7m
Casualty	11.3m
All Creatures Great and Small	10.9m
Howards Way	10.2m
The Ginger Tree	9.9m
Mother Love	8.6m
The Paradise Club	7.7m
The Justice Game, 2	6.4m

Sadly, many of BBC Scotland's recent dramas would not survive in a more competitive market place. *Playing for Real*, a series on Subbuteo skulduggery in Falkirk, averaged 3 million. *Tutti-Frutti*, despite the well deserved raves and great word of mouth – 3.3 million.

Down Where the Buffalo Go	4.8m
The Dark Room	4.7m

Dunroaming Rising	3.8m
Unreported Incident	3.3m
Wholly Healthy	
Glasgow	2.5m
Airbase	2.3m
Normal Service	2.2m
The Party	1.0m

Measured by network standards, BBC Scotland has only moderate ratings success – *The Justice Game*, written by John Brown.

These millions are a crude but still meaningful measure. Network controllers look more at percentage share against other channels and the strength of opposition. And, obviously, you get more millions watching in peak times on winter evenings, than on summer evenings.

Channel Four does not do much series drama. Jeremy Isaacs said he could not afford much and invested in Film on Four instead. Michael Grade, however, is switching towards series with *The Manageress* (4.1m) and *Traffic* with Bill Paterson (3.2m). *Woman of Substance* was Jeremy Isaacs rare smash hit in 1985 – station bookstall stuff, but huge for Channel Four (12.9 million). *Far Pavilions* from Goldcrest, another potboiler (4.8 million) – low by ITV/BBC network standards but, like *The Manageress*, a relative success for Channel Four.

For comparison, a list of the performances of some Scottish-made drama on Channel 4.

Extras A 1987 play by Scottish Television written by Alex Norton, 3.8 million. Good by Channel Four standards.

Blood Red Roses Three parter by John McGrath in 1986, 2.7 million.

Brond 1987 Three parter by Gareth Wardell and Paddy Higson, 2.1 million.

The Steamie Again a play by Scottish, in 1988, 2.0 million. Half its audience were in Scotland so only one million out of fifty million English, Welsh and Irish viewers tuned in.

Border Warfare By John McGrath in 1990, 550,000 viewers. Sadly, even Scots did not watch. Only 67,000 viewers in Scotland for a theatrical performance that clearly did not translate well to television.

Again, they are all worthwhile pieces of work, all fully justified by Channel 4's public service remit, but few propelled by popular appeal.

In Channel Four's *Film on Four*, some flat performances from Scottish movies with a couple of exceptions.

Heavenly Pursuits by Charlie Gormley	5.5m
Another Time, Another Place by Mike Radford	3.8m
Living Apart Together by Charlie Gormley	2.3m
Ill Fares the Land by Bill Bryden	2.1m
Conquest of the South Pole in 1990	
by Gareth Wardell and Gillies McKinnon	1.2m

The new Glasgow. Dennis Lawson as Dominic Rossi, flamboyant Glasgow lawyer who finds himself unmasked in a conspiracy in BBC's *The Justice Game*. A four part thriller written by John Brown, this series successfully hit on mood and style in terms of changing perceptions of the Glasgow of Garden Festivals and Cities of Culture.

Hero by Barney Platts Mills (first Scottish Gaelic feature, 1982)   0.4m

There are some miracles of economy in that list, some heroic acts of patronage, all worthwhile in their way, but again too few with popular appeal.

Last year at Scottish Television we spend hundreds of thousands of pounds on script development. Out of a dozen new projects – most won't get made, but we don't know which. No independent producer in Scotland can yet afford to invest speculatively on that scale. BBC Scotland probably cannot afford it either. Indeed, I doubt if Scottish Television can afford it! But you develop or die. Let me explain from present experience what is involved for a small company like ours. Working with Iain Smith, a Scottish feature film producer in London, Scottish Television Films Enterprises has in development now:

Rough Trade with Liz Lochead and Gillies McKinnon. A S Neill (a biopic about the old Scots prophet of free schools) by Kara Wilson, with Michael Relph producing.
McRory's Children, an adventure set in the Highlands, being developed by Iain Smith and David Reilly.
Oktober, a thriller by best selling novelist Stephen Gallagher, Mike Newell directing.

200

Hero was the first Gaelic feature film. Set in a mythical Scotland it was directed by Barney Platts-Mills.

Television projects include:

a three or four part life of Ingrid Bergman with Danish independents Nordisk who made *Babette's Feast,* called *As Time Goes By.*
Dream Patrol thirteen part animation series with a Scots graduate of the National Film School. Animation is an area of rapid growth in Europe but the money for the *Dream Patrol* would come from PBS in America if our £50,000, three-minute pilot gets an ITV commission.

Television series are just as costly:

Scotia Nostra written by Glasgow's Murray Smith, three part comedy gangster series, turned down by ITV, written off at £50,000.
Ramensky, a three or four part series by Alex Norton about the legendary Glasgow safe-blower and his wartime exploits. We actually had an ITV commission but late delivery mean we lost the 1990 ITV slot and competition is now a lot tougher in 1991. Another £50,000 worth of good work looking for a home.
The Advocates, another three part series written by Alma Cullen to be directed by Peter Barber-Fleming. About two women lawyers

201

Take the High Road was launched in 1980 and remained sufficiently successful in network audience to see it into the '90s. It is being re-vamped to appeal to a younger audience, not without controversy. Morag Stewart (Jeannie Fisher), Fiona Cunningham (Caroline Ashley) and Isabel Blair (Eileen McCallum) are some of the mainstays of Scottish Television's main soap.

Edinburgh. Another development which, thankfully, we will put into production.

And there are a dozen other projects, some with independents attached. Scots producers must do what any ambitious business in this position would do make things the consumers, our UK viewers, will watch in numbers large enough to pay the bill. A start can be made by analysing the characteristics of the different markets in ITV, Channel Four and BBC 1 and 2 and on satellite. Then, the expensive bit, invest in research and development of new products working with creative talents with expertise in popular programming. The best growth strategy for Scottish drama producers is to focus on making quality programmes with popular appeal for the UK. It won't be easy, it certainly won't be cheap, but success will give us the income to build a more durable competitive production base in Scotland. One caveat: if we succeed in professionalising our approach to wider markets, in creating more popular series, it should not be at the expense of indigenous Scottish drama. The challenge is to expand beyond our borders, while simultaneously finding ways of telling stories to ourselves that don't need the approval of UK network patrons.

Telling stories to local audiences should also encourage the craft of writing, breeding confidence from familiarity. Experimentation at home could help offset the homogenising pressures of the competitive international markets. Most importantly, it would serve our audience by encouraging a discourse that is more distinctively Scottish. A decade ago there was more local space for television drama in Scotland than there is now. For BBC Scotland 1980 was a memorably productive year with some classics initiated during the tenure of Alistair Hetherington as Controller. Some series from that year were *Walls of Jericho, The Treachery Game, Square Mile of Murder, Cloud Howe* and *The House with Green Shutters*. Single plays included *The Silly Season, Her Mother's House and The Good Time Girls*. There were also two 'opt outs' commissioned just for Scotland. These are dramatic options which have disappeared. *Andrina* was a story adapted from George Mackay Brown by Bill Forsyth. *The Drystane Dyker* was by James Duthie.

Scottish Television back in 1980 had one single play, the ITV network *Between the Covers* and the wonderful six part *Charles Endell Esquire* with Iain Cutherbertson. *Airport Chaplain*, a religious drama series, (a rare genre which reminds me of the brainstorming sessions trying to combine action-adventure with authority figures and producing titles like *Soho Vet* and *Underwater Rabbi*) never flew again.

1980 also saw the first 52 episodes of a new drama serial for the network, *Take the High Road*. Now approaching its 800th edition this Lomond-side 'soap' is the most consistently popular Scottish-made programme (twice weekly it takes a 60 per cent audience share) and it has become the biggest dramatic enterprise ever undertaken in Scotland. But as well as launching *Take the High Road* in 1980, Scottish Television like BBC Scotland was also making local dramas – half a dozen hours called *Preview*.

There were, in all, six series of *Preview* – 33 half hour plays. Scottish actors like Fulton McKay, Alex Norton, Maureen Beattie, Phyllis Logan, John Gordon-Sinclair, Chic Murray, Dorothy Paul and Maurice Roeves, appeared in *Previews* between network or fill contracts. Writers got a chance on *Preview*: Michael Wilcox, Janice Hally, Alan Spence, James Grahan, Catherine Lucy Czerkawska and a young Edinburgh scribbler, Glen Chandler, who went on to write *Taggart*.

Purely Scottish productions like these were lost in the otherwise welcome advance into networking in the eighties which produced the *Taggarts, Tutti Fruttis, Blood Red Roses* and *The Steamie*. It is perhaps time to bring them back. A comparison from across the sea is illuminating. Ireland, poor but free, is caught in a similar dilemma over the production of fiction. Radio Telefis Eireann, the state broadcaster, and Irish drama producers have conducted a spirited debate that should concern Scots producers of films and television drama.

By the mid-eighties RTE's drama policy was being widely criticised. Critics said RTE had been seduced by prospects of co-production, that they had turned away from the gritty, messy problems of contemporary reality in favour of glossy art house features, safe adaptations and soft-centred nostalgia. Sadly, critics alleged, most producers with dramatic stories to tell about Ireland worked in current affairs, not in drama. So away with costly, reactionary film and on to radical raw video the argument ran. Single plays were demanded which attacked relevant social issues more quickly than lumbering star studded vehicles. Local Irish drama was also seen as a ladder for home grown talent, whereas

The Steamie was a very successful stage play which transferred well to the small screen. Adapted by Tony Roper from his own play, *The Steamie* was an affectionate and funny look at an important but vanished part of Scottish working class women's lives. The publicity still shows Kate Murphy, Eileen McCallum, Sheila Donald and Dorothy Paul.

co-production was likened to a greasy pole with a platform at the top accessible only to established talent. Actors Equity demanded a policy of home produced drama for Irish screens, written, directed, performed and fully controlled by Irish people.

The Irish even launched a brave, doomed experiment, Community Access drama. Today their problems are largely unresolved and they are denied most of the opportunities which Scots have through their UK network connections. Be assured, Scotland produces a wider, deeper, better range of drama than Ireland. However we might address some of the issues RTE debated with such fervour, because as one commentator argued, 'drama is of particular importance in its power to make sense of the world, to purge the soul and illuminate contemporary social problems through the ritualised process of public enactment.' Well, up to a point. Without going that far we might ask in Scotland: where is the dramatic treatment of poll tax agitation? Where is the satirical script about 'cultural subsidy junkies'? Where is the hoot about Glasgow hype? In the year of the Grand Slam and the World Cup where is the woman writer psychoanalysing Scotsmen's childlike obsession with balls?

The Irish experience demonstrates that television drama with traditional crewing and international production values is simply too
expensive for most small countries. In Scotland, as elsewhere, we
now have the benefit of cheaper, more responsive equipment and
more flexible working arrangements. Another encouraging factor is
the emergence of a range of young talents in Scotland. The growth of
the independent sector encourages that process. Troublesome talent can
no longer be completely shut out by the gatekeepers in a broadcasting
duopoly. While it is essential for the growth of network production
in the future to maintain a critical mass of technical expertise and
resources of the kind we have at Scottish Television or BBC Scotland,
most producers, writers, and directors with something to say need the
freedom to follow opportunities. Because it lacked network production
centres of any consequence Scotland in the past could never sustain the
freelance talent which made much of the premium drama programming
in England. The growth of the independent sector will help Scotland
compete in the 1990s when the present politicking and lobbying
becomes less relevant than working together. In recent years too
much creative energy has had to be diverted into setting up produc-

A Wholly Healthy Glasgow was a BBC
television version of Iain Heggie's
prize-winning play. Set in the Adonis
Health Club it featured Gerard Kelly, Paul
Higgins and Tom Watson as Charley
Hood, Murdo Caldwell and Donald Dick.
Murdo has visions of a 'wholly healthy
Glasgow' by 1990 but Charley is more
interested in the punters' money and
Donald in something called 'apres
massage'.

205

tion business or rowing over the convulsions in public broadcasting policy.

To conclude in the 1990s, in the decade of deregulation, the challenge for Scottish film and television producers is to move simultaneously in and out. Turning out into that UK market to use zest and craft to push our share up from a meagre 3.5 percent, increasing our share of the British market by making fiction programmes more British viewers want to watch.

Turning in towards the home audience, where our Scottishness is not a *problem* but a *priority*, in an attempt to make our own drama on our own terms.

In the 1990s let us see if we can find the resources and originality to tell ourselves some lively stories, stir some controversy and perhaps expose some home truths. If we don't work together now after three decades of ineffectual division then television in Scotland will atrophy into a parochial, impoverished, service. If there is no strong base for television there will be no real future for Scottish feature film either.

Declarations of Independence

Robin McPherson

> . . . it is a question not of in-dependence but of dependence and inter-dependence . . . From such a perspective it becomes possible to begin unravelling the basic premises of 'independence': to ask not 'How independent?' but rather 'Dependent on what?' (Blanchard and Harvey: *The Post-War Independent Cinema* – in Curran and Porter: *British Cinema History* p226)

In the nineties the term 'independent producer' has come to be associated with the 700-odd UK production companies, 70 or so of them in Scotland, making programmes for Channel Four, the BBC and ITV, and who are not owned or controlled by any of the latter. Before Channel Four existed an independent producer was a person or a company making (or trying to make) films outside of the few remaining film studios and, generally, without any fixed financial backing.

The 'independent cinema', on the other hand, has a wider meaning, connotations of being independent in a larger sense, or as Blanchard and Harvey put it, independent of 'something':

> . . . that 'something' is the dominant products, practices and values of the mainstream film industries in England (sic) and the United States.

That sense of independent as implying a wholesale alternative to the dominant forms of cinema and, latterly, television, was for a long time associated with a desire to challenge and create an alternative to the mainstream film industry; to the institutions of broadcasting; and to the narrative and other conventions of both film and television. Now the connotations of 'independent producer' are very different, at best encompassing a wider range of people, practices and product, at worst epitomising the Thatcherite agenda-setting that characterised the eighties.

It's a long way from this:

> Because it can be done, it has to be done. Film is expensive, very expensive, the commerce fucks up the art and will go on doing so. But we can cope with that if we use our energy right. We can make our own approaches to industry, local authorities,

207

Dancers, directed by Brian Crumlish in 1980. A film which looked at the lives and performances of strippers and go-go dancers in Edinburgh. The male dancer in the still is entertaining a specially gathered audience of female dancers, quite successfully it seems.

government bodies, this that and the other trust, individuals. Do it ourselves and we can use the profits from the films we have to make our bread and butter survival to finance the films we have to make for the other kind of survival. But we have to do it together. For starters we're all members of the same union. (Douglas Eadie, producer/writer: 'We can't say meanwhile any more', *Scottish International* September 1973)

To this:

Walk into Soho's Groucho club on any weekday evening and you will see a collection of ambitious young men and women earnestly discussing their 'projects', the appalling prices of designer clothes and second homes in Shropshire. It is a pound to a peanut that they will be making their money in the independent television business. Though they would drown in their Mexican lagers rather than admit it, they are Thatcher's children through and through: beneficiaries of – and storm-troopers for – her relentless attacks on the BBC and ITV networks. ('Thatcherites of the small screen', *Economist* Feb 3 1990)

If the *Economist* is to be believed independent producers have gone from being members of the same union to being members of the same club. Well, perhaps in London, but in Scotland things are different aren't they?

Scottish film production has historically, in the main, depended on commercial sponsorship and state subsidy. As the poor relation of a British film industry struggling to sustain a home-market and fight off the dominance of Hollywood, Scottish filmmaking from the fifties to the seventies was struggle for survival. While filmmaking in the metropolitan south and, increasingly, in the English regions began to address a range of aesthetic and political agendas, and in that sense began to diversify into a number of distinct 'independent practices', Scotland's filmmaking community, smaller and more homogeneous, was, by the mid-seventies, still struggling to find any kind of consistent expression, far less to explore the creative and organisational frontiers that were being explored by the avant-garde, Arts Labs, film co-ops, Free Cinema, structuralists and so on.

In that sense the Scottish scene of the seventies was very different to England, where the existence of both 'mainstream' independent and 'alternative' filmmaking reflected the relative opulence of wider commercial opportunities on the one hand and greater public funding on the other. Even in the run-up to the launch of Channel Four, part child of the 'independent' film movement, part child of Tory aspirations to the free market in television, Scotland's filmmakers were addressing a different set of concerns, influenced as much by the devolution debate as by the imminent prospect of the fourth channel. Despite vigorous efforts by a few notable groups and individuals to mobilise a cultural debate about what *kind* of Scottish cinema we might aspire to, what *kind* of television Scotland might produce, the enduring questions remained how to sustain *any* kind of filmmaking and how to develop television production per se. In this respect, as in many others, Scotland's independent filmmakers inhabited (and still do) an underdeveloped country, strong in national aspirations, starved of the resources to realise them.

From London's Cinema Action and The Other Cinema to Amber Films in Newcastle, the beginning of the seventies gave voice to diverse strands of independent filmmaking throughout England, a movement which found collective expression in the Independent Filmmakers Association. Established in 1974, the IFA promoted independent filmmaking and lobbied the BFI, Regional Arts Associations and played a key role in the creation of Channel Four's initial policy of support for independent film. The IFA never, however, had a presence in Scotland. A reflection, perhaps, of the absence of the constituency which, until its demise 1990, it represented. On the other hand the Association of Independent Producers, representing the more commercial end of independent filmmaking, particularly those engaged in low and medium budget feature production, did have a presence in Scotland in the late seventies, indicating the presence of a more

Channel 4's *Into Nicaragua*, directed by Brian Crumlish of Cormorant Films over 1985–7, looked at Scottish medical aid in the beleaguered Central American country. The still shows a young woman Sandinista who was providing protection for refugees near Mulukuku.

Cameraman Phil Shingler and director David Halliday look serious and look the part in their battledress for the Channel 4 documentary on the militarisation of Scotland of Scotland, *Northern Front*. An Edinburgh Film Workshop Trust production.

mainstream oriented filmmaking community.

The critical mass of filmmaking, concentrated in London but spreading to other parts of England, facilitated the emergence of an 'independent' cinema, one which attempted to integrate production, distribution and exhibition and break the stranglehold of the vertically integrated commercial cinema by creating a parallel structure. With funding from Regional Arts Associations, the BFI and other bodies, these groups emerged in contrast to the mainstream film industry with clearly separate identities. At one level they were attempting to substitute dependence on the market for dependence on the local and national state, a strategy which in the early seventies seemed to have great potential. In 1973, for example, the ACTT adopted a policy of nationalising the film industry and two years later the Terry Committee was set up by the Labour Government to consider the future of the British film industry.

Scotland had, in a sense, no mainstream industry to spawn an 'alternative'. It had a collection of small production companies and freelance personnel who relied on direct and indirect sponsorship, a relationship which could at best aspire to being one of 'relative independence', as one of the leading producers of the time recalls:

> . . . looking back they seem very innocent times. Films of Scotland tried to operate the idea of having a body between the sponsor and the film-maker to act as a buffer between the two, hopefully to help the sponsor to think as much like a patron as possible as opposed to commercial sponsor but at the same time try and break that direct contact where the sponsor was leaning on the filmmaker's shoulder and saying a shot of this and a shot of that and the manager's house . . . (Laurence Henson)

210

Scotland's filmmakers in the sixties and seventies remained economically and creatively dependent on a mix of freelance work for BBC
and STV and the Films of Scotland/HIDB breadline, leavened by the
occasional Children's Film Foundation feature.

> . . . you'd get your annual handout from Films of Scotland and
> a 'Yes, OK, well IFA have done a road movie this year, so they
> can do a bridge movie next year. All the companies got their wee
> handout, were supposed to be content with that and go away and
> make it and then come back to Films of Scotland to do the next
> one. And there was a desire, I think fairly generally, to make films
> with more substance than that. But at the same time people were
> learning a craft, and had learned it really pretty well. (Paddy
> Higson, independent producer and founder of Blackcat Studios
> in Glasgow)

In 1976 a key event, Film Bang, brought Scotland's film producers
and freelance personnel together in an attempt to raise the profile of
Scottish film-makers and address the terms of their dependency on
such a limited range of finance.

In 1976 filmmakers were still very much dependent on the sponsored
film and, consequently, the space to develop a more personal, more
creative practice or to assert the idea of a national cinema remained
very limited:

John Sessions in the eponymous *Gramsci*
written by Doug Eadie who co-produced it
with director Mike Alexander. A Pelicula
Films production for Channel 4, *Gramsci*
wrought a serious performance from
Sessions who is best known for his comedy
routines. The documentary sections were
shot in location in Italy but production
designer Andy Harris recreated Gramsci's
prison in Bari in the studio at Blackcat in
Glasgow so convincingly that many
viewers thought that they too were made on
location.

> The Highlands and Islands Development Board played a very
> important part and also a very sad part, they meant everyone
> could buy their equipment and make films for them, but it was
> still very much the marvellous scenics – waiting for the dawn
> to come up and then everything cemented together with purple
> prose by Adam Maclean. (Murray Grigor, writer and director)

But despite the continuing need to secure a throughput of work from
Government and industry, the cultural options were aired during Film
Bang:

> There were actually two quite distinct groups within it. There
> was the group that was wanting to be far more political, which I
> think was probably led by Doug Eadie. There was the other side
> of it which was in a sense trying to give ourselves a bit more of a
> profile, and a bit more public awareness . . . there were all sorts
> of things that actually came out of it, because the Training Trust
> came along after that. The Production Fund started up in a very
> small way, and we as the filmmakers began to infiltrate the Film
> Council committees. (Paddy Higson)

Film Bang was closely followed by a special issue of *New Edinburgh
Review* enigmatically titled *Scottish Cinema?*. This blast of analysis and

rhetoric was the nearest Scotland at that time had come to a filmmakers' manifesto.

Colin Young, Director of the National Film School, wrote of Film Bang in the *Review*:

> . . . in a country the size of Scotland it shouldn't be possible to get all the filmmakers together in one room.
>
> In all industrialised countries there is by now a lot of sponsored documentaries, educational film production and some work in advertising. What is so odd about Scotland is that there is so little work by film artists, so little personal film narrative – whether in documentary or in fiction . . .

One expression of the gap between Scotland's independent filmmakers and the other elements of independent film culture had been their uneasy relationship with the Edinburgh International Film Festival. In large part its 'constituency' has been composed more of London-based film theorists than Scottish-based filmmakers – reflecting, amongst other things, the Festival's commitment in the seventies to the development of film theory and criticism.

> . . . we always used to bemoan the fact that not a lot of them seemed to be interested in the festival, maybe because the very strength that it was gaining on the theoretical front was anathema to these Scottish practical filmmakers who wanted to make films. Some of the older guard couldn't see where all this was going. And some of the younger ones weren't interested in theory at all and couldn't see how the politics of all that could inform their own lives or affect their own work in some way. (Jim Hickey, Director of the Festival 1982 – 1989)

However, while the film 'theorists' were appealing for more involvement by producers in the wider debates concerning film culture, at least some of the latter identified too much culture and too little ambition – amongst both filmmakers and the funding institutions – as a more pressing problem:

> The major element that is missing from Scottish film thinking is ambition. Those who are best placed to help us raise our sights (ie the Scottish Film Council, and Films of Scotland), have consistently fought shy of film production – preferring to dabble in film culture or in sponsored documentary.
>
> Film makers themselves are guilty of the same lack of drive. (Steve Clark-Hall, producer)

But even this critique relied on state intervention as a key component for any development of film in Scotland:

We must look to the national funding operations, merchant banks, the National Film Finance Corporation, the British Film Institute, until such time as a Film Board, or a revitalised Films of Scotland comes into being.

Where Film Bang and the *Scottish Cinema* edition of NER put the case for developing Scotland's embryonic film-industry in more politically neutral terms, the 1977 Cinema in a Small Country conference tried to raise questions of Scotland's cultural identity and the need for a truly Scottish cinema, not just Scottish filmmaking.

> The Labour Government was talking about restructuring the British film industry and bringing together a kind of arts arm and industry arm and with that and devolution in the air we thought it was time to get a Scottish chunk of it – it was a piece of opportunism really. Just the fact that it happened was important rather than what was said during the course of it. But it was all predicated on devolution and the one thing we thought would come out of devolution would be vastly increased spending on the arts which would include film and everything would be hunky dory. (Douglas Eadie)

But in a foretaste of the years to come, the simple need for growth undermined the drive to address a broad cultural agenda:

> . . . we were all of us fairly wary of one another and to that extent the consensus that we achieved was all at the level of the need for structure and finance rather than much discussion of the culture of it or the themes – it wasn't film-led, it wasn't like the French *nouvelle vague*. (Douglas Eadie)

Cinema in a Small Country did, however, have some impact on the body then most likely to take on the role of funding film production in Scotland, the Scottish Film Council:

> . . . that was an event that crystalised the change, the realisation that there was a generation of filmmakers in Scotland who were not simply going to follow in the tracks of previous generations, the small companies that had specialised in making industrial films, educational films and so on. That was partly a quite conscious ideological movement within Scottish filmmaking by people like Douglas Eadie and Charlie Gormley but it also foreshadowed the change, the death of the short film for the cinema, video taking over a medium for corporate or educational work. Looking back I blush that it never occurred to me (prior to 1977) that there were Scottish filmmakers. (John Brown, then Assistant Director, SFC)

The opportunities offered by the impending fourth channel seem to have

been overshadowed in Scotland by the prospect of feature production at
last becoming more than a forlorn dream:

> I think older, more senior ones like Charlie Gormley and Bill
> Forsyth, still saw cinema as the thing. Others including myself
> were quite happy to work in 16mm with a greater likelihood of
> getting stuff on television. (Douglas Eadie)

Yet the reality of independent production in Scotland, as opposed to
the cinematic aspirations of Forsyth, Gormley, Smith and others, was
of a group of producers working mainly in documentary, corporate film
and video, commercials and instructional film – modes of production
with more in common with television than feature film production.

It seems that it was only with the 1979 failure of the devolution
campaign to secure a Scottish Assembly that Scottish producers woke
up to the true potential of the fourth channel. And with a Conservative
Government newly installed the prospects of any major extension to
state support for the cinema seemed a long way off.

The arrival of Channel Four in 1982 was indeed a watershed in
the development of independent production in Scotland. Having been
slow to spot its potential Scotland's independent producers made up
for lost time when it came to chasing commissions:

The Jazz Apple is a Pelicula Films
production for Channel 4. Two one-hour
documentaries, these films starred Joe
Temperley who was born in Lochgelly and
is based in New York. A baritone sax player
whose career stretches from Buck Clayton
to Wynton Marsalis, Temperley made an
excellent and respected guide to the New
York jazz scene.

> I think right at the beginning of C4 there was an important
> sense that C4 needed Scotland as much as Scotland needed
> C4 to be seen to be fulfilling its own brief. Outside of London
> Scotland had the biggest concentration of film and TV people,
> independents, certainly in terms of ACTT membership that was
> the case. So contracts came quite fast, for example, Mike and I
> got the thirteenth contract, for *How to be Celtic*; Murray Grigor
> got a very early contract for *Scotch Myths*. (Douglas Eadie)

Combined with the success of Bill Forsyth's first two features and
signs that others were going to continue the momentum of feature
production (Charlie Gormley; Mike Radford) the first wave of Channel
Four contracts contributed to an air of great optimism and a relatively
high-profile debate about the future of film and television in Scotland.
The debate had two dimensions. One was the continued pressure for the
extension of film funding directed at the institutions – the Scottish Film
Council and the Scottish Arts Council. The other was a cultural debate
about representations of Scotland in the cinema and on television (their
history and future prospects) – fueled by the new channel's distinctive
remit to innovate and represent previously marginalised interests.

On the film side the anomalous position that the SFC, with a remit to
promote film culture in Scotland, had no money to do so in terms of film
production, and the SAC had no such remit but did have some money,
of a sort, became the focus for a push to set up a joint film-funding
body. The SFC's 1979 decision to put up £5000 for production was

Mr Sinclair, the Airdrie bingo caller, the character who introduces Big Star in a Wee Picture's *Halfway to Paradise*. A tongue-in-cheek approach to popular music made this show a welcome addition to TV for young people.

a 'symbolic' move to press the SED and the SAC into supporting a fund. The end result was that the SAC and SFC set up a combined film panel and in 1982 the hybrid body established between the two was replaced by a new organisation, the Scottish Film Production Fund, which took over the existing budget, later swelled by Channel Four money in 1986.

It could be argued that the high hopes of 1979-82, centred around the creation of a Scottish feature-making industry, obscured the cultural options facing the existing industry, such as it was, and diverted attention from the breadth of activity in which independent producers, whether by choice or necessity, were engaged – both their strengths and their weaknesses.

Between Film Bang in 1976 and the arrival of Channel Four in 1982 a consensus of sorts had been established around the idea that Scotland's filmmaking potential should be sold on its merits, without the need for an explicit positive discrimination on either cultural or economic grounds. This assertion of independence was mobilised in relation to Channel Four but echoed earlier efforts to establish a Film Production Fund:

. . . when Channel Four was coming into being a group took a very specific decision not to try and go for any kind of Scottish quota because we were convinced that would quickly lead to a kind of ghetto. In exactly the same way a couple of years before that, when the SFC in its embarrassment at its having no money came to us and said would we join them in a campaign to have the BFI production fund in London apportioned so that 13% or

215

whatever came up to Scotland we turned that down, again because we felt that was ghettoising us. (Douglas Eadie)

In both instances the idea of a complex, shifting sense of independence in which dependence on a particular institution or form of support is acknowledged in dynamic terms, as something to be used rather than suffered was displaced by the notion of independence in a meritocracy, bravely ignoring the historical imbalances and distortions implicit in the structures of both cinema and television:

> People didn't want to be marginalised, that's one of the reasons people turned the quota idea down, there was also the other considerable factor which was that Jeremy Isaacs, a Scot, was running Channel Four and was violently opposed to any kind of quotas. What he was saying every time we had meetings was don't go for quotas go for the bread and butter, put in more proposals for finance programmes, long running series, which will allow you to set up an industry. (Anita Oxburgh, producer)

Others were less hostile to quotas, however:

> This is where I part company with the rest of the people working in film in Scotland. They decided they wanted to be macho and stand up with the rest of them in London and try it. It was probably the biggest mistake and probably shows the lack of political acumen behind it, but that's very typical about the arts in Scotland – they do lack political clout and acumen. I have a certainty that what we should have had was an S4C. (Gareth Wardell, producer/director)

The underlying disquiet amongst Scottish producers evident by 1987 mirrored, to a degree, the growing campaign by the Independent Programme Producers Association (IPPA) to get the Government to institute a quota for independent production on BBC and ITV. The campaign was couched as much in the language of the free market as of cultural diversity, a (successful) strategy to appeal to both a wide cross-section of independent producers and the public at the same time as the free market ideologues in the conservative Government. Robin Crichton argues that the access debate was initiated by Scottish producers:

> I led a delegation down to the House of Commons which actually was the start of the whole independent debate. It was pre-Peacock and we said we want the right to work in our own country, we have no access to BBC or STV, these are the kind of programmes we make and they were absolutely astonished.
> The arguments were cultural, industrial and quite economic as well. I said 'look, we're doing all this kind of work, and we're denied

the domestic market, that is wrong' and the MPs were shocked. They didn't realise it, and it resulted in the adjournment debate, which got all-party support, for giving us access to BBC and STV and within eighteen months of that debate, then the legislation went through, the 25% deregulated production. (Robin Crichton, director)

The arrival of Channel Four, the access debate and now the Broadcasting Act, have all put independent production for television high on the political agenda. Even producers whose primary interest is in the production of feature films acknowledge that television, or at least television money, is crucial to the future of film production – if only because a throughput of television production is crucial to sustaining a viable core of producers, technicians and facilities in Scotland.

At the same time the technology, economics and politics of the audio-visual industries are challenging the conventional model of independent production – a cottage industry of individuals and small companies whose primary commitment is to pursuing a certain notion of creative independence which, in Scotland for example, has been dominated by documentary filmmakers producing for television and a small group of (occasional) feature-producers.

The independent sector in Scotland however, like that of the rest of the UK, faces great change and the newer generations of independent producers are in many instances pursuing a quite different agenda to that suggested by Film Bang, Cinema in a Small Country or Scotch Reels. A crucial issue is the question of whether a range of small, politically and culturally diverse production companies can be sustained in the midst of pressure towards conglomeration and 'lowest common denominator' production. The downside of pressing for a 'free market' in communications is that the market may reject the regional, national and cultural diversity that many independent producers aspire to:

> Well that's what everyone says, that that's how its going to be, that the era of the two man company is over, that the only way is the larger grouping . . . (Douglas Eadie)

> I think that that's true – I think that as companies they won't survive but the individuals probably will. I think the astonishing thing about the film industry that you're looking at now is that a good proportion of them have been around for a very long time. You'd be hard put to get that proportion in London or indeed anywhere else. (Penny Thomson, producer/director of the Scottish Film Production Fund)

But as television production becomes a substantial 'cultural industry which, like publishing, encompasses everything from small back-room independents' to multi-national conglomerates, what wider definitions

Muriel Gray chats to Glenda Jackson in *Walkie Talkie*, a Gallus Besom and Skyline Film and Television Production. A talk show with an interesting format, *Walkie Talkie* involved the gallus besom Gray walking in a location chosen by the interviewee and chatting about both place and career.

of independence can persist beyond survival in the market-place?

Historically independent producers in Scotland have played a prominent role in the film and television union ACTT, partly reflecting the mixed identity of independent producers who can be employer one day and employee tomorrow. As a consequence the union in Scotland, as elsewhere, has been instrumental in promoting not just the interests of film technicians, producers and directors as workers, but also in raising the wider concerns of Scottish film culture at every level from training to funding. Thus Film Bang in 1976 represented the linking of a cultural and industrial agenda:

> . . . the union ACTT was an important aspect in that because in breaking away from the Films of Scotland code we were all a bit exposed and individually and collectively pretty weak and so it was important to become unionised so we were pushing through the ACTT recognition as a Scottish regional shop which enabled us to have the weight of the union behind us when we were fighting people like Forsyth Hardy. So Film Bang was in a sense the demonstration of that. (Douglas Eadie)

However as the nature of independent production in Scotland changes, many producers now identify more closely with IPPA, the Trade Association of independent producers, than with ACTT. It has become the principal vehicle for lobbying broadcasters, local and central Government, and as a contact point for other bodies from the SDA to the STUC.

To the degree that IPPA Scotland reflects the different political and cultural agendas of independent producers it is a site of both consensus and conflict – a reflection perhaps of the complex identity of independent producers who criss-cross the boundary between commerce and culture, capital and labour, dependence and independence. As an organisation which represents the collectivity of independent producers IPPA is faced with the task of constructing a broad consensus amongst a diversity of members, creating a 'we' to present to the outside world. One contribution to a 1988 debate within IPPA illustrates this tension well:

> So who's *we*? Again, in order to find out we must be more prepared than we have been to test our self-definition and aspirations/ambitions against how the public sees us and against what (if anything) it expects/demands of us. If we don't or can't, the carrying on as before (the pursuit of the deal) may be a more honest expression of what we are both as individuals and as an association – than the pursuit of the ideal (which) is our job, our work, to make films and programmes that reflect the values and concerns of the society we live in . . . In our relationship with the Scottish public we are not keepers . . . and we're not servants: we are members, responsible members . . . Professional and trade definitions and agreements must flow from that kind of basic statement of social position.

An organisation like IPPA struggle, however, to rise above the common denominator of economic self-interest:

> I don't think we've really got there yet, to get the kind of collective lobbying together with any kind of consensus – certainly in terms beyond the most basic of needing more money for Scotland. (Douglas Eadie)

Another contribution to the debate defines independent producers as:

> . . . those who have stayed outwith the established duopolies because of a desire to remain more closely in touch with their own communities . . . in order to make programmes dictated by a more individual philosophy than that propagated by these authorities . . . It is important that we begin to define ourselves as representatives of our society with a responsibility towards it.

In one sense both these contributions are arguing against a notion of independence which divorces the individual producer from the wider community – an idea which has never found a secure home in the film world and which television has traditionally interpreted in terms of the Public Service Broadcasting ideal – with all the problems that entails. It is an idea which the Film and Video Workshop movement took to its heart in the seventies and has since attempted to institutionalise through the creation of a network of non-profit organisations which, while less dependent on commercial pressures, remained dependent on a mix of public funding and support from Channel Four.

Workshops in Scotland have, like the rest of the independent sector, suffered from the same chronic lack of resources which has debilitated the development of a wider Scottish independent film culture. In 1990, as Channel Four, the BFI and other funders pull out of the Workshop sector it has had to redefine its independence, a process which involves retaining an independent cultural practice whilst acknowledging the need to engage more with the market.

Having struggled in the sixties to sustain any kind of filmmaking sector, Scotland's independent producers spent the seventies engaged in an effort to establish mechanisms of public support for film production which would allow the development of a Scottish film industry, using public funds to seed commercial productions and develop indigenous talent. In the sense that their previous dependence on the sponsored film would be replaced by a greater degree of creative freedom, there was indeed a move towards some aesthetic independence, even if the price of that would have been the creation of a new dependence on a quasi-state funding system. The partial success of that strategy in the early eighties coincided precisely, however, with a decline in public funding of film and television and the end of any prospect of devolution.

Faced with the prospect of a virtual standstill in the public arena, the arrival of Channel Four was welcome relief providing as it did an initial boost in both economic and, to a degree, creative terms. Despite reservations many independent producers adopted, or at least accepted, the more industrial and market-led identity that the changing political and economic climate of the eighties fostered and which is accelerating into the nineties. A consensus of some sort was established around the economic agenda, mobilised now, for example, in efforts to establish a Scottish Screen Commission charged with developing Scotland's film and television industry infrastructure – from training to production and distribution.

Now, however, the burst of growth in the eighties and the optimistic air which it engendered is once again open to question as the cultural and political issues resurface. Can the market provide a space for creative innovation in the age of multi-channel TV? What kind of cinema can a small country like Scotland support, if any? Where can new filmmakers develop and experiment? What role can or will Government, both locally and centrally, play in the development of a national film and television culture beyond intervention in the industrial infrastructure driven by commercial criteria? And how can independent producers (or at least those who wish to) redefine their independence in ways which allow them to remain closely in touch with their own communities?

These are not a million miles from the questions asked by Scotland's independent producers in the early seventies. Aside from honourable exceptions such as the 1988 'Television in a Small Country', the process of answering these questions has barely begun.

Scotland, Europe and Identity

Philip Schlesinger

Today we face an unprecedented challenge to long-standing patterns of cultural and political identity in Europe. The confrontation between two politico-economic systems that has characterised the post-war years has broken down before our very eyes.

Nothing could have symbolised this more dramatically than the breaches – both literal and powerfully metaphorical – that appeared in the Berlin Wall in November 1989. None who have lived through the Cold War, and recall its chilling moments of high confrontation, could fail to be moved by the currents of democratisation in Eastern Europe. However, by the same token, no one who remembers the disastrous circumstances that led up to the post-war partition of Europe could fail to be concerned about what kind of new order is to be constructed, and how.

For European cinema and television, the issues raised by current changes on our continent offer a rich seam of investigation both for fiction and documentary production. For those living and working in Scotland, where the political dimension of nationhood and national identity is once again firmly on the agenda, but in quite a new continental context, it is difficult to imagine that a far-reaching cultural engagement with the questions to be posed in the coming decade can be long avoided.

Pressure Points

The following pressure points are of particular note in our perceptions of change in Europe:

the accelerating (if at times uneven) attempt to bring about economic and political integration in the European Community, a process which also has implications for culture;

the complete disintegration of the socialist camp in the wake of the Gorbachev reform programme.

in both East and West the question of the nation and its right to self-expression has forcefully re-entered the political agenda, although in different ways.

the acceleration of European Community integration has provoked questions about national sovereignty and democratic representation. But these questions do not stop with the existing state system. In Scotland, as is well known, far-reaching questions about the precise constitutional structure of the United Kingdom seem now to be unavoidable. Whether we talk of a Scottish Assembly or of 'Scotland in Europe' matters considerably in terms of the scope of the changes implied, but neither home rule nor national separatism can be dismissed as trivial in its impact upon the British state.

to complicate matters further, the question of German reunification is now widely acknowledged to be the principal political issue in the construction of a new European order acceptable to NATO and the crumbling Warsaw Pact alike.

The issues provoked by these momentous changes, which challenge the skills of diplomacy and statesmanship in far-reaching ways, are both politico-economic and cultural. On the one hand we are talking about a potential recasting of the structures of political and economic power in Europe, in ways that have wider, global implications. On the other, and this cannot be escaped, we must consider how we *think* about these structures and their interrelations. For cinema and television this places us squarely in the domain of how the new Europe is going to be *represented* to the multifold audiences that comprise European society.

The reshaping of Europe will engage us in far-reaching processes of remembering and forgetting. We must remember what is common to European culture and society and we have to forget what has divided it. We may, of course, choose – as an alternative – to remember divisions and forget commonalities. This is already all too apparent, not least in the renaissance of anti-semitism in many parts of Europe. I suspect that reactionary nationalist forms of adaptation to crisis will be powerfully attractive for many, for they offer reassurance at a time when navigation is rather difficult. How to handle this difficult problem is going to be a major challenge for filmmakers and broadcasters alike.

The task then is to remember and forget, but also to project, to imagine new alternatives and possibilities. It is a task to which the audio-visual media – and particularly so the medium of film – are exceedingly well adapted. Thus far, it is television actuality coverage which has held centre stage, most notably in its representations of the revolutions of 1989 and their aftermath. The breach of the Berlin Wall and the last public appearance of Nicolae Ceaucescu are moments not soon forgotten. In elaborating the possible grand designs of the future, though, it is the press that has taken the lead, and of its nature that tends to be a rather cerebral exercise addressed to elites.

During the turbulent events of the past year or so, one could hardly doubt the key importance of all the means of communication in conveying images and interpretations of change for widely differing audiences. In these times of rapid political transformation, the importance of cross-national processes of communication has assumed a heightened importance, and the responsibilities of the interpreters of change has increased accordingly.

It is unlikely that we can continue to assume that the citizen-viewer sees the world as a relativistic cultural collage. The interpretation of the 'message' is not uniform.

The emerging European space, rather than offering a cultural collage, seems one in which many sharp assertions of national identity based upon divergences of interest are the order of the day: one has but to think of the secessionist movements in the Baltic states and their acute difficulties with the Soviet central state power, of the tendency to fragment into hostile constituent national groupings in Yugoslavia, of the lethal enthno-religious hatreds of the Caucasus, or of the large Hungarian minority and its history of persecution in Romania. Talk of post-nationalism has been premature.

We are obliged to think of peoples and places whose existence has long been obscured by the crude antagonistic grand design of the Cold War. Now maps abound designating actual and potential trouble-spots where ethnic and religious divisions have resumed their potency. In one recent newspaper survey from the Atlantic almost to the Urals no less than forty-six locations were identified in the European 'patchwork of tensions'. There is little risk in predicting that given the continued messiness of European borders – when judged, that is, by the mythic nationalist criterion of a perfectly aligned state and culture – there will be many strains inherent in the new European order.

Collective Identities

National identities cannot be conflated with the boundaries of particular states, for polity and culture do not smoothly align with one another. States such as Britain and Spain, for instance, are multi-national and contain significant identity-conferring regional differences, a fact of which one could hardly be unaware if resident, say, in Scotland or Catalonia. Besides, one must also not neglect the significance of supra-national, trans-national and international bodies as locuses within which the articulation of intellectual projects takes place. It is precisely at such levels that many of the grand designs for the European future are being elaborated.

Collective identities are sustained by a dual process: one of inclusion that provides a boundary around 'us', and one of exclusion that distinguishes 'us' from 'them'. It is a common characteristic of social classifications to draw lines between 'friends', 'enemies' and 'neutrals'. At the extreme, such processes can be deadly (genocide being the limiting case) and, at the very least, they are often tenacious in ways that are far from trivial.

These rather general observations bear upon contemporary European

223

reality and its interpretation. Post-war socio-political space has been divided into alignments of Friends and Enemies, with broad labels of difference attached: Democracy vs Totalitarianism; Capitalism vs Communism; East vs West. These simplistic verities clouded internal differences within the two great camps and made pariahs within each of those who hankered for something substantially different (although, of course, McCarthyism and the Gulag cannot be equated). The weight of post-war international politics suppressed claims to commonality and abolished the idea of a Centre in a Europe divided into West and East, Good and Evil.

Discourses on Europe

The processes of political and economic change currently under-way are producing competition at the level of political discourse, and it is here, in the fashioning of new interpretations, that those involved in audio-visual production have a major contribution to make. With different force, and with different appeal depending on where we are situated in the European mosaic, we are being asked to 'imagine' or visualize a number of different Europes. This process is likely to accelerate and intensify, and offers a major opportunity for creative exploration. There are several distinctive fields in which debate is taking place, although they clearly interrelate.

Inside the European Community, there has been a conflict, whose precise resolution remains rather unclear, between minimalism and maximalism. The minimalist discourse is best exemplified by Mrs Margaret Thatcher's by now notorious Bruges speech of September 1988, in which she said:

> the European Community is *one* manifestation of . . . European identity. But it is not the only one. We must never forget that east of the Iron Curtain peoples who once enjoyed a full share of European culture, freedom and identity have been cut off from their roots.

These words were spoken before the revolutionary changes that began to reshape the erstwhile East in 1989. As Budapest, Prague, Warsaw and Berlin once more begin to resume their places in a wider European constellation one may reflect that although what Mrs Thatcher said was true, it was certainly not innocent. In her view, a loosely affiliated Europe, wider than the projected Single Market of 1992, may both reclaim the East and give Britain a wider stage on which to play – and keep her distance. For Mrs Thatcher and those who, like her, stress national sovereignty, the key principle of 'willing and active co-operation between independent sovereign states is the best way to build a successful European community'. If there is a message here for the Euro-integrationists, there is also one for Scots. Looked at from a Caledonian vantage-point, there is an interesting (but hardly surprising) conflation here between state and nation at the same time as it is insisted that nationhood, national customs, traditions and identity be maintained against 'some identikit European personality' and 'super-state'. '*Which* nation?' is an unavoidable question.

Although the minimalist view defending national sovereignty and cultural integrity commands some support, it now seems unlikely to prevail fully against the forces for political integration ranged across EC Europe. In April 1990, a further major step in pursuit of the integrationist vision was undertaken when President Mitterand and Chancellor Kohl proposed accelerating the drive towards political union. Precisely what this means in terms of institutional development is open to question, and the eventual outcome will be the product of much horse-trading. Nevertheless, it is not too far-fetched to suppose that the national-state level will become less important as an instance of sovereignty and decision-making in the coming years. In part, behind this latest push lies the need to create a viable framework for containing the enlarged German state that will be a consequence of the absorption by the Federal Republic of the GDR.

EC maximalism envisages a 'social Europe' or Euro welfare state offering an opening, it seems increasingly likely, to an integrated political and defence community. Spokesmen for this point of view present a different image of the future from that of the homogenising 'identikit Europe'. Jacques Delors, President of the European Commission, for instance, has talked in homely terms of the creation of a 'European Village', whereas for his part, Felipe Gonzalez, the Spanish Prime Minister, has gestured towards a 'European space'.

It must be said that the precise constitution of this 'space' remains in need of detailed specification. Certainly, since the 1980s there has been an effort (largely bureaucratically inspired by Brussels) to find a cultural character for the Twelve, most notably under the label of a 'European audio-visual space', defined in many respects against the importation of US television programmes or by the stamp of satellite footprints. At one level this has been a mini-exercise in industrial subsidy and half-hearted proto-protectionism. As is now dramatically apparent, with accelerating investment by capitalist multi-media enterprises, EC media space increasingly occupies the territories of the former East as well, so in many respects that project will have to be thoroughly rethought.

Of late, a second field of discourse has intersected with debates internal to the EC in the shape of the Soviet call for a 'Common European Home'. It is plainly a slogan that has stirred the political imagination: Jacques Delors has said that he shares this vision; James Baker, US Defense Secretary, claims that the New Europe of the Freedoms holds the key to the European House of the Future.

The new rhetorics offer more comfort than the old but they also obscure many problems of socio-economic and political reorientation. The reform process in the East may be seen as a relative historic victory for bourgeois democracy and capitalist efficiency. But in becoming fixated with the crisis of the East, we are apt to forget that the West is hardly problem-free. Poverty, unemployment, inequality, racism, homelessness and unresolved political differences still exist. The global capitalist economy is still subject to cyclical fluctuations, and in a world in which we are compelled to recognise our interdependence, we cannot ignore how the North-South divide and major ecological problems are likely to shape our future.

Returning more directly to the question of collective identity, one might note that the emergent so-called Europe of the Freedoms, is one in which one is also freer to migrate (as has been most dramatically been demonstrated by the flight from the GDR in 1989). Large-scale population movements (which engender increased socio-economic demands upon host countries and associated political problems) have a tendency to put defensive conceptions of national and cultural identity on the political agenda. Racism and discrimination against incomers are ever-present dangers.

Boundaries of Belonging

The question of inclusion and exclusion lies at the heart of collective identity. Putting it differently, one is forced to ask *where* Europe stops. In the recent debate about Central Europe, the focus has been upon whether or not Russia can rightly be seen as 'European'. One may expect this matter to remain on the agenda. Lines of inclusion and exclusion also criss-cross the relations between Islam and Europe.

In Britain, the emergence of Islam as a politico-cultural force offering a potent source of collective identification for sections of the Asian community, was latterly crystallised by the Salman Rushdie affair. As is well known, sections of the British Muslim community were mobilised against the novelist Rushdie in the wake of the Ayatollah Khomeini's denunciation of *The Satanic Verses*; the effect of this edict was to sentence him to death and send him into hiding under police protection, where he still remains. This episode raised central questions of cultural identity, with the dominant view proclaiming Islamic fundamentalism to be an eruption of an alien tradition within the body politic. Compelled by the need to defend its public space, much of the intelligentsia rallied round the threatened writer in a defence of the liberal conception of authorship, which certainly (and rightly) sees the cultural producer as needing to be free from threat of intimidation or violence.

But that is only part of the story. Having provided a focus for the accumulated resentments of the Muslim immigrant community at the discrimination and marginalisation that it has suffered, the Rushdie case has also crystallised a much wider problem, namely how the international politics of Islam may at times be articulated inside Western polities. Behind these tensions lies the sensitive question of labour migration into the more affluent western European states and the establishment within the wider societies of ethnic sub-cultures with highly distinctive communal identities. In the near future, the

This enigmatic and alluring image of Lucia Lanzarini by Jean Mohr was chosen as *Play Me Something's* poster. There had been debate about using an image which tells the story; this cropped black and white clearly does not. The poster helps to position – and promote – the film as a European art house film.

EC is likely to have to face dealing with Turkey's manifest desire for accession. The issue poses with considerable sharpness the question of the relation between 'Europeanness' and Islam.

The matter also assumes greater significance a time when Pope John Paul II and other leading figures in the Catholic church argue that 'Christianity is at the very roots of European Culture' and that 'Europe has no identity without Christianity'. The denunciation of materialism and the evocation of Christian spirituality as a solution to Europe's identity crisis in the wake of 'the death of Marxism' has also come from Anglican quarters. One can only conjecture how future relations between the various Christian denominations and between Christians and the non-Christian faiths who are excluded from these projections will evolve.

The Stuff that Films are Made Of

There are enough themes in the matters touched upon above to keep documentarists and the makers of fiction films busily at work in Scotland (and for that matter, in the rest of Europe) for the next decade. But apart from whether there are good stories to be told, more importantly, the problem of an adequate national infrastructure for Scottish audio-visual production still has to be resolved, although undoubtedly some positive steps have been taken in this direction. The problem of what the content of the national film culture of a smallish nation should be is still unresolved. (It is, of course, no more resolved in the United Kingdom as whole.) Although the debate about surmounting the 'kailyard/tartanry' inheritance is much less intense today, it does not seem to have exhausted its pertinence completely as fashioning representations of identity that handle the subject of

227

'Scottishness' with confidence and flair remains a tricky task.

Examples of how to accomplish this are not exactly plentiful. Without wishing to claim more that an illustrative purpose, one can take as a convenient starting-point Timothy Neat's recent film *Play Me Something* – which won a major prize at the Barcelona Film Festival in 1989 – as this not only deals with the question of cultural and political identities in different settings, but has also been critically received (in line with its makers' intentions) as being both 'European' and 'Scottish'.

Play Me Something was directed by Neat from a script co-written with the well-known novelist and art critic John Berger. The story is taken from Berger's book, *Once in Europa*, a collection of tales which deals with the experiences of the European peasantry in this century. Berger quite self-consciously turned himself into a 'European' writer by expressly deciding to leave England thirty years ago, when as he has said 'the idea of Europe wasn't as present as it is now, and England seemed isolated from Europe in its own enclosed psychologically regressive world'. For his part, Neat has a track record of producing documentaries dealing with Scottish culture, such as, for instance, the work of the Gaelic poet Sorley MacLean. It is hardly surprising, then, to find the question of identity at the heart of *Play Me Something*. The central theme is the role of story-telling within a given cultural group and how, offering points of identification for an audience, this might inspire its members to become active participants in the telling of the tale, and even transform their lives. Translated to another level of analysis, we are talking about the communal transmission and modification of culture. While I do not necessarily share the film's optimism, I do certainly think that it addresses many of the right questions in a sensitive and imaginative way.

Play Me Something's anchorage point is the Hebridean island of

Charlie Barron in Piazza San Marco, Venice, 1987, a year before the Barra filming. *Play Me Something* was a two phase production, for financial reasons. Tim Neat, the film's director, shot 16mm footage which was successfully used to impress backers to release the necessary further funding. The 1987 trip also allowed research into farm locations in the Dolomito Mountains.

228

Barra, where it constantly returns to the waiting-room of the island's tiny airport. There, a story-teller, in the tradition of the Highland senachie, played by Berger, entertains a group of passengers awaiting a flight to Glasgow that has been delayed by fog. He has been quasi-magically summoned into existence by the television repair man (played by Edinburgh Scottish Studies academic Hamish Henderson) whose arrival by horse and cart to repair the malfunctioning airport television set effectively opens the film and whose departure closes it.

Play Me Something was writer John Berger's first acting role. Wanting to be seen as a character in the film as opposed to John Berger, art critic, he called himself 'The Secretary'. He hoped to portray a character not specific to time or place who pulls stories from the air.

But within the waiting-room narrative there is another. Clad in the respectable feast-day garb of the Italian rural worker, a dark hat, dark suit, collar and tie, John Berger's story-teller, arriving from nowhere, peremptorily addresses the waiting-room listeners with a simple but gripping love story set a thousand miles away in that still magical city, Venice. He relates a tale about Bruno, an Italian mountain peasant, who journeys to Venice with the fellow members of his village band, and who decides on impulse to visit the Communist Party's *Festa dell'Unita* held on the nearby island of Giudecca. On the way, Bruno meets a young woman, Marietta, who works in a chemist's shop in Mestre, with whom he has a one-day love affair. They are divided by cultural difference, by his rurality and her urbanity. She smells of perfume, he of the cowshed. She believes passionately in socialism and progress, he harbours a peasant suspicion for big ideas and regimentation. They talk, drink, dance, make love in a boat. However their differences are too great for anything more to come of it, despite their desires, and he leaves for home in the mountains with his fellow musicians.

Play Me Something (Marietta's request to Bruno before they part) is a complex and skilfully realised film which moves between different levels of narrative and employs a mix of visual styles. The scenes in Barra are shot in colour with a deliberate and lingering eye, closing up on the actors, conveying intimacy in the shared experience of the story and tracking their reactions as it is told. The story-teller is constantly interrupted by singing, commentary, jokes, analogies brought to the surface by the stirrings of memory. His influence is most apparent in the way his story provokes the initial steps in a love affair between a young couple, a hairdresser and a motorbike enthusiast, who await the delayed Glasgow flight.

But the site of action shifts constantly. Black and white documentary-style footage conveys the primitive texture of mountain peasant life, placing Bruno, without actually showing him, in the village, the byre, the hen coop. Similar framing is used to give a taste of the life of the Italian urban worker, the milieu from which Marietta springs. The love story itself is told by a sequence of telling photographs of the couple by Berger's long-standing collaborator, the Swiss photographer Jean Mohr. This works remarkably well as a visual counter-point to the oral telling of the tale. These photographs are themselves interwoven with colour footage of the bustle of the Venice *vaporetti*, the workers' *festa*, the patterning of light upon the movement of the water.

What we have, then, and herein no doubt lay the appeal to the

229

Charlie Barron (Bruno) is an agricultural worker and handyman in Fife, Lucia Lanzarini (Marietta) is an Italian actress found at a 1987 casting session in Florence. Marietta and Bruno have just made love in the boat at the workers' festival.

Barcelona jury, is a simple love story located in one of Europe's most magical settings. This is evoked from within a quintessentially Scottish island scene, where self-conscious use is made of the traditions of Celtic story-telling. The marginal rural settings of Italy and Scotland are brought into a common frame, a 'European' one, as are Venice's tidal city and Barra's tidal airport. At one level we are being told that the power of a tale well-told can compare, contrast and also transcend cultures, to produce transformative effects upon those who attend in the right way.

Given the ability of *Play Me Something* to address some of the 'European' issues discussed earlier, the cavalier treatment the film has received in Britain, and even in Scotland, is regrettable, particularly when contrasted with its much merited acclaim on the continent. Reading the critical responses, one is struck, saving a few honourable exceptions, at just how trivialising these have been.

Of particular interest to Scottish critics has been the presence of well-known local names in the cast. Actress Tilda Swinton (playing the hairdresser), the writer Liz Lochhead and the scholar Hamish Hamilton have all been discussed in the up-market press. Of particular interest in the popular end of the market has been the presence of Timothy Neat's friend, Charlie Barron, cast as the Italian peasant figure in the tale within the tale unfolded by the story-teller. It is

230

Scottish content in this sense (the actors, production staff, the setting, the evocation of local tradition) that have made it a 'Scottish film'. It is perfectly reasonable to discuss Scottishness in this way, but in hailing the film as a 'Scottish success story' no broader discussion of why this should happen more by accident than design has really begun. Must such work be condemned to a marginal existence?

Moreover, there was a somewhat troubling ambiguity about much comment, an undertone of critics often having to demonstrate, even protest, the film's Scottish credentials. Interestingly, whereas for writers in the Spanish and French press, the film was unequivocally 'Scottish' and its director a 'Scot', in Scotland for most it was the nuances of difference that were compelling. Timothy Neat was described frequently as 'Cornish' and as 'Scottish-based'. The director himself, presumably to some extent out of sensitivity to this dimension, has stressed his Celtic roots as a broader way of embracing Scottishness. Neat talks of Celtic culture as being 'about a lifestyle, a human interaction of music, song and story . . . the cinema is the one most suited to capturing an entire lifestyle, and so I realised that it would have real potential in representing and speaking for this basis of Celtic culture'.

The film was indeed critically evaluated as 'European'. It is currently a good thing to be (at least in some circles), and certainly a way of leap-frogging London and the obscuring presence of England. However,

Hamish Henderson drives Alison Carruthers across the Barra sands on the last day's shoot at the beginning of the film. Henderson's first acting role, he plays a 'TV repairman' who magics up the storyteller played by John Berger. The cart and horse had to be imported from Oban, the track had to be laid and the helicopter aerial shots of the beach were taken: the most expensive day in the whole £330,000 budget.

just what this means is, without doubt, somewhat arbitrary. Above all, it was *Play Me Something*'s art house sensibility that appealed to critics home and abroad: the qualities commented upon (as 'un-Scottish' and 'un-British' and therefore as 'European') were its formal innovativeness, the interplay between documentary and fictional modes of representation, its intellectuality. One can readily understand this, but does it not oversimplify? For some, what made *Play Me Something* 'European' is its rootedness in a region. This may be taken as a riposte to the bureaucratic grand design of a 'European audio-visual space', which some interpret as inevitably bringing about a 'Euro-soap' homogeneity – that is an American model of industrialised production distant from the vital roots of culture. To argue this is to discover 'Europe' through the local, the intimate, and the organic workings of a distinctive culture. Certainly 'Europe' has many levels. But at what point are we still really talking about Europe as such?

These postures are but the opening moves in what ought to be a complex and far-reaching debate. I hope this can now really begin to take off, because a lot is at stake, and not just talk about films and television programmes. Underlying it all, is an exploration of the wider relations between cultures and political orders, and the decisions we take about these can have the most profound effects on our lives.

None of this is tremendously clear-cut, to tell the truth. To evoke variously the European, the Scottish, the Celtic dimensions is at the same time to be doing two things. First, it is to refer to various levels of cultural reality all of which are themselves continually being redefined. And second, far from innocently, making such reference is to play with the cards of identity. And these are especially potent today. Whereas, on the one hand, such identifying labels allow the producers of an audio-visual culture to discuss artistic products, on the other hand they also permit the outlining of a series of potential markets.

The only hopeful European future, I think, is one in which we can use our actual plural identities as resources, acknowledge that we be allowed to move freely between them, and refuse the beguiling invitation to find something utterly compelling and essential in each and every one of them. National identities and patriotic self-identification have an important place in such a view, as points of departure. But it also follows that, at the same time, they are but stages in a wider cultural journey that looks ahead and not behind.

Note

This essay draws freely on work in progress. Many of the arguments and issues are more full elaborated in *Innovation* (Vienna) 1988, *The New European* (London) Autumn 1989, and in *Telos* (Madrid) September 1990.

Scotland in Feature Film: a Filmography

Janet McBain

This compilation has been prompted by the desire to present as complete a listing as possible of the many ways in which Scots and Scotland have been portrayed in fictional cinema and to offer a body of information on which to base discussion and argument.

The principal criteria in selecting titles for inclusion in this filmography were: Scotland used as an identified setting or backdrop to the story; Scots characters, either at home or abroad, playing a central or at least significant role in the narrative. Scots 'authorship' alone is not necessarily enough to warrant inclusion. The content has to reflect some aspect of 'Scottishness'.

This means that the several versions of Robert Louis Stevenson's story *Dr Jekyll and Mr Hyde* will not figure in this list despite the fact that the original characters were loosely based on Edinburgh's infamous Deacon Brodie. Equally these criteria allow for the inclusion of the adaptation of Neil Paterson's story *The Kidnappers*, which although set in Canada, reflects the experiences of Scottish immigrants.

Each title in this listing has been released for cinema exhibition or some measure of public screening. Films produced exclusively for television broadcast such as Scottish Television's *Taggart* drama *Loveknot* have not been included, whereas some which at first glance might appear to be solely broadcast material have been included, for example *Heavenly Pursuits* (Film Four International) which had limited cinematic release prior to transmission.

In general film archives' catalogues and published sources do not index feature films by location, a factor that has presented considerable difficulties in trying to compile a fully comprehensive listing. Staff in film archives worldwide have been most helpful in this rather daunting research and if there are any omissions to this list the blame should be laid at my door rather than my colleagues' in the archival institutions.

Entries have been arranged chronologically according to year of release and contain the following information (where this can be ascertained).

TITLE
Alternative title and country of use
Country of origin
Colour or black & white
Running time   Silent films have been listed either in 35 mm footage or number of reels
                  Sound films are in minutes
pc   Production company
p, ap   Producer, associate producer
d   Director
sc   Screenplay
s   Source of story e.g. play or novel, with author and title of work if different from film titles
lp   Leading players
Summary   Prefaced by a simple descriptive classification e.g. *Comedy, Drama*

Titles up to and including 1928 are assumed to be silent, and from 1929 onwards assumed to be sound unless specified differently in the entry.

 * An asterisk after the title indicates no known copy of the film exists in the UK. This does not necessarily mean that for films without an asterisk there is a viewing print currently in distribution.

Selected entries include quotes from *Monthly Film Bulletin* (*MFB*) and *Variety* (*VAR*). These are not intended as definitive critical statements but rather to give the reader a sense of the reaction to the films at the time of their release.

Silent Scream (1989) the dream horse

1898
SCOTCH REEL*
GB B & W 70'
pc Levi Jones & Co
Four Scotsmen dance traditional reel.
THE HIGHLAND FLING*
GB B & W 75'
pc Leviathan Films
Children dance in Highland dress.
HIGHLAND FLING*
GB B & W 75'
pc Riley Bros
Members of the Black Watch in dance
display.
HIGHLAND REEL
GB B & W 75'
pc Riley Bros
Members of the Black Watch in dance
display.

1899
A GRETNA GREEN WEDDING*
GB B & W 60'
pc R W Paul
Comedy. Girl's father arrives too late to
stop wedding.

1900
THE FLYING SCOTS*
GB B & W 175'
pc Warwick Trading Co
lp The Three Missouris
Comedy. Acrobats dressed as Scots.

1903
THE EFFECTS OF TOO MUCH
SCOTCH*
GB B & W 160'
pc Gaumont, *d* Alf Collins
Trick. Scot undresses after drinking
session and his clothes come to life.

1904
THE ADVENTURES OF SANDY
MACGREGOR*
GB B & W 300'
pc Clarendon, *d* Percy Stow
Comedy. Scotsman tries to undress on
beach without being seen.

1905
THE EIGHTEEN PENNY LUNCH*
GB B & W 190'
pc Walturdaw
Trick. Scotsman's sausage transforms
into a dog.
MCNAB'S VISIT TO LONDON
GB B & W 300'
pc Alpha trading Co, *d* Arthur Cooper
lp Arthur Cooper
Comedy. Scots golfer wrecks relative's
house in search for lost ball.

1908
THE SKIRL OF THE PIBROCH*
GB B & W 140'
pc Walturdaw, *d* Dave Aylott
Comedy. Boy plays bagpipes and makes

everybody dance.
HARRY LAUDER IN A HURRY*
GB B & W 325'
pc Gaumont, *d* Alf Collins
lp Harry Lauder
Comedy. Scots performer takes his time
despite efforts of callboy and stage
manager to hurry him up.
MACBETH*
US B & W
pc Vitagraph, *s play* Wm Shakespeare
THE CHIEFTAIN'S REVENGE *
alt A TRADEGY IN THE HIGH-
LANDS OF SCOTLAND*
US B & W 415'
pc Vitagraph
MARY STUART*
France B & W 840'
pc Pathé

1909
THE AMOROUS SCOTCHMAN*
GB B & W 133'
pc Empire Films
Comedy. Scotsman flirts with host's
portly cook.
GRETNA GREEN*
GB B & W 75'
pc Walturdaw
Chase. Parents pursue elopers in vain
to border.
LOCHINVAR*
US B & W 790'
pc Edison, *s poem* Sir Walter Scott
MACBETH*
Italy B & W
pc Cines, *s play* Wm Shakespeare
KENILWORTH*
US B & W 985'
pc Vitagraph, *s novel* Sir Walter Scott
lp Florence Turner
THE IMP OF THE BOTTLE*
US B & W 750'
pc Edison, *s story* R L Stevenson
THE BRIDE OF LAMMERMOOR*
alt A TRAGEDY OF BONNIE
SCOTLAND*
US B & W 540'
pc Vitagraph, *s novel* Sir Walter Scott

1910
MACBETH*
France B & W
pc Pathe, *s play* Wm Shakespeare
MARIE STUART*
France B & W
pc Pathé, *d* Albert Capellani, *sc* Michael
Carré, *s* Victor Hugo
lp Jeanne Delvair, Jacques Grétillat,
Henry Krauss
AULD ROBIN GRAY
US B & W 770'
pc Vitagraph, *d* Larry Trimble, *s poem*
Lady Ann Lindsay
lp Florence Turner, Maurice Costello
Romance. Young girl forced to marry
older man in order to support parents,
finds her true love.

1911
ROB ROY*
GB B & W 2500'
pc United Films, *p* James Bowie, *d*
Arthur Vivian, *s novel* Sir Walter
Scott
lp John Clyde, Theo Henries, Durward
Lely
Adventure. 1715. Outlawed clan leader
falls foul of royal justice.
(First British 3-reel feature)
AN ADVENTURE OF ROB ROY *
GB B & W 995'
pc Gaumont
Adventure. Soldier kills own kidnapped
child, mistaken for outlaw's.
THE HIGHLANDER*
GB Col 600'
pc Natural Colour Kinematograph Co,
d Theo Bouwmeester
Romance. Girl marries another despite
Scots fiancé serving abroad.
MACBETH*
GB B & W 1360'
pc Co-operative Cinematograph Co, *s*
play Wm Shakespeare
lp Frank Benson, Constance Benson
Drama.
A COMRADE'S TREACHERY*
GB B & W 580'
pc B & C
War. India. Soldier shot in the back
by rival is saved from death by
Highlander.
GREAT SCOT ON WHEELS*
GB B & W 450'
pc Clarendon, *d* Percy Stow
Chase. Fat man on roller skates.
LOCHINVAR*
US
pc Thanhouser, *s poem* Sir Walter
Scott
MARIE STUART ET RIZZIO*
alt GB: MARY QUEEN OF SCOTS
France B & W 910'
pc Gaumont
lp Renée Carl, Luitz Morat, Bréon

The Heart of Midlothian (1914) Flora Morris, Violet
Hopson and John MacAndrews

1911

AULD LANG SYNE
US B & W 1380'
pc Vitagraph, *d* Larry Trimble
lp Tess Johnstone, Florence Turner,
Helene Costello, Harry Morey, Jean (the
'Vitagraph dog')
Romance. The eternal triangle ends in
mutual reconciliation.

1912

GRETNA GREEN*
GB B & W 700'
pc Heron Films, *p* Andrew Heron, *d*
Mark Melford
lp Mark Melford
Chase. Elopers chased by parent who
arrives at smithy too late.
PETER'S RIVAL*
GB B & W 325'
pc Cricks & Martin, *d* Edwin J
Collins
Comedy. Two rivals in contest for a girl
who loves a Scot.
SANDY'S NEW KILT
GB B & W 800'
pc B & C, *d* Dave Aylott
lp William Gladstone Haley
Comedy. Family shortens father's new
kilt during the night.
THE LITTLE MINISTER*
US B & W
pc Vitagraph, *s novel* J M Barrie
lp Clara Kimball Young
THE LADY OF THE LAKE *
US B & W
pc Vitagraph, *s poem* Sir Walter Scott
lp Harry T Morey, Ralph Ince, Edith
Storey, Earle Williams
FAVOURITE OF MARY STUART*
France B & W
pc Eclair
MAIRI, THE ROMANCE OF A
HIGHLAND MAIDEN
GB B & W 1140'
p, d & sc Andrew Paterson
lp Evelyn Duguid, Dan Munro, Jack
Maguire
Drama. Young girl caught up in rivalry
between excise man and smuggler.

1913

A STORM IN A TEACUP;*
GB B & W 725'
pc Hepworth, *d* Warwick Buckland
lp Flora Morris, Claire Pridell, Ruby
Belasco
Crime. Man posing as journeyman saves
beloved from burglars.
THE FATE OF A KING*
GB B & W 1926'
pc Britannia Films, *d* A E Coleby
History. King ignores witch's warning
and is done to death.
ROB ROY*
US B & W 3 reels
pc Eclair
lp Robert Frazer

MARY STUART*
US B & W
pc Edison, *s play* Friedrich Schiller
lp Mary Fuller, Miriam Nesbitt
MARY STUART*
France B & W 840'
pc Pathé

1914

PIMPLE'S HUMANITY*
GB B & W 690'
pc Folly Films, *d, s* Fred Evans, Joe
Evans
lp Fred Evans
Comedy. Scotsman fights treacherous
friend.
BLACK RODERICK THE
POACHER*
GB B & W 2025'
pc Big Ben Films -Union,
d H O Martinek
Crime. Gamekeeper exonerates laird who
has been framed.
THE SHEPHERD LASSIE OF
ARGYLE*
GB B & W 3000'
pc Turner Films, *d* Larry Trimble, *s*
Hector Dion
lp Florence Turner, Rex Davis
Drama. Shepherd's daughter is struck
dumb seeing her dog save her from
an attack by laird's mad brother.
A DAUGHTER OF BELGIUM*
GB B & W 1350'
pc Barker, *d* F Martin Thornton,
s Rowland Talbot
War. Belgium. Highland soldiers save
girl who is avenging deaths of her
father and her lover.
BRAVO KILTIES*
GB B & W 1066'
pc Barker, *d* F Martin Thornton,
s Rowland Talbot
War. Belgium. Soldier defends post office
until relieved by Highlander troops.
A DAUGHTER OF FRANCE*
GB B & W 2000'
pc Crusade
War. Wounded soldier dies in saving
French girl who then brings Highlander
troops to save village.
THE HILLS ARE CALLING*
GB B & W 1150'
pc Hepworth, *d* Cecil Hepworth
lp Tom Powers, Alma Taylor
Romance. Scots violinist spurned by
London socialite returns to his Scottish
home.
CLANCARTY*
GB B & W 1760'
pc London, *d* Harold Shaw
lp Lillian Logan, Walter Gray
Adventure. Period. Banished lord saves
King from Jacobites.
THE HEART OF MIDLOTHIAN*
GB B & W 4275'
pc Hepworth, *d* Frank Wilson, *s novel*
Sir Walter Scott

lp Flora Morris, Violet Hopson, Alma
Taylor
Drama. Edinburgh. 1736. Crofter's
daughter has child by outlaw and
is condemned to death when it is
stolen by midwife's mad daughter.
A WOMAN'S TRIUMPH*
US B & W 4 reels
pc Famous Players, *d* J Searle Dawley,
s novel Sir Walter Scott *Heart of Midlothian*
lp Laura Sawyer, Betty Harte, Hal
Clarendon
Drama. Effie gets involved with gang of
smugglers and is saved from sentence
of death by sister Jeanie.
MACBETH*
Germany B & W
pc Film Industrie Gesellschaft, *s play*
Wm Shakespeare

1915

PIMPLE IN THE KILTIES*
GB B & W 900'
pc Folly Films, *d, s* Joe & Fred
Evans
lp Fred Evans
Comedy. Pimple joins a Scottish regiment
and becomes a war hero.
MACDOUGAL'S AEROPLANE*
GB B & W 530'
pc Phoenix, *d, s* James Read
lp James Read
Comedy. Scotsman builds his own
aeroplane which then explodes.
THE LITTLE MINISTER*
GB B & W 3920'
pc Neptune, *d* Percy Nash, *s play*
J M Barrie
lp Joan Ritz, Gregory Scott
Romance. Period. Laird's fiancé poses as
gypsy and falls in love with the village's
new minister.
THE LITTLE GYPSY*
US B & W 5 reels
pc Fox, *d* Oscar D Apfel, *s novel* J M
Barrie *The Little Minister*
lp Dorothy Bernard, Thurlow Bergen,
Raymond Murray

Lochinvar (1915) Godfrey Tearle and Peggy Hyland

LOCHINVAR*
GB B & W 2100'
pc Gaumont, *d, sc* Leslie Seldon-
Truss, *s poem* Sir Walter Scott

236

lp Godfrey Tearle, Peggy Hyland
Romance. Period. Laird abducts his
loved one the night before her enforced
marriage.
AT THE TORRENT'S MERCY*
GB B & W 3500'
pc B & C, *d* H O Martinek
lp Percy Moran, Ivy Montford
Drama. Gamekeeper's daughter saves
beloved from drowning at hands of a
poacher.
THE CAMPBELL'S ARE COMING*
US B & W 4 reels
pc Universal, *d* Francis Ford
lp Francis Ford, Grace Cunard, Duke
Warne
War. 1857. Mary McLean leaves her
sweetheart to go to India as a
teacher, and is caught up in the
Indian mutiny.

1916
SANDY AT HOME
GB B & W 605'
pc Transatlantic, *d, s* Will Page
lp Will Page
Comedy. Scot left to look after wife's
and sister's babies.
SANDY'S SUSPICION
GB B & W 600'
pc Transatlantic, *d, s* Will Page
lp Will Page
Comedy. Suspicious husband follows wife
to cafe.
HIS HIGHNESS*
GB B & W 2000'
pc Club Comedies, *p* George Green,
d Mr Foote
Comedy. Glasgow.
ANNIE LAURIE*
GB B & W 3800'
pc Hepworth, *d* Cecil M Hepworth,
s Alma Taylor
lp Alma Taylor, Stewart Rome
Romance. Laird weds country girl who
then falls in love with his nephew.
ON THE BANKS OF ALLAN
WATER*
GB B & W 4125'
pc Clarendon, *d* Wilfred Noy, *s* Reuben
Gillmer
lp Basil Gill, Violet Leicester
Romance. Bard's son marries miller's
daughter but stress caused by class
differences almost cause her suicide.
MACBETH*
US B & W
pc Triangle, *s play* Wm Shakespeare
THE WAR BRIDE'S SECRET *
US B & W 6 reels
pc Fox, *d* Kenean Buel
lp Virginia Pearson, Walter Law, Glen
White
Drama. WWI. Scots lass marries lover
who is sent to the front. Pregnant and
believing him to be killed in action she
marries elderly farmer who graciously
makes way for returning hero.

PEGGY*
US B & W 7 reels
pc New York/Kay Bee, *d* Thomas
Ince
lp Billie Burke, William H Thompson,
William Desmond, Charles Ray
Comedy. Peggy, New York society
favourite, returns to Scottish homeland
and despite her 'offensive' lifestyle
she gradually earns the respect of the
villagers.
THE BALLET GIRL*
US B & W 5 reels
pc Wm A Brady Pictures Plays, *s novel*
Compton Mackenzie *Carnival*
lp Alice Brady, Holbrook Blinn, Robert
Frazer
Drama. Jennie Raeburn, daughter of
aerial dancer, makes stage debut and
gets caught up in the dangerous social
world of the theatre.

1917
THE CALL OF THE PIPES*
GB B & W 5000'
pc Regal Films, *d* Tom Watts
lp Ernest A Douglas
War. Scot wins VC saving rival and
returns home in time to save blind
father from eviction.
AULD LANG SYNE
GB B & W 4400'
pc B & C, *d, s* Sidney Morgan
Drama. Girl takes blame when brother
steals necklace from her husband.
WHAT EVERY WOMAN KNOWS*
GB B & W 5100'
pc Barker-Neptune, *d* Fred S C Durrant,
s play J M Barrie
lp Hilda Trevelyan
Romance. Porter, educated in return for
marrying rich man's daughter, learns
love after entering Parliament.
AULD ROBIN GRAY*
GB B & W 4500'
pc Ideal, *d* Meyrick Milton
lp Langthorne Burton, Miss June
Romance. Shipwrecked sailor returns
home in time to save beloved from
marrying another.
KIDNAPPED*
US B & W 5 reels
pc Forum Films for Edison, *d* Alan
Crosland, *s novel* Sir Walter Scott
lp Raymond McKee, Joseph Burke
KITTY MACKAY*
US B & W 5 reels
pc Vitagraph, *d* Wilfred North, *s play*
Catherine C Cushing
lp Lilian Walker, Jewel Hunt
Comedy. Sweet-natured girl, mistreated
by her adopted aunt and uncle, finds
true parents and falls in love.
THE PRIDE OF THE CLAN*
US B & W 7 reels
pc Artcraft, *d* Maurice Tourneur
lp Mary Pickford, Matt Moore, Warren
Cooke

The Little Minister (1922) Alice Calhoun and James
Morrison.

Drama. Margaret McTavish takes
command as chieftain of the clan
after the death of her father.
THE BOTTLE IMP*
US B & W 5 reels
d Marshal Neilan, *s novel*
R L Stevenson
lp Sessue Hayakawa, Lehua Waipahu

1918
A ROMANY LASS
GB B & W 6378'
pc Harma Photoplays, *d* F Martin
Thorburn, *s* Reuben Gillmer
Romance. Colonel's son conquers cow-
ardice by fighting rival for gypsy.
HEAR THE PIPERS CALLING*
GB B & W 5000'
pc Grenville-Taylor, *d* Tom Watts,
s H Grenville-Taylor
Romance.
BONNIE MARY*
GB B & W 5000'
pc Master Films, *p* Low Warren, *d* A
V Bramble, *s* Herbert Pemberton
lp Miriam Ferris, Leon Belcher
Romance. Feuding laird and farmer
reconciled by children's marriage.
THE MASTER OF GRAY*
GB B & W 5000'
pc Monarch, *d & s* Tom Watts
lp Athalie Davis, Harry Clifford
Romance. 1860. Wild girl seduced by
laird weds old man who drowns himself
on learning that she loves another.
KILTIES THREE*
GB B & W 5819'
pc Gaiety, *p & d* Maurice Sandground,
s Bernard Merivale
lp Bob Reed, Rowland Hill
War. Edinburgh industrialist weds
German spy's widow who becomes
nurse.
BONNIE ANNIE LAURIE*
US B & W 5 reels
pc Fox, *d* Harry Millarde, *s song* Lady
John Scott

237

lp Peggy Hyland, William Bailey
Drama. Annie Laurie, betrothed to
Donald who is fighting in France,
takes care of man washed up on
shore, and falls in love.
PATRIOTISM*
US B & W 6 reels
pc Paralta, d Raymond West
lp Bessie Barriscale, Charles Gunn
War. Spy drama surrounding Scots-
woman who turns her home into
hospital for convalescing soldiers.
THE MAN AND THE MOMENT*
GB B & W 5850'
pc Windsor, d Arrigo Bocchi, s novel
Elinor Glyn
lp Manora Thew, Hayford Nobbs
Romance. American heiress weds laird
to meet conditions of a will.
MAID O'THE STORM*
US B & W 6 reels
pc Paralta Plays, d Raymond B West
lp Bessie Barriscale, George Fisher,
Herschell Mayall
Drama. McTavish, a fisherman, rescues
baby washed up on shore, who grows
up to become celebrated dancer.

1919
YE BANKS AND BRAES*
GB B & W 5000'
pc Regal, d Tom Watts
lp Ethel Douglas Ross, John Jenson
Romance. Scots girl disappointed in love
by deceitful nobleman.
IN THE GLOAMING*
GB B & W 5000'
pc Broadwest, p Walter West, d Edwin
J Collins, s J Bertram Brown
lp Violet Hopson, Jack Jarman
Drama. Speculator escapes jail, makes
good abroad, and returns to find wife
wed to former lover.
THE HARP KING*
GB B & W 5000'
pc Ace Film Producing Co, d & sc
Max Leder
lp Nan Wilkie, W R Bell
Romance. Daughter of laird falls in love
with musician.

Comin' Thro' the Rye (1923) Alma Taylor and Shayle
Gardner

BONNIE BONNIE LASSIE*
US B & W 6 reels
pc Universal, d Tod Browning
lp Mary McLaren, David Butler
Comedy. Alison Graeme journeys from
Scotland to America and meets a young
billboard painter.
THE MAN BENEATH*
US B & W 5 reels
pc Haworth, d William Worthington
lp Sessue Hayakawa, Helen Jerome
Eddy
Crime. Hindu scientist visits Scotland
and falls in love with Kate, but
their plans are thwarted when he gets
involved with members of the Black
Hand Society.
THE WHITE HEATHER*
US B & W 6 reels
pc Tourneur, d Maurice Tourneur,
s play Raleigh and Hamilton
lp H E Herbert, Ben Alexander
Drama. Lord Angus Cameron's marriage
to Scots aristocrat is thwarted by his
secret marriage years before to the castle
housekeeper.

1920
THE ROMANCE OF ANNIE
LAURIE*
GB B & W 2000'
pc Lancashire Film Studios, d Gerald
Somers, s play Alfred Denville
lp Joan Gray, Allan McKelvin
Romance. Laird, married to madwoman
elopes with daughter of landowner.
A RACE TO SCOTLAND*
GB B & W 2000'
Crime. (Two episodes of American
serial, filmed in London, Liverpool
and Glasgow.)
FAITH*
US B & W 5 reels
pc Fox, d Howard Mitchell, sc J A
Roach
lp Peggy Hyland, J Parks Jones
Drama. Set in 'old Scottish village' near
Edinburgh. Faith healer's son falls in
love with daughter of laird.
THE FOURTEENTH MAN*
US B & W 6 reels
pc Paramount, d Joseph Henabery
lp Robert Warwick, Bebe Daniels
Comedy. After a quarrel at a Scottish
war soldier wounds another man and
has to flee.
THE BEST OF LUCK*
US B & W 6 reels
pc Screen Classics, d Ray C Smallwood,
s story Anthony Hope
lp Kathryn Adams, Jack Holt
Drama. Leslie MacLeod, an American,
comes to Scotland after buying her
ancestral castle and is wooed by
two suitors.
THE WHITE CIRCLE*
US B & W 5 reels
pc Paramount, d Maurice Tourneur,
s novel R L Stevenson The Pavilion on

the Links
lp Spottiswoode Aitken, Janis Wilson
Drama. London banker flees to Scottish
castle for protection against an Italian
secret society.

c 1920
ALL FOR THE SAKE OF MARY
aka I LOVE A LASSIE, MACK'S
FIRST LOVE
GB B & W 1400'
pc Harry Lauder Prods
lp Harry Lauder, Effie Vallance
Romance. Scot goes to South Africa to
seek fortune, and returns home to claim
his sweetheart.

1921
IN HIS GRIP*
GB B & W 5945'
pc Gaumont-British Screencraft, d C C
Calvert, s novel David Christie Murray
Drama. Glasgow. Unscrupulous
guardian and bogus brother try
to steal girl's diamonds.
CHRISTIE JOHNSTONE*
GB B & W 5151'
pc Broadwest, p Walter West, d Norman
Macdonald, s novel Charles Reade
lp Gertrude McCoy, Stewart Rome
Romance. 1850. Bored laird saves
fisherlassie's lover from drowning.
FOOTBALL DAFT*
aka FITBA DAFT (Glasgow)
GB B & W 2000' Re-issue 1923
pc Broadway Cinema Prods. d Victor
W Rowe, s sketch James Milligan
lp Jimmy Brough
Comedy. Temperance observer
mistakenly drinks whisky thinking it to
be vinegar.
BESIDE THE BONNIE BRIER
BUSH*
GB B & W 570'
pc Famous Players – Lasky, d Donald
Crisp, s play James MacArthur,
Augustus Thorne
lp Donald Crisp, Mary Glynne
Romance. Fiancé of rich girl is in love
with peasants.
BUNTY PULLS THE STRINGS*
US B & W 7 reels
pc Goldwyn, d Reginald Barker, s play
Graham Moffat
lp Leatrice Joy, Russell Simpson,
Raymond Hatton
Comedy. Bunty, sister of a bank robber
and daughter of a stern church elder in
a Scottish village intercedes on behalf
of her brother and manoeuvres events
to a satisfactory conclusion.
SENTIMENTAL JOURNEY
US B & W
pc Goldwyn
WHAT EVERY WOMAN KNOWS*
US B & W 7 reels
pc Paramount, d William de Mille,
s play J M Barrie
lp Lois Wilson, Conrad Nagel

Comedy. Railway porter becomes MP thanks to wife's sponsorship.

THE LITTLE MINISTER
US B & W 6 reels
pc Paramount, *p* Adolph Zukor, *d* Penrhyn Stanlaws
lp Betty Compson, George Hackathorne
Melodrama. The weavers of Thrums, enraged by reduction of prices for their products, rise against the manufacturers.

COURAGE*
US B & W 2444'
pc Sidney A Franklin Prods, *p* Albert A Kaufmann, *d* Sidney A Franklin *lp* Naomi Childers, Sam de Grasse
Drama. Inventor wrongly imprisoned for murder of Scots steel mill owner.

GET YOUR MAN*
US B & W 5reels
pc Fox Films, *d* George SC Hill
lp Buck Jones, William Lawrence, Beatrice Burnham
Melodrama. Spurned Scots coal miner goes to Canada and becomes a mountie.

SENTIMENTAL TOMMIE*
US B & W 8 reels
pc Famous Players-Lasky, *p* Adolph Zukor, *d* John S Robertson, *s* novels J M Barrie *Sentimental Tommie* and *Tommie and Grizel*
Melodrama. Villagers in Thrums ostracise child Grizel until arrival of newcomer with whom she falls in love.

THE FORTUNE OF CHRISTINE MCNAB*
GB B & W 6200'
pc Gaumont-Westminster, *d & sc* P Kellino, *s novel* Sarah McNaughton
lp Nora Swinburne, David Hawthorne
Comedy. Heiress spurns titled fiancé to return to soldier sweetheart.

1922
THE LILAC SUNBONNET*
GB B & W 6100'
pc Progress, *p* Frank Spring, *d & sc* Sidney Morgan, *s novel* S R Crockett
lp Joan Morgan, Warwick Ward
Romance. Girl wins cleric's approval by revealing she is daughter by runaway marriage.

ROB ROY
GB B & W 6100'
pc Gaumont-Westminster, *d & sc* P Kellino, *s* Alicia Ramsey
lp David Hawthorne, Gladys Jennings
Adventure. 1712. Clan chief exacts revenge on laird who outlawed him.

THE WEE MACGREGOR'S SWEET-HEART*
GB B & W 5300'
pc Welsh, Pearson, *d & sc* George Pearson, *s* stories J J Bell
lp Betty Balfour, Donald Macardle
Romance. Girl weds sweetheart despite snobbish aunt.

MARY QUEEN OF SCOTS*
GB B & W 1000'
pc B & C, *p* Edward Godal, *d* Edwin Greenwood
From series *The Romance of British History*

THE LITTLE MINISTER*
US B & W 6 reels
pc Vitagraph, *p* Albert E Smith, *d* David Smith
lp Alice Calhoun, James Morrison
Melodrama. Newly appointed minister to village of Thrums falls in love with gypsy.

THE MAN FROM GLENGARRY*
Canada B & W 6 reels
pc Ottawa, *p* Ernest Shipman, *d* Henry MacRae, *s* book Ralph Connor *The Man From Glengarry*
lp Anders Randolph, Warner P Richmond, Harlan E Knight, Marion Swayne
Melodrama. Heads of lumber camps meet in fight. Scot 'Big Macdonald' is killed and son swears revenge.

MACBETH*
GB B & W 1175'
pc Master, *d* H B Parkinson, *s play* Wm Shakespeare
lp Russell Thorndike, Sybil Thorndike
Drama. One of a series *Tense Moments From Great Plays.*

1923
BONNIE PRINCE CHARLIE*
GB B & W 6540'
pc Gaumont-British Screencraft, *d* C C Calvert, *s* Alicia Ramsey
lp Gladys Cooper, Ivor Novello
History. 1746. The Young Pretender is betrayed by rival after defeat at Culloden.

YOUNG LOCHINVAR
GB B & W 5300'
pc Stoll, *d & sc* P Kellino, *s poem* Sir Walter Scott & *novel* J P Muddick
lp Owen Nares, Gladys Jennings
Adventure. Girl, forced to marry rival's son, is saved by her lover.

Young Lochinvar (1923) director Kellino

THE FAIR MAID OF PERTH*
GB B & W 5500'
pc Anglia Films
p Jack Buchanan, *d* Edwin Greenwood, *s novel* Sir Walter Scott
lp Russell Thorndike, Sylvia Caine
Adventure. Chief's daughter is saved by beloved from unscrupulous laird.

THE ROMANY*
GB B & W 5800'
pc Welsh-Pearson, *p* George Pearson, *d* F Martin Thornton, *s* Elliot Stannard
lp Victor McLaglen, Irene Norman
Adventure. Gypsy chief saves runaway girl from rich fiancé.

THE LOVES OF MARY QUEEN OF SCOTS*
GB B & W 7684'
pc Ideal, *d & s* Denison Clift
lp Fay Compton, Gerald Ames
History. 1542-87. Widowed queen weds Scots nobleman. Is later executed for plotting against Queen of England.

COMIN' THRO' THE RYE
GB B & W 7900'
pc Hepworth, *d* Cecil M Hepworth, *s* novel Helen Mathers
lp Alma Taylor, Shayle Gardner
Romance. 1862. Fake wedding announcement intended to break up relationship, to the benefit of jealous girl's friend.

LITTLE MISS NOBODY*
GB B & W 5750'
pc Carlton Productions
d & sc Wilfred Noy, *s play* John Graham
Comedy. Lodgers pose as earl's family to dupe wealthy relative.

1925
LIVINGSTONE
GB B & W 9600' Re-issue 1933
pc Hero, *d & s* M A Wetherell
lp M A Wetherell, Molly Rogers, Henry Walton
History. Africa. 1871. Biography of the Scots explorer.

MARY QUEEN OF TOTS*
US B & W
p Hal Roach
'Our Gang' comedy.

THE SPORTING VENUS*
US B & W 5900'
pc Metro-Goldwyn *d* Marshall Neilan
lp Blanche Sweet, Ronald Colman, Lew Cody
Romance. Aristocrat falls in love with Scots medical student in opposition to family. Returns to student's Scottish cottage to find him wealthy and in possession of family estate.

1926
THE FAIR MAID OF PERTH*
GB B & W Sound
pc DeForest Phonofilms, *d* Miles Mander
lp Louise Maurel
Drama

THE LIFE OF ROBERT BURNS*
GB B & W 7600' Re-issue 1928
pc Scottish Film Academy, *d* Maurice
Sandground
lp Wal Croft
History. Biography of Ayrshire poet.
From series *Immortals of Bonnie Scotland.*
THE LIFE OF SIR WALTER
SCOTT*
GB B & W 7600'
pc Scottish Film Academy. Re-issue
1928
d Maurice Sandground
History. Biography of novelist. From
series *Immortals of Bonnie Scotland.*
THOU FOOL
GB B & W 5100'
pc Stoll, *d* Fred Paul, *s novel* J J Bell
Drama. Scots shopkeeper ruins ex-
employer, whose daughter marries man
made rich by father's tips.
THE LADY FROM HELL*
US B & W 6 reels
pc Stuart Paton Prods, *d* Stuart Paton
lp Roy Stewart, Blanche Sweet
Western melodrama. Scots officer arrives
in US and becomes foreman of ranch.
Returns to Scotland to marry sweetheart
but is falsely accused of murder of ranch
owner and is extradited.
BACHELOR BRIDES*
US B & W 6 reels
pc De Mille Pictures, *d* William K
Howard
lp Rod La Rocque, Eulalie Jenson
Comedy. American heiress about to
marry laird of Duncreggan Towers
castle gets involved in theft of jewels
and claims by another woman that
laird fathered her child.

Huntingtower (1927) Bolshevik and Gorbals Boys

A KISS FOR CINDERELLA*
US B & W 10 reels
pc Paramount
d Herbert Brenon, *s play* J M Barrie
lp Betty Bronson, Tom Moore

1927
HUNTINGTOWER*
GB B & W 7192'
pc Welsh-Pearson-Elder, *d* George
Pearson, *s novel* John Buchan
lp Sir Harry Lauder, Vera Voronina,
Pat Aherne
Adventure. White Russian saved from
Bolsheviks with aid of Gorbals boys.
MCFADDENS FLATS*
US B & W 8 reels
pc Asher-Small-Rogers, *p* Edward Small
d Richard Wallace, *s* Gus Hill
lp Charlie Murray, Chester Conklin,
Edna Murphy
Comedy. Two fathers fall out over
different ambitions for their offspring.
ANNIE LAURIE*
US B & W 9 reels
pc MGM, *d* John S Robertson
lp Lillian Gish, Norman Kerry
Romance. Set against background of
feuding Campbells and Macdonalds.
MARIA STUART*
Germany B & W 7866'
pc National, *d* Friedrich Feher, *sc*
Leopold Jessner, Anton Kuh
lp Magda Sonja, Fritz Kortner,
Friedrich Feyer

1928
THE LADY OF THE LAKE*
GB B & W 5168' Sound added July
1931.
pc Gainsborough, *p* Michael Balcon,
James A Fitzpatrick, *s poem* Sir Walter
Scott
lp Percy Marmont, Benita Hume
Adventure. Exiled girl saves king from
outlaws

1929
AULD LANG SYNE*
GB B & W 6800' Silent. Sound added
Sept 1929.
pc Welsh-Pearson-Elder, *d & sc* George
Pearson, *s* Hugh E Wright
lp Sir Harry Lauder, Dorothy Boyd,
Pat Aherne
Drama. Scots farmer visits London and
finds his son a boxer and his daughter
a nurse.
THE PLAYTHING*
GB B & W 78 mins
pc B I P, *d* Castleton Knight, *s play*
Arthur Black
lp Estelle Brody, Heather Thatcher
Romance. Scot seeks revenge on society
lady who rejected him.
THE BLACK WATCH*
US B & W 8000'
pc Fox Film Corp, *d* John Ford, *s*
S Mundy *King of the Khyber Rifles.*

lp Victor McLaglen, Myrna Loy
Adventure. Capt King of the Black Watch
assigned to secret mission in India,
averts revolt by tribesmen.
CHINA BOUND*
US B & W 7 reels. Silent
pc MGM, *d* Charles Reisner
lp Karl Dane, George K Arthur,
Josephine Dunn
Farce. Scotsman takes daughter to China
to prevent romance with employee,
who subsequently rescues both from
revolutionaries.

1930
TERRORS*
GB B & W 47 mins
pc Erie O Smith, *p, d & s* Erie
O Smith
Fantasy. Scots boys tell how they
tunnelled to Australia and frighten
prehistoric monsters with bagpipes.
TAM O'SHANTER
GB B & W 9 mins
pc BIP, *d* R E Jeffrey, *s poem* Robert
Burns
lp Gilbert McAllister
THE LOVES OF ROBERT BURNS
GB B & W 96 mins
pc B & D, *p & d* Herbert Wilcox, *s*
Reginald Berkeley
lp Joseph Hislop, Dorothy Seacombe
Musical. 1786. Biographical treatment
of the poet.
SEVEN DAYS LEAVE*
US B & W 90 mins
pc Paramount, *d* Richard Wallace, John
Cromwell, *s play* J M Barrie *The Old
Lady Shows Her Medals*
lp Gary Cooper, Beryl Mercer
War. Scots charwoman claims Canadian
soldier of Black Watch as her son.
THE COHENS AND KELLYS IN
SCOTLAND*
US B & W 8 reels
pc Universal, *d* William J Craft, *p* Carl
Laemmle
lp George Sidney, Charlie Murray
Farce. Cohen and Kelly go to Scotland to
buy plaids thinking to make fortune.
THE LADY OF THE LAKE*
US B & W (synch music score) 5
reels
pc Fitzpatrick, *d* James A Fitzpatrick
s poem Sir Walter Scott
lp Percy Marmont, Benita Hume,
Lawson But
Romantic melodrama.

1933
THEIR NIGHT OUT
GB B & W 46 mins
pc BIP, *d & sc* Harry Hughes, *s play*
George Arthurs, Arthur Miller
lp Claude Hulbert, Renee Houston
Comedy. Mistaken identity as husband
pays for illicit night out with Scots
girl.

TILL THE BELLS RING
GB B & W 46 mins
pc BSFP, *d* Graham Moffat, *s Play*
Graham Moffat, *sc* Graham Moffat
lp Graham Moffatt, Margaret Moffat,
Winifred Moffat
Comedy. Scot attempts to win spinster
he believes to be wealthy.

The Secret of the Loch (1934) Frederick Paisley and
Gibson Rowland

The Thirty Nine Steps (1935) Madeleine Carroll, Robert
Donat and Alfred Hitchcock

1934

THE SECRET OF THE LOCH
GB B & W 80 mins
pc Wyndham, *p* Bray Wyndham, *d*
Milton Rosmer
lp Seymour Hicks, Nancy O'Neil
Fantasy. Diver discovers prehistoric
monster in Loch Ness.
THE RUGGED ISLAND
GB B & W 44 mins
pc Zenifilms, *p* John Gifford, *d* Jenny
Brown
lp John Gilbertson, Enga Stout
Drama. The prospect of emigration
divides a young crofting couple.
THE LITTLE MINISTER
US B & W 110 mins
pc RKO, *p* Pandro S Berman, *d* Richard
Wallace, *s play* James Barrie
lp Katharine Hepburn, John Beal, Alan
Hale, Donald Crisp
Romance. 1840. The gypsy girl with
whom the minister falls in love is really
the local laird's wayward daughter.

The Rugged Island (1934) John Gilbertson

WHAT EVERY WOMAN KNOWS*
US B & W
pc MGM, *d* Gregory La Cava, *s play*
J M Barrie
lp Helen Hayes, Brian Aherne
RED ENSIGN
alt US: STRIKE!
GB B & W 69 mins
pc Gaumont, *p* Jerome Jackson, *d*
Michael Powell, *s* Michael Powell,
Jerome Jackson
lp Leslie Banks, Carol Goodner, Frank
Vosper
Drama. Clydebank. Shipbuilder
launches new boat despite rival's
attempts to prevent it.

1935

MCFADDENS FLATS*
US B & W 65 mins
pc Paramount, *d* Ralph Murphy, *s play*
Gus Hill
lp Walter C Kelly, Andy Clyde, Richard
Cromwell
Comedy. Quarrel between bricklayer and
barber affects their children.
THE THIRTY-NINE STEPS
GB B & W 86 mins Re-issue 1939,
1942
pc Gaumont, *p* Ivor Montagu, *d* Alfred
Hitchcock, *s novel* John Buchan
lp Robert Donat, Madeleine Carroll,
Godfrey Tearle
Crime. A framed man is helped by a
girl as they are chased across Scotland
by a spy ring.
FLAME IN THE HEATHER*
GB B & W 66 mins
pc Crusade, *p* Victor M Greene, *d &*
sc Donovan Pedelty, *s novel* Esson
Maule *The Fiery Cross*
lp Gwenllian Gill, Barry Clifton
Adventure. 1745. Scots chieftain's daugh-

ter is saved by English infiltrator.
BONNIE SCOTLAND*
US B & W 80 mins
pc MGM, *p* Hal Roach, *d* James
Horne
lp Stan Laurel, Oliver Hardy
Comedy. Parody of *Lives of a Bengal Lancer*.
Two Americans journey to Scotland to
collect non-existent inheritance, join the
army and end up in India.

1936

MARY OF SCOTLAND*
US B & W 123 mins
pc RKO, *p* Pandro S Berman, *d* John
Ford, *sc* Dudley Nichols
lp Katharine Hepburn, Fredric March,
Donald Crisp
History. Mary Stuart refuses to give
up claim to the English throne and
is eventually executed.
DAVID LIVINGSTONE*
GB B & W 71 mins
pc Fitzpatrick Pictures, *d* James A
Fitzpatrick, *s & sc* K Williamson
lp Percy Marmont, Marion Spencer
History. Africa 1871. Explorer searching
for source of the Nile is found by
American.
WEDDING GROUP
GB B & W 69 mins
pc Fox British, *p* Leslie Landau, *d* Alex
Bryce, Campbell Gullan
lp Fay Compton, Barbara Greene
Romance. 1855. Daughter of the manse
follows soldier to the Crimea as a
nurse.
HIGHLAND FLING
GB B & W 68 mins
pc Fox British, *p* John Findlay, *d*
Manning Haynes, *s* Alan d'Egville
lp Charlie Naughton, Jimmy Gold
Comedy. Efforts to locate missing will

241

Mary of Scotland (1936) John Ford, Katharine Hepburn and Douglas Walton

during Highland Games.
ANNIE LAURIE*
GB B & W 82 mins. Re-issue 1943.
pc Mondover, *p* Walter Tennyson, Wilfred Noy, *d* Walter Tennyson
lp Will Fyffe, Polly Ward, Bruce Seton
Musical. Bargee's adopted daughter becomes successful dancer.
BORN THAT WAY*
GB B & W 64 mins
pc Randall Faye, *d* Randall Faye, *s* V C Clinton-Baddeley, Diana Bourbon
lp Elliot Mason, Kathleen Gibson
Comedy. Scottish spinster looks after absent-minded brother-in-law's children.
THE END OF THE ROAD*
GB B & W 71 mins
pc Fox British, *d* Alex Bryce, *s* Edward Dryhurst
lp Harry Lauder, Ruth Haven
Musical. Travelling minstrel loses savings after daughter dies.
THE GHOST GOES WEST
GB B & W 85 mins
pc London Films, *p* Alexander Korda, *d* René Clair, *sc* Robert E Sherwood, Geoffrey Kerr
lp Robert Donat, Elsa Lanchester, Jean Parker, Eugene Pallette
Comedy. Millionaire buys Scottish castle and transports it stone by stone to America, complete with ghost.

1937
AULD LANG SYNE*
GB B & W 72 mins
pc Fitzpatrick Pictures, *p* & *d* James A Fitzpatrick, *s* & *sc* K Williamson
lp Andrew Cruikshank, Christine Adrian
History. 1780. Biography of poet, Robert Burns.

SPRING HANDICAP
GB B & W 68 mins
pc ABPC, *p* Walter C Mycroft, *d* Herbert Brenon
lp Will Fyffe, Marie O'Neill
Comedy. Miner's predilection for betting and bookmaking creates domestic tension.
THE EDGE OF THE WORLD
GB B & W 80 mins. Re-issue 1948.
pc Rock Studios, *p* Joe Rock, *d* Michael Powell
lp Niall MacGinnis, Belle Chrystal, John Laurie, Finlay Currie
Drama. Foula. Life and death on desolate Shetland isles based on the true life experience of the evacuation of St Kilda.
WISE GUYS*
GB B & W 87 mins Re-issue 1943.
pc Fox British, *p* Ivor McLaren, *d* Harry Langdon, *s* Alison Booth
lp Charlie Naughton, Jimmy Gold
Comedy. Edinburgh. Couple must find £500 so that they can inherit a relative's loan company.
STORM IN A TEACUP
GB B & W 87 mins. Re-issue 1943, 1946.
pc London – Victor Saville, *p* Victor Saville, *d* Victor Saville, Ian Dalrymple, *s play* Bruno Frank
lp Vivien Leigh, Rex Harrison, Sara Allgood
Comedy. Reporter seeks revenge on ambitious provost for his callous treatment of a widow's dog.
SAID O'REILLY TO MCNAB
GB B & W 85 mins
pc Gainsborough, *p* Edward Black, *d* William Beaudine, *s* Howard Irving Young
lp Will Mahoney, Will Fyffe
Comedy. Irish entrepreneur and Scots

businessman promote slimming pills.
FINE FEATHERS*
GB B & W 68 mins
pc British Lion, *p* Herbert Smith, *d* Leslie Hiscott, *s* Michael Barringer
lp Renee Houston, Donald Stewart
Musical. Paris. Scots shopgirl in guise of mistress of a foreign prince.
WEE WILLIE WINKIE*
US B & W 99 mins
pc 20th Century Fox, *d* John Ford, *s story* Rudyard Kipling
lp Shirley Temple, Victor McLaglen, Cesar Romero, C Aubrey Smith
Drama. Period. Indian frontier, Sgt Macduff's daughter becomes heroine of her father's Highland Regiment.

1938
MARIGOLD*
GB B & W 73 mins
pc ABPC, *p* Walter C Mycroft, *d* Thomas Bentley, *s play* Charles Garvice & Allen Harker.
Romance. 1842. Girl flees from arranged marriage to discover that her mother was an actress.
MFB 'The story moves in a leisurely manner in keeping with its pleasant old-world atmosphere. It has refreshing wholesomeness and fragrance.'
OWD BOB
GB B & W 78 mins
pc Gainsborough, *p* Edward Black, *d* Robert Stevenson, *s novel* Alfred Olivant
lp Will Fyffe, John Loder, Margaret Lockwood
Drama. Cumberland. Old Scots farmer's dog accused of killing sheep.
MFB 'Fyffe gives a really brilliant performance as the drunken, quarrelsome, crafty old Scot whom one cannot help liking despite his character.'

242

THISTLEDOWN*
GB B & W 79 mins
pc WB-FN, *p* Irvin Asher, *d* Arthur
Woods, *s* John Meehan Jnr, J O
C Orton
lp Aino Bergo, Keith Falkner
Musical. Scots landowner becomes
suspicious of his foreign bride's
virtue.
KIDNAPPED – THE ADVENTURES
OF DAVID BALFOUR*
US B & W 93 mins
pc 20th Century Fox, *p* Kenneth
MacGowan, *d* Alfred L Werker,
s novel R L Stevenson
lp Warner Baxter, Freddie
Bartholemew, Arleen Whelan
Adventure. During the Jacobite rebellion
a young boy is sold by uncle as a slave,
and is helped by outlaw.
*MFB 'Alan and his followers may not be
entirely convincing as Scottish rebels, but they
are impressive rebels and fighters.'*

1939
THE SPY IN BLACK
GB B & W 82 mins. Re-issue 1944.
pc Harefield, *p* Irving Asher, Alexander
Korda, *d* Michael Powell, *s novel* J Storer
Clouston, *sc* Emeric Pressburger
lp Sebastian Shaw, Marius Goring
War. Orkneys. 1917. Spy posing as
German spy posing as schoolmistress
catches U-boat captain acting as spy.
*MFB 'The atmosphere is realistic and
convincing, the photography noteworthy.
Pictures of Scapa Flow, of the Orkney
Islands, and of the Fleet are particularly
effective.'*
SHIPYARD SALLY
GB B & W 79 mins
pc 20th Century Prods, *p* Robert T
Kane, *d* Monty Banks, *s* Gracie Fields,
Tom Geraghty, Val Valentine
lp Gracie Fields, Sydney Howard,
Morton Selten
Musical. Clydeside pub landlady poses as
American singer to save shipyard from
closure.
*MFB 'An excellent team assists Gracie,
who works hard and has a variety of
songs to sing.'*
HOOTS MON!
GB B & W 77 mins
pc WB-FN, *p* Sam Sax, *d* Roy William
Neill
lp Max Miller, Florence Desmond,
Hal Walters
Comedy. Cockney comedian and Scots
impressionist, rivals in love.
*MFB 'For those who like dialogue that flickers
like lightning, magnificent fooling and broad
humour this is definitely a picture to see.'*
STANLEY AND LIVINGSTONE*
US B & W 101 mins
pc 20th Century Fox, *p* Kenneth
MacGowan, *d* Henry King
lp Spencer Tracy, Richard Greene,
Cedric Hardwicke, Charles Coburn,

Nancy Kelly
History. Henry Stanley's expedition to
find David Livingstone in Africa.
RULERS OF THE SEAS*
US B & W 96 mins
pc Paramount, *p & d* Frank Lloyd
lp Douglas Fairbanks Jnr, Margaret
Lockwood, Will Fyffe
Drama. Period. Steam versus sail in the
race to cross the Atlantic from Greenock
to New York.
*MFB '. . . the real stars are Will Fyffe
and the sea.' '. . . his love for his invention
and for strong drink will not quickly be
forgotten.'*

1940
THEY CAME BY NIGHT*
GB B & W 72 mins
pc 20th Century Productions, *p* Edward
Black, *d* Harry Lachman, *s play* Barre
Lyndon
lp Will Fyffe, Phyllis Calvert
Crime. Scots jeweller infiltrates gang
responsible for brother's suicide.
DAS HERZ DER KÖNIGIN
Germany B & W 9799'
pc Tonfilmstudio Carl Froelich for UFA,
d Carl Froelich
lp Zarah Leander, Willy Birgel
History. The story of Mary, Queen
of Scots 'with anti-English, pro-Nazi
tones'. (Catalogue of Forbidden German
Features 1951.)

1941
JEANNIE
GB B & W 101 mins. Re-issue 1949.
pc Tansa Films, *p* Marcel Hellman, *d*
Harold French, *s play* Aimée Stuart
lp Barbara Mullen, Michael Redgrave,
Wilfrid Lawson
Romance. Vienna. Salesman woos Scots
girl and saves her from unscrupulous
suitor.
*MFB 'Full marks must be given to a
collie-dog for its histrionic abilities and to
the minor human characters, each of whom
performs his allotted task with a little more
than adequacy.'*
HATTER'S CASTLE
GB B & W 102 mins. Re-issue 1947.
pc Paramount British, *p* Isadora
Goldsmith, *d* Lance Comfort, *s novel*
A J Cronin
lp Robert Newton, Deborah Kerr,
Emlyn Williams
Drama. 1879, Dumbarton. Tyrannical
hatter dominates father.
SHINING VICTORY*
US. B & W
pc First National, *p* Jack L Warner,
d Irving Rapper, *s play* A J Cronin
Jupiter Laughs
lp James Stephenson, Geraldine
Fitzgerald, Donald Crisp
THE GHOST OF ST MICHAEL'S
GB B & W 82 mins. Re-issue 1944,
1947, 1955.

pc Ealing, *ap* Basil Dearden, *d*
Marcel Varnel, *s* Angus Macphail,
John Dighton
lp Will Hay, Claud Hulbert
Comedy. Skye. Teacher with evacuees
catch spies in a 'haunted' castle.
COTTAGE TO LET
GB B & W 90 mins. Re-issue 1948.
pc Gainsborough, *p* Edward Black,
d Anthony Asquith, *s play* Geoffrey
Kerr
lp Leslie Banks, Alastair Sim, John
Mills
Crime. Evacuee thwarts spies' plot to
steal aircraft secrets.
*MFB 'The only minor blemish was that the
Scottish atmosphere was never realistic.'*
ATLANTIC FERRY*
alt US: SONS OF THE SEAS
GB B & W 108 Mins
pc Warner, *p* Max Milder, *d* Walter
Ford
lp Michael Redgrave, Valerie Hobson,
Griffith Jones
Drama. 1840. Scots engineers and
shipbuilders in race to cross the
Atlantic by steam-ship.

1942
BACK ROOM BOY
GB B & W 82 mins
pc Gainsborough, *p* Edward Black, *d*
Herbert Mason, *s* Val Guest, J O C
Morton
lp Arthur Askey, Moore Mariott
Comedy. Scientist catches remote spy in
Scots lighthouse.
*MFB '. . . the man who sends out the
pips on the BBC goes gay one night and
syncopates the rhythm. This irresponsible story
was evidently only written to serve as a vehicle
for Arthur Askey and he gives all that is
expected of him in the shape of wisecracks,
madcap chases and so on.'*

1943
THE SHIPBUILDERS
GB B & W 89 mins
pc British National, *p & d* John Baxter,

The Shipbuilders (1943) Clive Brook

The Brothers (1947) Maxwell Reed and Patricia Roc

s George Blake
lp Clive Brook, Morland Graham,
Finlay Currie
Drama. 1931-9. Clydeside shipbuilder
and loyal rivetter fight to keep Britain a
sea power and to maintain the yards.
ON APPROVAL
GB B & W 80 mins
pc Verity, *p & d* Clive Brook, *s play*
Frederick Lonsdale
lp Clive Brook, Beatrice Lillie, Googie
Withers
Comedy. Edwardian duke and American
rent Scottish keep for trial marriage.
*MFB 'Complete success was probably
impossible in view of the essentially dated
and theatrical character of the original.'*

1944
MY AIN FOLK*
GB B & W 75 mins. Re-issues 1946,
1949.
pc Butcher, *p* F S C Baker, *d* German
Burger
lp Mabel Constanduros, Moira Lister,
Norman Prince
Musical. Glasgow. Factory girl's
relationship with wireless operator
in Merchant Navy.
*MFB 'This is a homely, sentimental
production rather overloaded with Scottish
songs, all of which, however, are pleasantly
rendered. Moira Lister and Norman Prince
are an appealing young couple, though the
latter has some difficulty with his Scottish
accent . . .'*
GIVE ME THE STARS*
GB B & W 90 mins
pc British National, *p* Fred Zelnik, *d
& sc* Maclean Rogers
lp Will Fyffe, Leni Lynn, Jackie
Hunter
Musical. 1939. American cures her Scots
grandfather of alcohol problem.

1945
I KNOW WHERE I'M GOING
GB B & W 92 mins. Re-issue 1949.
pc Archers, *p, d & s* Michael Powell,
Emeric Pressburger
lp Wendy Hiller, Roger Livesey, Pamela
Brown, Finlay Currie

Romance. Hebrides. Bride en route to
her wedding falls for poor laird while
stranded in storm.
*MFB 'The great strength of this most
entertaining film lies in its affectionate and
sympathetic handling of the Highland setting:
its great weakness lies in its story.'*
THE BODY SNATCHERS*
US B & W 77 mins
pc RKO, *p* Val Lewton, *s novel* R L
Stevenson
lp Henry Daniell, Boris Karloff, Bela
Lugosi
Drama. 19th-century Edinburgh. Doctor
obtains specimens for medical research
from grave robbers who turn to murder
when supplies run short.

1947
THE SILVER DARLINGS
GB B & W 84 mins
pc Holyrood, *p* Karl Grune, William
Elder, *d* Clarence Elder, Clifford Evans,
s novel Neil Gunn
lp Clifford Evans, Helen Shingler, Carl
Bernard
Adventure. Hebrides islanders turn to to
herring fishing to make a living.
*MFB '. . . a refreshing film of an unusual
and well-treated subject.'*
COMIN' THRO' THE RYE
GB B & W 61 mins
pc Advance, *p* Arthur Dent, *d* Walter
C Mycroft
lp Terence Alexander, Olivia Barley
Musical. 1780. The loves of poet, Robert
Burns.
THE BROTHERS
GB B & W 98 mins. Re-issue 1948.
pc Triton, *p* Sydney Box, *d* David
Macdonald, *s novel* L A G Strong
lp Patricia Roc, Will Fyffe, Maxwell
Reed, Finlay Currie
Drama. Servant girl caught between
rivals for her attention.

1948
CASTLE SINISTER
GB B & W 49 mins
pc Unicorn, *p & sc* Howard Borer, *d*
Oscar Burn
lp Mara Russell-Tavernan, Robert
Essex, Karl Mier, Allistair Hunter
Crime. Marchioness' stepson discovers
spy in British army
*MFB '. . . a confusion of plot, poor direction,
general miscasting and some acting that can
hardly be called professional, are the main
weaknesses.'*
THE GREED OF WILLIAM HART
GB B & W 78 mins
pc Bushey, *p* Gilbert Church, *d* Oswald
Mitchell, *s novel* R L Stevenson
lp Tod Slaughter, Henry Oscar, Aubrey
Woods
Crime. Edinburgh, 1820. Resurrection-
ists kill innocent to sell body to
surgeons.
BONNIE PRINCE CHARLIE
GB B & W 136 mins
pc London – BLPA, *p* Edward Black, *d*
Anthony Kimmins, *s* Clement Dane
lp David Niven, Margaret Leighton,
Judy Campbell, Jack Hawkins
History. 1745. Pretender fails in his bid to
restore Stuarts to the British throne.
*MFB 'The photography of the magnificence
of the Scottish landscape is almost as fresh
and lovely as Margaret Leighton's portrayal
of Flora MacDonald.'*
THE HILLS OF HOME*
aka GB: MASTER OF LASSIE*
US Colour 95 mins
pc MGM, *d* Fred Wilcox, *sc* William
Ludwig
lp Edmund Gwenn, Tom Drake, Donald
Crisp, Janet Leigh
Drama. A doctor returns to his Scottish
village to practise medicine and brings
his faithful collie.

Bonnie Prince Charlie (1948) David Niven

244

MACBETH
US B & W 89 mins
pc Republic, *p & d* Orson Welles
lp Orson Welles, Jeanette Nolan, Dan
O'Herlihy
KIDNAPPED*
US B & W 81 mins
pc Monogram, *p* Lindsley Parsons,
d William Beaudine, *s novel* R L
Stevenson
lp Roddy McDowall, Sue England, Dan
O'Herlihy
Adventure. Young Scot comes to claim
inheritance from uncle who has him
kidnapped and shipped off to slavery.

1949
FLOODTIDE
GB B & W 90 mins
pc Aquila, *p* Donald B Wilson, *d*
Frederick Wilson, *sc & s* George
Blake
lp Gordon Jackson, Rona Anderson,
John Laurie, Jimmy Logan
Drama. Clydebank. Shipyard apprentice
trains as naval architect and falls in
love with boss's daughter.
*MFB '. . . a story conventionally absurd,
unpretentiously told . . . thanks to capable
direction and camerawork the Glasgow
background is convincing.'*
WHISKY GALORE!
alt USA: TIGHT LITTLE ISLAND
GB B & W 82 mins
pc Ealing, *p* Michael Balcon, *d* Alexander
Mackendrick, *sc* Compton Mackenzie,
Angus McPhail, *s novel* Compton
Mackenzie
lp Basil Radford, Joan Greenwood,
James Robertson Justice, Gordon
Jackson
Comedy. Hebrides, 1943. Islanders salvage crates of whisky from shipwrecked
vessel.
MFB '. . . a refreshing sense of comedy and an

understanding of Anglo-Scots relationships.'
THE HASTY HEART
GB B & W 107 mins
pc ABPC, *p & d* Vincent Sherman,
sc Ronald MacDougall, *s play* John
Patrick.
lp Ronald Reagan, Patricia Neal,
Richard Todd
War. Burma, 1945. Attitudes to arrogant
Scot change when it is learnt that he
is dying.
*MFB '. . . pedestrian transcription of the
sentimental stage play.'*

1950
THE GORBALS STORY
GB B & W 74 mins
pc New World, *p* Ernest Gartside, *d
& sc* David McKane, *s play* Robert
McLeish
lp Howard Connell, Betty Henderson,
Russell Hunter, Roddy McMillan
Drama. Glasgow. Tension in tenement
community almost leads to murder.
MFB '. . . one respects its aims.'
MADELEINE
GB B & W 114 mins
pc Pinewood-Cineguild, *p* Stanley
Haynes, *d* David Lean,
lp Ann Todd, Norman Wooland, Ivan
Desny, Leslie Banks
Crime. Glasgow, 1857. Society lady
accused of murdering her lover.
*MFB '. . . beautifully, elegantly made . . .
what is served up on the screen is cold, remote
and intolerable.'*

1951
FLESH AND BLOOD*
GB B & W 102 mins
pc Harefield, *p* Anatole de Grunwald, *d*
Anthony Kimmins, *s play* James Bridie
The Sleeping Clergyman
lp Richard Todd, Glynis Johns, Joan
Greenwood
Drama. Glasgow, 1867-1927. Family
suffer from the affects of heredity.

Happy-Go-Lovely (1951) Vera-Ellen

HAPPY-GO-LOVELY
GB Col 97 mins
pc Excelsior, *p* Marcel Hellman, Bruce

Humberstone, *sc* Val Guest, Arthur
Macrae
lp David Niven, Vera-Ellen, Cesar
Romero
Musical. Edinburgh. Chorus girl meets
millionaire during the Edinburgh
Festival.

1952
YOU'RE ONLY YOUNG TWICE
GB B & W 81 mins
pc Group 3, *p* John Grierson, Barbara
K Emery, *d* Terry Bishop, *s play*, James
Bridie *What Say They*
lp Duncan Macrae, Joseph Tomelty,
Patrick Barr, Diane Hart
Comedy. Glasgow. Irish poet poses
as University gatekeeper and creates
trouble for the principal.
*MFB '. . . an irresponsible, lunatic kind
of entertainment.'*

The Brave Don't Cry (1952) Jack Stewart and Eric
Woodburn

THE BRAVE DON'T CRY
GB B & W 90 mins
pc Group 3, *p* John Grierson, *d* Philip
Leacock, *sc* Montagu Slater
lp John Gregson, Meg Buchanan,
Andrew Keir, Fulton Mackay
Drama. Over one hundred men rescued
after 36 hours in Scottish coal mine.
*MFB '. . . made with deliberate sobriety
and much technical care . . . an estimable
achievement.'*
CASTLE IN THE AIR*
GB B & W 90 mins
pc Hallmark, *p* Edward Dryhurst, Ernest
Gartside, *d* Henry Cass, *s play* Alan
Melville
lp David Tomlinson, Helen Cherry,
Margaret Rutherford
Comedy. Poor laird's castle subject of
rival bids for ownership.

1953
LAXDALE HALL
alt US: SCOTCH ON THE ROCKS
GB B & W 77 mins
pc Group 3, *p* John Grierson, Alfred
Shaughnessy, *d* John Eldridge, *s novel*
Eric Linklater
lp Ronald Squire, Kathleen Ryan,
Raymond Huntley
Comedy. Hebrides. Village's five car
owners refuse to pay tax until road
is built.

245

Laxdale Hall (1953) Raymond Huntley

MFB 'Whitehall, as usual, retires vanquished
and partly won over from this encounter with
tradition, whimsicality and the simple life.'
JOHNNY ON THE RUN
GB B & W 68 mins
pc International Realist for Children's
Film Foundation, p Victor Lyndon, d
Lewis Gilbert, Vernon Harris
lp Eugeniusz Chylek, Sidney Tafler,
Michael Balfour
Drama. Runaway Polish orphan gets
involved with jewel thieves.
MFB '. . . a stronger sense of pathos
in the scenes of the orphan's isolation and
unhappiness than we are used to in children's
films (Saturday audiences ought to be made
to cry more often).'

THE MASTER OF BALLANTRAE
US Col 88 mins
pc WB-FN, d William Keighley, s novel
R L Stevenson
lp Errol Flynn, Roger Livesey, Anthony
Steel, Beatrice Campbell
Adventure. 1745. Rebel becomes buccaneer
thinking his brother has betrayed him.
MFB 'With Errol Flynn cast for the part
of Jamie, it is perhaps not surprising
that the original characterisation is largely
corrupted.'

ROB ROY – THE HIGHLAND
ROGUE
US Col 81 mins
pc Walt Disney , p Perce Pearce. d
Harold French
lp Richard Todd, Glynis Johns, James
Robertson Justice
Adventure. 1715. Clan chief rebels against
King.
THE MAZE*
US Col 80 mins 3-D
pc Allied Artists, p Richard Heermance,
d William Cameron Menzie
lp Richard Carlson, Veronica Hurst,
Michael Pate
Horror. Two weeks before his wedding
groom is called to uncle's castle in
Scotland. Bride and her aunt worried
by his disappearance follow him to
Scotland and uncover 200 year old
family secret in the castle maze.
THE KIDNAPPERS
alt US: THE LITTLE KIDNAPPERS
GB B & W 95 Mins
pc Rank, p Sergei Nolbandov, Leslie
Parkyn, d Philip Leacock, s story Neil
Paterson Scotch Settlement
lp Duncan Macrae, Adrienne Corri,
Jon Whiteley, Vincent Winter
Drama. Nova Scotia, 1900. Orphans
steal a baby when stern grandfather
refuses them a dog.

1954
THE MAGGIE
alt US: HIGH AND DRY
GB B & W 92 mins
pc Ealing, p Michael Truman, d & s
Alexander Mackendrick
lp Paul Douglas, Alex Mackenzie, James
Copeland, Abe Barker
Comedy. Glaswegian Puffer crew outwit
American businessman.
MFB '. . . very successful in capturing the
particular mixture of canniness and humour,
petty deceitfulness and honesty.'
DEVIL GIRL FROM MARS*
GB B & W 76 mins
pc Gigi, p Harry Lee, Edward J
Danziger, d David Macdonald, s John
C Maher
lp Hugh McDermott, Hazel Court,
Patricia Laffan
Fantasy. Nyah, Queen of Mars comes
with robot to abduct Scottish males for
breeding purposes.
MFB '. . . after much argument she is
persuaded that more suitable males are to
be found in London . . . everything, in its
way, is perfect.'
TROUBLE IN THE GLEN
GB Col 91 mins
pc Everest, p & d Herbert Wilcox, s
Maurice Walsh
lp Margaret Lockwood, Orson Welles,
Forres Tucker, Victor McLaglen
Comedy. New Argentinian laird creates ill
feeling in Scotland rural community.
MFB '. . . the whole tone of the film

is as synthetic as its remarkable picture of
the Highlands . . . the predominant colour
being an acid shade somewhere between yellow
and green.'
SEAGULLS OVER SORRENTO*
alt US:CREST OF THE WAVE*
GB B & W 92 mins
pc MGM British, p & d John & Roy
Boulting, s play Hugh Hastings
lp Gene Kelly, John Justin, Bernard
Lee, Jeff Richards
War. British and American naval
personnel test new torpedo on remote
Scots isle.
THE END OF THE ROAD*
GB B & W 76 mins
pc Group 3, p Alfred Shaughnessy, d
Wolf Rilla, s radio play James Forsyth
lp Finlay Currie, Duncan Lamont,
Naomi Chance
Drama. Retired engineer, frustrated by
retirement, wanders off with small
grandson.
MFB '. . . the script ranges from passages
of banality to flashes of near brilliance . . . a
dignified and accomplished performance from
Finlay Currie.'

Brigadoon (1954) Cyd Charisse and Gene Kelly

BRIGADOON
US Col 108 mins
pc MGM, p Arthur Freed, d Vincente
Minelli, sc Alan Jay Lerner, s play Alan
Jay Lerner
lp Gene Kelly, Cyd Charisse, Van
Johnson
Fantasy. Two Americans find ghost
village in Scotland which awakens
only once every hundred years.

1955
GEORDIE
GB Col 129 mins
pc Argonaut, p Frank Launder, Sidney
Gilliat, d Frank Launder, s novel David
Walker
lp Alastair Sim, Bill Travers, Norah
Gorsen
Comedy. Weak Scot takes body building

Geordie (1955) Alastair Sim

course and becomes Olympic champion at Melbourne.
A MAN CALLED PETER
US B & W 119 mins
pc TCF, *p* Samuel G Engel, *d* Henry Koster, *sc* Eleanore Griffin, *s book* Catherine Marshall
lp Richard Todd, Jean Peters, Marjorie Rambeau
Biography. The life of Peter Marshall, a Scottish clergyman who became chaplain to the US Senate.
MFB '. . . the Cinemascoped Marshall Manse demonstrates the paying concern that personal religion must be.'

1956
THE LITTLE SINGER*
GB B & W 60 mins
pc Elder Films, *p* Jack Elder, *d* Clarence Elder, *s book* Isabel Cameron *The Little Singer*
lp Louise Boyd, Campbell Hastie, Evelyn Lockhart, Archie Neal
Drama. Moral tale concerning young girl who wishes to sing in the St Andrew's Halls, Glasgow but whose family's debts put her ambition at risk.
X THE UNKNOWN
GB B & W 78 mins
pc Hammer, *p* Anthony Hinds, *d* Leslie Norman
lp Dean Jagger, Edward Chapman, Leo McKern
Horror. Radioactive seeping mass erupts in the Scottish Highlands.

1957
LET'S BE HAPPY
GB Col 107 mins
pc Marcel Hellman, *d* Henry Levin, *sc* Diana Morgan, *s play* Aimee Stuart *Jeannie*
lp Vera-Ellen, Tony Martin, Zena Marshall, Robert Flemyng
Musical. Edinburgh. Poor laird woos American girl in belief that she is heiress. Re-make of *Jeannie*.
MFB '. . . an elaborate musical, losing most of its charm on the way . . . Edinburgh in festival time provides an unusual, if not exotic, setting.'
THE KID FROM CANADA*
GB B & W 57 mins
pc Anvil Children's Film Foundation, *p* Ralph May, *d* Kay Mander, *s* John Eldridge
lp Christopher Braden, Bernard Braden, Bobby Stevenson
Children. Canadian braggart proves courage by rescuing shepherd.
MFB 'Stylish and highly satisfactory film, well-written and well-acted by real Scots and real Canadians.'

1958
ROCKETS GALORE
GB Col 94 mins
pc Rank, *p* Basil Deardon, *d* Michael Relph, *s novel* Compton Mackenzie
lp Finlay Currie, Jeannie Carson, Donald Sinden
Comedy. Hebridean islanders resist rocket base intrusion.
MFB '. . . puts too much faith in its collection of rusty character studies and determinedly Gallic (sic) whimsy.'

The Thirty Nine Steps (1959) Kenneth More

1959
THE THIRTY-NINE STEPS,
GB Col 93 mins
pc Rank, *p* Betty E Box, *d* Ralph Thomas, *s novel* John Buchan
lp Kenneth More, Taina Elg, Brenda de Bansie
Crime. Spy ring trapped by framed man after chase across Scotland.

THE UGLY DUCKLING
GB Col 84 mins
pc Hammer, *p* Tommy Lyndan-Hayes, *d* Lance Comfort, *s novel* R L Stevenson *Dr Jekyll and Mr Hyde*
lp Bernard Bresslaw, Reginald Beckwith, Jon Pertwee
Comedy. Under influence of great grandfather's potion a pharmacist turns to burglary.

The Bridal Path (1959) Joan Fitzpatrick and Pekeo Ainley

THE BRIDAL PATH
GB Col 95 mins
pc Vale, *p* Frank Launder, Sidney Gilliat, *d* Frank Launder, *s novel* Nigel Tranter
lp Bill Travers, Bernadette O'Farrell, George Cole, Duncan Macrae
Comedy. Hebridean islander suffers from mistaken identity whilst seeking mainland wife.
MFB 'Bill Travers . . . striding dourly up hill and down dale to the songs of the Campbeltown Gaelic Choir.'
BATTLE OF THE SEXES
GB Col 84 mins
pc Prometheus, *p* Monica Danischewsky, *d* Charles Crichton, *s story* James Thurber *The Catbird Seat*
lp Peter Sellers, Robert Morley, Constance Cummings
Comedy. Edinburgh. Conservative businessman tries to kill American woman who threatens the firm.
MFB '. . . a disappointment to anybody looking for genuine native material.'
JOHN PAUL JONES*
US Col 126 mins
pc Warner, *p* Samuel Branstan, *d & sc* John Farrow
lp Robert Stack, Charles Coburn, Bette Davis
Biography. American war of independence. Young Scotsman rises to great heights in the American navy.
KIDNAPPED
US Col 97 mins
pc Walt Disney, Hugh Attwool, *d &*

sc Robert Stevenson, s novel R L
Stevenson
lp Peter Finch, James MacArthur,
Bernard Lee
Adventure. 1751. Jacobite rebel saves
youth from being kidnapped by uncle.
MARIA STUART*
Austria 106 mins
pc Thalia, d Alfred Stöger
lp Judith Holzmeister, Liselotte
Schreiner
History. Record of performance of play
by Friedrich Schiller.

1960
THE YOUNG JACOBITES
GB B & W Serial 8 episodes
pc Rayant for the Children's Film
Foundation, p Anthony Gilkinson, d
John Reeve, s Kenneth Macfarlane
lp Francesca Annis, Jeremy Bulloch,
Frazer Hines
Children. Skye. Stone transports children
back in time where they can help Bonnie
Prince Charlie escape to France.
MFB '. . . full of well constructed excitement
. . . free of any temptation to impose Scotland
too strongly.'
TUNES OF GLORY
GB Col 107 mins
pc HM Films, p Albert Fennell, Colin
Lesslie, d Ronald Neame, s novel James
Kennaway
lp Alec Guiness, John Mills, Dennis
Price, Kay Walsh
Drama. Edinburgh. Disciplinarian
introduces changes to alcoholic
commander's regiment with tragic
results.
MFB '. . . an interesting melodrama. . .
unfortunately one cannot put it higher than
that.'
DEPTH CHARGE
GB B & W 55 mins
pc President, p James Mellor, d Jeremy
Summers, sc Kenneth Talbot, Jeremy
Summers
lp Alex McCrindle, David Orr, Elliot
Playfair

Tunes of Glory (1960) Alec Guiness

Adventure. Boatman helps expert dismantle depth charge caught by fishing
trawler.
MFB '. . . agreeable pocket-feature.'

Depth Charge (1960) David Orr and Elliot Playfair

THE FLESH AND THE FIENDS*
alt US: MANIA*
GB Col 97 mins
pc Triad, p Robert Baker, Monty
Berman, d John Gilling
lp Peter Cushing, June Laveric, Donald
Pleasance
Crime. Edinburgh, 1820. Resurrec-
tionists commit murder to supply
anatomists with corpses.
MFB '. . . the studio set fails to capture
the grim atmosphere pervading many of
Edinburgh's closes even today.'

1961
GREYFRIARS BOBBY
US Col 91 mins
pc Walt Disney, p Hugh Attwool, d Don
Chaffey, s novel Eleanor Atkinson
lp Donald Crisp, Laurence Naismith,
Alexander Mackenzie
Drama. Edinburgh. Period. Skye terrier
keeps vigil over old shepherd's grave
and is given freedom of the city.
MFB '. . . an engaging display of charm
for children and susceptible adults.'
DON'T BOTHER TO KNOCK
alt US: WHY BOTHER TO KNOCK
GB Col 88 mins
pc Haileywood, p Frank Godwin, d Cyril
Frankel, s novel Cliff Hanley Love From
Everybody
lp Richard Todd, Nicole Maurey, Elke
Sommer
Comedy. An Edinburgh travel agent's
philandering catches up with him when
several ladies arrive at his flat at the
same time.
MACBETH
US/GB Col 108 mins
pc Grand Prize, p Phil C Samuel,
d George Schaefer, s play Wm
Shakespeare
lp Maurice Evans. Judith Anderson,
Michael Hordern

Drama. Thane's wife urges him to
murder his way to the throne.
MFB 'Scotland of the travelogues.'

1962
THE AMOROUS PRAWN
alt US: THE PLAYGIRL AND THE
WAR MINISTER
GB B & W 89 mins
pc Covent Garden, p Leslie Gilliat,
d Anthony Kimmins, s play Anthony
Kimmins
lp Ian Carmichael, Joan Greenwood,
Cecil Parker, Dennis Price
Comedy. Absent general's wife poses as
widow and his staff pose as servants
to bored American lodgers.
MFB '. . . the climax is a glorious
romp.'
THE FAST LADY
GB Col 95 mins
pc Independent Artists, p Julian Wintle,
Leslie Parkyn, d Ken Annakin, s story
Keble Howard
lp James Robertson Justice, Leslie
Phillips, Stanley Baxter
Comedy. Bashful Scot learns to drive,
captures bank robbers and wins the
hand of his beloved.

1963
THE WITCHES CURSE*
alt MACISTE ALLE'INFERNO*
Italy Col 78 mins
pc Panda for l'Industria Cinematografica
Italiana, p Luigi Carpentieri, d Riccardo
Freda
lp Kirk Morris, Helene Chanel, Vira
Silenti
Horror. 17th Century. In the Scottish
village of Loch Lake a woman
condemned as a witch leaves a
curse on the village, which affects
the lives of her descendants.

1964
THREE LIVES OF THOMASINA
US Col 97 mins
pc Walt Disney, p Hugh Attwool, d
Don Chaffey, s novel Paul Gallico
lp Patrick McGoohan, Susan
Hampshire, Karen Dotrice
Drama. 1912. 'Witch girl's' love cures
injured cat.
MFB '. . . glutinously sentimental.'
CULLODEN
GB B & W 71 mins
pc BBC, p, d & sc Peter Watkins
lp George McBean, Alan Pope
History. 1746. Reconstruction of the
battle of Culloden and its aftermath.
MFB 'Watkins aims to pose urgent questions
about an episode in British history in a
"new light". But his radical (for its
time) mise-en-scène also raises questions,
largely ignored in Watkins' later work,
about the intervention of the film-maker in
history . . .'

1966

AMBUSH AT DEVIL'S GAP
GB Col Serial 6 episodes
pc Rayant for Children's Film Foundation, p John Durst, d David Eastman,
sc David & Kerry Eastman
lp Chris Barrington, Sue Sylvaine,
Stephen Brown
Children. Group of children thwart
crooks' attempts to steal invention.

1967

FLASH THE SHEEPDOG
GB Col 58 mins
pc IFA (Scotland) for Children's Film
Foundation, p J B Holmes, d,sc Laurence
Henson, s novel Kathleen Fidler
lp Earl Younger, Ross Campbell, Alex
Allan
Children. Orphan trains uncle's sheepdog
to win trials.

TWO WEEKS IN SEPTEMBER*
alt France: A COEUR JOIE*
GB/France Col 95 mins
pc Francos-Les Films du Quadrangle-
Pomereu-Kenwood, p Francis Cosne, d
Serge Bourguignon, sc Vahe Katcha
lp Brigitte Bardot, Laurent Terzieff,
Jean Rochefort
Drama. Genial laird lends French model
and amorous London photographer
Scottish castle for romantic interlude.
MFB 'Bardot: "happiness is just drops of
water" . . . supremely ludicrous amalgam
of all the clichés of women's magazines.'

UP THE MACGREGORS*
Italy/Spain Col 93 mins
pc Produzione D S – Jolly-Talia.
p Dario Sabatello, d Frank Grafield,
lp David Bailey, Agatha Flory, Leo
Anchoriz
Western comedy. Ranchers of Scots descent
and Irish family join forces against
Mexican bandits.

1968

CARRY ON . . . UP THE
KHYBER
GB Col 88 mins
pc Adder, p Peter Rogers, d Gerald
Thomas, sc Talbot Rothwell
lp Sidney James, Kenneth Williams,
Charles Hawtrey
Comedy. India, 1895. Uprising is
provoked by Scottish soldiers' dress.
MFB '. . . the bluest and funniest of the
series for some time.'
VAR '. . . and the reputation of the British
is rocked when the local rulers suspect that the
dreaded Scottish Devils in Skirts, members of
the intrepid Third Foot and Mouth regiment,
actually wear drawers under their kilts.'

THE BIG CATCH
GB Col 55 mins
pc IFA for Children's Film Foundation,
p Laurence Henson, Eddie McConnell,
d Laurence Henson, s Laurence Henson,
Charles Gormley
lp David Gallacher, Ronald Sinclair,

Andrew Byatt
Children. Scots children rescue boy cut
off by tide.

SEVEN GUNS FOR THE
MACGREGORS
Italy/Spain Col 94 mins
pc Produzione D S – Jolly- Estela, p
Dario Sabatello, d Frank Grafield
lp Robert Woods, Manuel Zarzo, Nick
Anderson
Western comedy. Ranchers of Scottish
descent get involved with bandits on
the Mexican frontier.

1969

THE PRIME OF MISS JEAN
BRODIE
GB Col 116 mins
pc 20th Century Fox, p Ronald Fryer, d
Ronald Neame, sc Jay Presson Allen, s
novel Muriel Spark
lp Maggie Smith, Robert Stephens,
Gordon Jackson, Celia Johnson
Drama. Edinburgh, 1930. Schoolteacher
exerts harmful influence on her girls.

RING OF BRIGHT WATER
GB Col 107 mins
pc Brightwater-Palomar, p Joseph Strick,
Edgar Schenck, d Jack Couffer, sc Jack
Couffer and Bill Travers, s book Gavin
Maxwell
lp Bill Travers, Virginia McKenna,
Peter Jeffrey
Animal. Ex-civil servant returns to the
Highlands to write a book and raise
Mij the otter instead.

SINFUL DAVEY
US Col 95 mins
pc Mirisch-Webb, p Walter Mirisch, d
John Huston, sc J R Webb, s book David
Haggart The Life of David Haggart
lp John Hurt, Pamela Franklin, Nigel
Davenport
Crime. 1821. True story of army deserter
turned highwayman.
MFB '. . . highly enjoyable for anyone who
is not in search of hidden significance.'

KH-4
GB B & W 12 mins
pc Smith Schorstein Assoc, d Jon
Schorstein
Glasgow. A young artist is seen making
his way through a city which has been
delivered into the hands of demolition
experts.

THE BODYGUARD
GB B & W 15 mins
pc BFI Production Board, d Michael
Alexander
The relationship between two brothers.
An allegory of human nature through
a succession of images of a boy and
his protector.

1970

THE FAMILY
GB B & W 26 mins
pc BFI Production Board/BBC Scotland,
d & sc Michael Alexander

lp The Alexander Family
Young man, dominated by wife's
close-knit family, withdraws into fantasy
world.

THE MACKENZIE BREAK
GB Col 106 mins
pc Brighton, p Jules Levy, d Lamont
Johnson, sc William Norton
lp Brian Keith, Helmut Griem, Ian
Hendry
War. U-Boat officers escape from POW
camp in Scotland.
MFB '. . . an unusually intelligent B-feature
in which even the Irish locations manage to
stand in for a credible Scotland.'

THE POET
GB Col 19 mins
pc Michael Alexander/BBC, d Michael
Alexander
Skit about interviews with poets.

THE PRIVATE LIFE OF
SHERLOCK HOLMES
GB Col 125 mins
pc Mirisch/Phalanx/Sir Nigel, p & d
Billy Wilder, s characters Sir Arthur
Conan Doyle
lp Robert Stephens, Colin Blakely, Irene
Handl, Christopher Lee
Crime. 1887. Detective gets involved with
secret submarine tests, camouflaged as
the Loch Ness monster.

1971

COUNTRY DANCE
alt US: BROTHERLY LOVE (1970)
GB Col 112 mins
pc Windward/Keep/MGM British, p
Robert Emmett Ginna, d J Lee
Thompson, s play James Kennaway
Household Guests and Country Dance
lp Peter O'Toole, Susannah York,
Michael Craig
Drama. Perth. Baronet's incestuous love
for his sister wreaks havoc in family.

BURKE AND HARE
GB Col 91 mins
pc Shipman/Armitage, p Guido Coen,
d Vernon Sewell, sc Ernle Bradford
lp Harry Andrews, Derren Nesbitt,
Glynn Edwards
Horror. Edinburgh, 19th century. Irishmen commit murder to supply surgeon,
Dr Knox, with corpses.
MFB '. . . less concerned with Dr Knox's
character than with presenting a series of
fetishistic interludes in the local brothel.'

KIDNAPPED
GB Col 107 mins
pc Omnibus, p Frederick H Brogger, d
Delbert Mann, s novel R L Stevenson
lp Michael Caine, Trevor Howard, Jack
Hawkins, Gordon Jackson
Adventure. Jacobite helps boy whose
uncle has him kidnapped.

THE DUNA BULL
GB Col 33 mins
pc IFA/Films of Scotland, p, d Laurence
Henson, s Forsyth Hardy, sc Cliff
Hanley

Burke and Hare (1971) director Vernon Sewell

lp Julie Cadzow, Richard Harbord, Victor Carin
Drama. Hebrides. Islanders' request for replacement for their only bull presents problems for civil servants.
MACBETH
US Col 140 mins
pc Playboy/Caliban, *p* Andrew Braunsberg, *d* Roman Polanski, *sc* Roman Polanski, Kenneth Tynan, *s play* Wm Shakespeare
lp Jon Finch, Francesca Annis, Martin Shaw
Drama. Period. Thane's wife urges him to murder king.
MFB '. . . in adapting Shakespeare to suit Hugh Hefner and themselves, Polanski and Tynan has served Macbeth very well.'
MY CHILDHOOD
GB B & W 48 mins
pc BFI Production Board, *p* Geoffrey Evans, *d & sc* Bill Douglas,
lp Stephen Archibald, Hughie Restorick, Jean Taylor Smith
Drama. Young boy grows up in deprived Scottish mining village.
MADAME SIN
US Col 90 mins
pc Cecil/ITC/Independent Artists, *p* Julian Wintle, Lou Morrheim, *d* David Greene, *sc* Barry Oringer, David Greene
lp Bette Davis, Robert Wagner, Denham Elliott
Crime. Ex-agent foils woman crook's plot to steal Polaris submarine.
MARY QUEEN OF SCOTS
US Col 128 mins
pc Universal, *p* Hal B Wallis, *d* Charles Jarrott, *sc* John Hale
lp Vanessa Redgrave, Glenda Jackson, Patrick McGoohan, Timothy Dalton
History. Queen of England executes Queen of Scots to safeguard succession to the throne.
THE DEVIL'S WIDOW
alt US: TAM LIN
GB Col 106 mins
pc Winkast, *p* Alan Ladd Jnr, Stanley Mann, *d* Roddy McDowall, *sc* William Spier, *s poem* Robert Burns *The Ballad of Tam Lin*
lp Ava Gardner, Ian McShane, Richard

Wattis, Cyril Cusack
Horror. Young man's love for daughter of the manse is jeopardised by the hold over him exercised by his wealthy patroness.
MFB '. . . enigmatic sense of menace out of stray allusions and apparitions that hover without ever really being explained or over-exploited: the snatches of Burns intimating the presence of diabolic machinations . . .'

WHEN EIGHT BELLS TOLL
GB Col 94 mins
pc Winkast, *p* Elliott Kastner, *d* Etienne Perier, *w*, *s novel* Alistair MacLean
lp Anthony Hopkins, Robert Morley, Nathalie Delon, Jack Hawkins
Adventure. Secret service agent sent to investigate pirating of gold bullion ships in Irish Sea.
MFB '. . . dour professionalism and emotional tensions well set off by the bleak vistas of the Western Highlands.'

1972
THE GARDENER
GB Col 10 mins
pc Pelicula/BBC, *d* Michael Alexander
A lonely young gardener dreams of death during his solitary routine.

1973
MAURO THE GYPSY
GB Col 58 mins
pc IFA(Scotland) for Children's Film Foundation, *p & d* Laurence Henson, *s* Ken Pople
lp Graeme Greenhowe, Fiona Kennedy, Andrew Byatt
Children. Gypsy boy saves girl from drowning.
MY AIN FOLK
GB B & W 55 mins
pc BFI Production Board, *p* Nick Nacht, *d & s* Bill Douglas
lp Stephen Archibald, Hughie Restorick, Jean Taylor Smith
Drama. Boy living with grandmother in Scots mining village learns man next door is his father.
MFB '. . . a very considerable work of art.'
THE WICKER MAN
GB Col 86 mins
pc British Lion, *p* Peter Snell, *d* Robin Hardy, *s* Anthony Shaffer
lp Edward Woodward, Britt Ekland, Diane Cilento
Horror. Policeman investigates death of a child and uncovers pagan practices on Scottish island.
MFB '. . . immensely enjoyable piece of hokum.'

1974
THE ALL-ROUNDER
GB Col 10 mins

pc Michael Alexander/BBC, *p & d* Michael Alexander
A handyman-gardener grits his teeth as he compulsively turns the simplest of household jobs into feats of daring and endurance.
THE CHEVIOT, THE STAG AND THE BLACK, BLACK OIL
GB Col 123 mins
pc 7:84 Theatre Co, *p* Graeme McDonald, *d* John Mackenzie, *s play* John McGrath
lp John Bett, David Maclennan, Dolina Maclellan, Elizabeth Maclennan, Alex Norton
History. Highland life as affected by economic change, from the Clearances to the exploitation of North Sea oil resources.
THE GREAT MCGONAGALL
GB Col 89 mins
pc Darlton, *p* David Grant, *d* Joseph McGrath, *s* Spike Milligan, *sc* Spike Milligan, Joseph McGrath
lp Spike Milligan, Peter Sellers, Julia Foster
Comedy. Dundee 1890. Poet foils attempt to murder the Queen.
MFB '. . . surely one of the most embarrassingly unfunny films ever to see the light of day.'
HOME AND AWAY
GB Col 30 mins
pc BFI, *p & d* Michael Alexander, *sc* Michael Alexander & Bill Douglas
Young boy leaves his island home to attend school on another island.

1975
DONALD OF THE COLOURS
GB Col 54 mins
pc Group 5, *d* Ron Miller
History. A young Cameron lad flees after the battlefield of Culloden taking with him the Clan standard.
THE GREAT MILL RACE
GB Col 32 mins
pc Edinburgh/Films of Scotland, *ap* Michael Pavett, *d* Robin Crichton, *sc* Clifford Hanley, *s story* Alasdair Gray
lp John Cairney, Russell Hunter, John Grieve, Leonard MacGuire, Ros Drinkwater
Drama. Borders textile manufacturers compete in race to make a suit from fleece in a single day.

1976
ECLIPSE
GB Col 85 mins
pc Celandine, *p* David Munro, *d & sc* Simon Perry, *s novel* Nichola Wolleston
lp Tom Conti, Gay Hamilton, Gavin Wallace
Crime. Man makes love to wife of historian, whom he has killed.
MFB 'This carefully crafted film (shot in Caithness and Sutherland) proceeds obliquely,

leaving a trail of beguiling suggestions about reality and fantasy . . .'
NOSEY DOBSON
GB Col 59 mins
pc Pelicula for Children's Film Foundation, *p* Cyril Randell, *d & s* Michael Alexander
lp Joe McKenna, James Morrison, Gary Rankin
Adventure. Boy acts detective and foils robbers.
MFB '. . . makes intelligent use of the Isle of Arran locations to lend a freshness to its simple narrative and rather flat characterisation.'

1977
BIG BANANA FEET
GB Col 77 mins
pc Viz/Unicorn, *p,d & s* Patrick Higson, Murray Grigor
lp Billy Connolly
Comedy. Glasgow comedian's performance at ABC Cinema, Belfast, October, 1975.
MFB '53% of the population of Belfast's got a willy, so what's wrong wi' it?'

1978
THE THIRTY-NINE STEPS
GB Col 102 mins
pc Media Management/Norfolk International, *p* Greg Smith, *d* Don Sharp, *s novel* John Buchan
lp Robert Powell, David Warner, Eric Porter, John Mills
Crime. 1914. Spies pursue framed man across Scotland.
MFB 'In fairness, it should be noted that Robert Powell as Hannay not only has to contend with a script that refuses to let him work out the mystery himself (he and Eric Porter's Lomas are told in an aside the location of the steps).'
THE TENT
GB Col 18 Mins
pc Pelicula
The contrasting reactions of a farmer and his adolescent son towards a young couple camping on their land.
LONG SHOT
GB B & W 85 mins
pc Mithras, *p, d & sc* Maurice Hatton
lp Charles Gormley, Neville Smith, Ann Zelda
Comedy. Edinburgh. Aspirant film-maker tries to raise finance for his projects.
MFB '. . . engaging shaggy dog tale for film buffs . . .'

1979
DEATHWATCH
alt France: LA MORT EN DIRECT
France/GDR Col 130 mins
pc Selta/Little Bear/Sara, *p, d & sc* Bertrand Tavernier
lp Harvey Keitel, Romy Schneider, Max van Sydaw
Science fiction thriller, set in Glasgow of the future. Woman, told she has only

three weeks to live, agrees to let her last days be televised.
MFB 'He makes both too much and too little of his locations, stressing the picturesque decay of Glasgow as if that would answer all questions about what is supposed to be going on in terms of social control, the manipulation of the media, the lobotomisation of the masses.'
MY WAY HOME;
GB B & W 78 mins
pc BFI Prod Board, *p* Judy Cottam, Richard Craven, *d & s* Bill Douglas
lp Stephen Archibald, Paul Kermack, Jessie Combe
Drama. Edinburgh 1950. Young man, released from children's institution, enters his National Service.
THAT SUMMER
GB Col 93 mins
pc Film In General, *p* Davina Belling/Clive Parsons, *d* Harley Cokliss
lp Ray Winstone, Tony London, Emily Moore
Drama. Torquay. Glasgow youths foil boy offender's attempt to win swimming contest.
MFB 'Why, for example, if Cokliss is genuinely concerned with the causes of deliquency, does he not concentrate his attention on the hard-case Scottish hooligans (a rather snide piece of parochial racism, incidentally), who blight the hero's pursuit of goodness . . .'
THE ADMAN
GB Col 20 mins
pc Pelicula, *p,d & sc* Mike Alexander
lp David Hayman, Alec Heggie, Angie Rew
An advertising executive's life is shattered when he becomes the lone witness to a robbery.
SHAKESPEARE'S MOUNTED FOOT
GB Col 43 mins
pc Breck, *p* Douglas Eadie, Mick Campbell, *d* Bert Eeles
lp Alex Norton, James Copeland, Russell Hunter
Comedy. Barnstorming theatrical troupe at the turn of the century travelling through North Country and Scottish borders.
NORTH SEA HIJACK
GB Col 100 mins
pc Cinema Seven, *p* Elliot Kastner, *d* Andrew V McLaglen, *sc & s novel* Jack Davies *Esther, Ruth and Jennifer*
lp Roger Moore, James Mason, Anthony Perkins, Michael Parks
Drama. Underwater expert foils plans to hijack oil-drilling rig.

1980
NEVER SAY DIE;
GB B & W 39 mins
pc National Film School, *p* Clyde Bridges, *d & sc* Sandy Johnson
Black comedy set against backdrop of

Glasgow.
THAT SINKING FEELING
GB Col 93 mins
pc Lake, *p, d & sc* Bill Forsyth
lp Tom Mannion, Eddie Burt, Richard Demarco, Alex McKenzie
Comedy. Glasgow. Unemployed youths form gang to steal stainless steel sinks from warehouse.

1981
GREGORY'S GIRL
GB Col 91 mins
pc Lake/Scottish TV, *p* Davina Belling, Clive Parsons, *d & sc* Bill Forsyth
lp John Gordon Sinclair, Dee Hepburn, Jake D'Arcy, Clare Grogan
Comedy. Cumbernauld. Schoolboy falls in love with girl who plays in the football team.
MFB '. . . (who could want to know how many tons of cornflakes pass daily down a motorway, except Bill Forsyth who likes cornflakes jokes) . . .'
GOODBYE UNCLE
GB Col 42 mins
pc Quinlan, *p, d & sc* Norman Pollock
Ambitious reporter gets involved in murder and terrorism.
CHARIOTS OF FIRE
GB Col 121 mins
pc Enigma/Allied Stars, *p* David Puttnam, *d* Hugh Hudson, *sc* Colin Welland
lp Ben Cross, Ian Charleson, Nigel Havers
Sport. 1924. True story of Scots missionary and Oxford graduate who compete in the Paris Olympics.
MFB '. . . tweed suits against a Highland backdrop, academic paraphernalia bathed in a perpetual amber glory – as if they must be reverentially caressed to summon the spirit of times past.'
DOLLAR BOTTOM
GB Col 33 mins
pc Rocking Horse/Paramount, *p* Lloyd Phillips, *d* Roger Christian, *s story* James Kennaway
lp Rikki Fulton, Robert Urquhart, Jonathan McNeil
Comedy. 1953. Boy starts insurance scheme against corporal punishment.
A SENSE OF FREEDOM
GB Col 88 mins
pc Scottish Television, *p* Jeremy Isaacs, *d* John Mackenzie, *s autobiography* Jimmy Boyle
lp David Hayman, Jake d'Arcy, Sean Scanlon, Alex Norton
Biography. The life of Jimmy Boyle, the Glasgow 'hardman'.
EYE OF THE NEEDLE
GB Col 113 Mins
pc Kings Road, *p* Stephen Friedman, *d* Richard Marquand, *s novel* Ken Follett
lp Donald Sutherland, Ian Bannen, Stephen McKenna

War. 1940. German spy, stranded on rain-soaked Scottish island, is foiled from transmitting secrets by crippled pilot's wife.

1982
HERO
GB Col 90 mins
pc MAYA/Channel 4, *p* Andrew St John, *D* Barney Platts-Mills
lp Derek MacGuire, Cardine Kenneill, Alaistair Kenneill, *s story* J F Campbell *Tales of the Western Highlands*
Romance. A mythical Scotland of the past. Young couple fall in love though she is married to another.
Gaelic with English subtitles.
MFB '. . . is a challenge to colonialism via its own back door, a defiance of the English language within the British Isles. And all the more curious (canny) that the vehicle for this should be a selection of Gaelic tales that could clearly be related to the Arthurian legends.'
SCOTCH MYTHS
GB Col 90 mins
pc Everallin/Channel 4, *p* Barbara Grigor, Murray Grigor, *d* Murray Grigor
lp John Bett, Juliet Cadzow, Walter Carr
Celebration of the romatic fantasies about things Scottish that have been invented by novelists, poets and musicians over the years.
ILL FARES THE LAND
GB Col 102 mins
pc Scottish & Global TV Enterprises, *p* Robert Love, *d & sc* Bill Bryden
lp David Hayman, Fulton Mackay, Jean Taylor Smith, Andrew McCulloch
History. 1930 The events leading up to the evacuation of the remote island of St Kilda as seen through the eyes of a young boy.

1983
ANOTHER TIME ANOTHER PLACE
GB Col 102 mins
pc Umbrella/Rediffusion/Channel 4 TV, *p* Simon Perry, *d* Michael Radford, *s novel* Jessie Kesson
lp Phyllis Logan, Giovanni Mauriello, Denise Coffey
War. 1944. Farmer's wife has affair with Italian POW working on their farm.
MFB '. . . there is Phyllis Logan's magnificent central performance, one all the more moving for its fastidious self-denial of every facile cliché inherent in such MacBovaryism.'
THE PRIVILEGE
GB Col 26 mins
pc High Road, *d* Ian Knox, Andrea Finlay, *s story* George Mackay Brown
Romance. Orkney 19th-century tenant farmers celebrate wedding.
LOCAL HERO
GB Col 111 mins

Another Time, Another Place (1983) Giovanni Mauriello and Phyllis Logan

pc Enigma/Goldcrest, *p* David Puttnam, *d & sc* Bill Forsyth
lp Burt Lancaster, Peter Riegert, Denis Lawson, Fulton Mackay
Comedy. Young American oil executive meets various difficulties when sent to coastal village to buy up land for new refinery.
LIVING APART TOGETHER
GB Col 98 mins
pc Legion/Film on Four, *p* Gavrik Losey, Paddy Higson, *d & sc* Charles Gormley
lp B A Robertson, Barbara Kellerman, Judi Tratt
Drama. Rock singer returns to home town of Glasgow to attempt reconciliation with wife.

1984
COMFORT AND JOY
GB Col 106 mins
pc Lake/ Thorn EMI/Scottish TV, *p* Davina Belling/Clive Parsons, *d & s* Bill Forsyth.
lp Bill Paterson, Eleanor David, C P Grogan, Alex Norton
Comedy. Radio Disc jockey gets involved in war between rival ice-cream manufacturers.
MFB 'The city of Glasgow . . . has been so streamlined by Chris Menges' neon-lit cinematography, and so peopled with cool, leggy cover girls, presumably to add what one must call, to distinguish it from the local variety, "imported colour", as to be all but interchangeable with New York or Dallas or any other of the movies' archetypal urban dreamscapes.'
FALL FROM GRACE
GB Col 55 mins
pc NFTS/SFPF, *p, d & sc* Ian Wyse
lp John MacIness, Tim Potter, Louis Mellis
1746. The efforts of a band of Jacobites to shelter Bonnie Prince Charlie after the battle of Culloden.
EVERY PICTURE TELLS A STORY
GB Col 83 mins
pc Flamingo/Channel 4/SFPF, *p* Christine Oestreicher, *ap* Paddy

Higson, Adam Kempton, *d* James Scott
lp Alex Norton, Phyllis Logan
Biography. Based on the life of painter William Scott, and his upbringing in Greenock and Enniskillen.

1985
RESTLESS NATIVES
GB Col 89 mins
pc Oxford Films/Thorn EMI, *p* Rick Stevenson, Andy Paterson, *d* Michael Hoffman, *sc* Ninian Dunnett
lp Vincent Friell, Joe Mullaney, Teri Lally
Comedy. Edinburgh. Two young men start to rob American coach parties and become celebrities.
MFB 'Sinking feelings set in early with this cheap and determinedly cheerful slice of forced frivolity and forged Forsythery. . . . Scotland's touristic geography has been quite radically rearranged for narrative convenience . . .'
VAR 'Premise of the film, an unlikely one, is that the tourists, mostly Yanks, don't mind having their money and valuables stolen by these two eccentrics; in fact, they seem to enjoy it so much that Scottish tourism actually increases.'
THE GIRL IN THE PICTURE
GB Col 91 mins
pc Antonine/NFCC, *p* Paddy Higson, *d* Cary Parker
lp John Gordon-Sinclair, Irina Brook, David McKay
Romance. A young photographer falls in love with the girl whose pictures he develops.
MFB '. . . this is a soft-hearted Scots romance that could do with some Glasgow grit.'
NOT FIXED
GB Col 18 mins
pc Quinlan, *p, d &sc* Norman Pollock
Young drug addict exacts revenge on pusher.
THE DOCTOR AND THE DEVILS
GB Col 93 mins
pc Brooksfilm, *p* Jonathan Sanger, *d* Freddie Francis, *sc* Ronald Harwood
lp Timothy Dalton, Jonathan Pryce, Twiggy
Horror. In 18th-century Edinburgh a surgeon starts to pay for bodies as specimens, and doesn't ask about their provenance.

1986
HEAVENLY PURSUITS
GB Col 91 mins
pc Island/Film Four International, *p* Michael Relph, *d & sc* Charles Gormley
lp Tom Conti, Helen Mirren, Brian Pettifer
Comedy. Catholic schoolteacher discovers hidden talent for performing miracles.
MFB '. . . the diminutive Father Cobb, so distressed by his awareness of Scotland as "a hard-headed country when it comes to

*believing'' that he grabs blindly at a miracle
which will surely swell his diminishing
congregation . . .'*
HIGHLANDER
GB/US Col 111 mins
pc EMI/Highlander, *p* Peter S Davis,
William N Panzer, *d* Russell Mulcahy,
sc Gregory Widden, Peter Bellwood,
Larry Ferguson
lp Sean Connery, Christopher Lambert,
Roxanne Hart, Clancy Brown
Fantasy. A 14th-century Highlander
apparently dies in battle but finds
he is immortal.
*MFB '. . . the historical episodes
which, despite the genial self-caricature
of Sean Connery's cameo appearance (his
Mediterranean courtier reacts with incredulous
revulsion at the prospect of eating haggis), all
too often descend to a token level of fancy-dress
flummery.'*
*VAR 'Lambert looks and acts a lot better
in a tartan and long, scraggly hair than as a
nearly non-verbal antiques dealer in SoHo.'*
PASSING GLORY
GB Col 40 mins
pc NFTS/SFPF, *p* Bill Hackman, *d*
Gillies Mackinnon
lp Fiona Chalmers, Alan Cummings,
Ida Schuster
The relationship between a rebellious
girl and her grandmother who fought
in the Spanish Civil War.
THE RIVETER
GB Col 33 mins
pc NFTS, *d & sc* John Kerr, *d* Michael
Caton-Jones
lp Andrew Barr, Ewen Bremner
A drunken, drifting failure flees from
Glasgow with his son to the Western
Isles.
BLOOD RED ROSES
GB Col 150 mins
pc Freeway Films, *p* Steve Clark-Hall,
d & sc John McGrath
lp Elizabeth MacLennan, James Grant,
Gregor Fisher, Dawn Archibald
Drama. One woman's lifelong struggle
on behalf of her fellow workers.
*MFB '. . . even in defeat Bessie is potent,
a bonny fighter . . . her story is a powerful
account of both solidarity and betrayal.'*

1987
LOSER'S BLUES
GB Col 18 mins
p, d & sc Norman Pollock
A bad night at the dogs for a young
steelworker who also has marital
problems to contend with.
MACBETH
France/Germany Col 136 mins
pc Dedalus/SFPC/TFI/Unitel, *p* Henry
Lange, *d* Claude d'Anna, *s play* Wm
Shakespeare
lp Leo Nucci, Johan Leysen, Shirley
Verrett, Philippe Volter
History. Adaptation of opera by Guiseppi
Verdi.

1988
FACTS OF LIFE
GB Col 33 mins
pc NFTS/SFPF, *p & sc* Amanda
Mckenzie Stuart, *d* Laura Sim
lp Natalie Robb, Paul Young, Eliza
Langland, Sheila Latimer
Edinburgh 1963. Eleven year old Alice
is fascinated by sex. Her mother's
involvement with her singing teacher
introduces Alice to more facts of life
than she had bargained for.

1989
SILENT SCREAM
GB Col 85 mins
pc Antonine for BFI, Film Four
International, SFPF, *p* Paddy Higson,
d David Hayman, *sc* Bill Beech
lp Iain Glen, Anne Kirsten
Biography, based on life and writings of
Larry Winters, inmate in the Special
Unit, Barlinnie prison, Glasgow.
VENUS PETER
GB Col 94 mins
pc BFI/Channel 4/SFPF/British
Screen/Orkney Islands Council
p Christopher Young, *d* Ian Sellar, *sc*
Ian Sellar, C Rush, *s novel* Christopher
Rush *A Twelvemonth and a Day*
lp Ray McAnally, David Hayman,
Sinead Cusack, Gordon R Strachan
Drama. 1940s. A small boy dreams of
the sea as a fishing community suffers
the pressure of economics and his
grandfather is forced to sell his boat.
*MFB '. . . the film has all the hopes and
promises of a voyage just begun in a life
with many more discoveries ahead.'*
*VAR 'The evocative background of the Orkneys
is a major asset to the film . . .'.*
PLAY ME SOMETHING
GB Col 72 mins
pc BFI/Film Four Internation-
al/SFPF/Grampian TV
p Kate Swan, *d* Timothy Neat, *sc*
Timothy Neat, John Berger
lp Tilda Swinton, Hamish Henderson,
John Berger, Liz Lochhead
A man entertains passengers waiting at
Barra airport with a tale of an Italian
peasant on a trip to Venice.
*MFB 'As well as paying tribute to the oral
tradition in European culture . . . Play Me
Something also explores various possibilities
of narrative construction in the cinema.'*
VAR 'Poetic, political and philosophical

The Big Man (1990) Liam Neeson

platitudes abound in Berger's tale-spinning.'
HARBOUR BEAT
Australia/GB Col 99 mins
pc Zenith/Palm Beach/Australian Film
Finance Corp, *p & d* David Elfick, *sc*
Morris Gleitzman
lp John Hannah, Steven Vidler
Crime. Glasgow cop is transferred to
Sydney and breaks up drug ring.

1990
THE BIG MAN;
GB Col 116 mins
pc Palace/BSB/Scottish Television, *p*
Stephen Woolley, *d* David Leland, *s
novel* William McIlvanney
lp Liam Neeson, Billy Connolly
Drama. Out of work miner is lured into
bare-knuckle fighting.
TIN FISH
GB Col 45 mins
pc NFTS, *p* Andrea Calderwood, *d*
Paul Murton
lp Jon Morrison, Matt Costello, Emma
Thomson
Clyde coast taxi driver airs his fears
about presence of US nuclear submarine
base.
ALABAMA
GB Col 45 mins
pc NFTS, *d* Jim Shields, *p* Kate Swan,
sc Jim Shields and Brian Keeley
lp Louise Beattie, Paul Birchard, Jake
d'Arcy
Comedy. *'A rich Dundeed cake of a
movie'*.
ASHES
GB Col 39 mins
pc NFTS, *sc & d* Douglas Mackinnon
lp Willie Blair, Paul Young, Alec
Heggie, Lloret Mackenna
Islander brought up in Glasgow takes
his father's ashes back to Skye and
tries to piece together his past.

253

Filmography Index

255

Acknowledgements

Many grateful thanks are due to Scottish Television whose generous hansell ensured an improvement in the quality of this book.

Gratitude is due to the book's contributor's who responded to my prods without plowter and my cuts without girnin. Carolyn McLean, Hazel McNaught and Kathleen Smith did all the real work, going VDU-blind and finger-weary in the process, but with no greetin. Heartfelt thanks to them. Janet McBain and Dan MacRae helped out with the captions.

Acknowledgements for the use of stills are due to:

Scottish Film Archive, British Film Institute, Edinburgh Film Guild, BBC Scotland, Scottish Television, Charlie Gormley, Kate Swan, Andrea Calderwood, BAFTA Scotland, Paddy Higson, Pinewood Studios, Empire Magazine, Chris Rush, Oasis Productions, Daily Record, Bill Forsyth, Dennis Davidson Associates, Jean Mohr, Murray Grigor, D C Thomson Ltd, Alan Crumlish, Cormorant Films, Pelicula Films, Tom Hilton, Penny Thomson, Big Star in a Wee Picture, Strathclyde Regional Archives, George Singleton, J K S Poole.

The principal source of information for the filmography (for British registered productions) is *The British Film Catalogue 1895-1985, a reference guide* by Denis Gifford. That meticulously researched volume made possible what would otherwise have been an inconceivable task.

For US registered productions the American Film Institute's *Index to Feature Films* for 1911-20, 1921-30, 1961-70 has been invaluable. Thanks are due to staff at the AFI and the Library of Congress for their assistance in researching the intervening decades.

Our thanks to the *Monthly Film Bulletin* and *Variety* for the use of the quotations.

Eddie Dick

Contributors

Neil Blain is Senior Lecturer in Communications at Glasgow College.
David Bruce is Director of the Scottish Film Council.
John Caughie is Senior Lecturer in the Theatre, Film and Television Studies Department at Glasgow University.
Eddie Dick is Media Education Officer at the Scottish Film Council.
Charlie Gormley is a writer and film director.
Murray Grigor is a writer and film director.
Alan Hunter is a freelance journalist.
David Hutchison is Senior Lecturer in Communications at Glasgow College.
Ian Lockerbie is Professor of French at Stirling University.
Colin McArthur is a freelance writer and researcher.
Janet McBain is Archivist of the Scottish Film Archive of the Scottish Film Council.
Gus Macdonald is Managing Director of Scottish Television PLC.
Robin McPherson is administrator and producer at the Edinburgh Film Workshop.
John Millar is Television Editor with *The Daily Record*.
Christopher Rush is a teacher and writer.
Philip Schlesinger is Professor of Film and Media Studies at Stirling University.
Adrienne Scullion is a post-graduate student at Glasgow University.
Andrew Young is Features Editor with *The Glasgow Herald*.